Church Talk Makes Men Walk

Church Talk Makes Men Walk

What the Research Shows and What to Do

WOODY L. DAVIS

Foreword by George G. Hunter, III

WIPF & STOCK · Eugene, Oregon

CHURCH TALK MAKES MEN WALK
What the Research Shows and What to Do

Copyright © 2017 Woody L. Davis. All rights reserved. Except for brief quotations in critical publications or reviews, no part of this book may be reproduced in any manner without prior written permission from the publisher. Write: Permissions, Wipf and Stock Publishers, 199 W. 8th Ave., Suite 3, Eugene, OR 97401.

Wipf & Stock
An Imprint of Wipf and Stock Publishers
199 W. 8th Ave., Suite 3
Eugene, OR 97401

www.wipfandstock.com

PAPERBACK ISBN: 978-1-5326-0297-9
HARDCOVER ISBN: 978-1-5326-0299-3
EBOOK ISBN: 978-1-5326-0298-6

Manufactured in the U.S.A.   JULY 5, 2017

Contents

List of Images | *vii*
List of Tables | *viii*
List of Figures | *x*
Permissions | *xiii*
Foreword by George G. Hunter, III | *xv*
Preface | *xvii*

---

1. The Missing Men | 1
2. So What Should We Do? | 20
3. The Words We Use | 40
4. What Should We Do about the Words We Use? | 68
5. The Topics We Choose | 84
6. So What Do We Do about the Topics We Choose? | 106
7. How We Talk | 135
8. So Now What Do We Do? | 160
9. Where Do We Go from Here? | 179

Appendix A   *Research on Gender across the Cultures* | *211*
Appendix B   *Perceptions of Christians* | *214*
Appendix C   *Gender Schemas and Self-Schemas* | *228*
Appendix D   *Detailed Comparison of Values Sought in Pastors vs. Industry Leaders* | *249*

Appendix E   Men, Gender Schemas and Responses to Christian Messages | 251

Appendix F   Responses of Men and Women to Masculine and Feminine Christian Message | 266

Bibliography | 271

Subject Index | 281

Scripture Index | 285

List of Images

Billy Sunday preparing to preach to a men's meeting in his Princeton, Illinois campaign in 1906. | 5

The Men's Bible Class of the First Methodist Episcopal Church of Vandalia, IL, May 7, 1911 | 6

Men's Class, First Christian Church Sunday School, Canton, OH, June 7, 1912 | 6

"Largest Bible class in the world, 1316," Men's Bible Class, First Methodist Episcopal Church, Lancaster, OH, April 18th, 1915 | 7

The Men's Bible Class of the First Methodist Episcopal Church of Westbrook ME, Feb. 15, 1917 | 7

Men's Bible Class, First Baptist Church, Charleston, WV, 1923 | 8

The Men's Bible Class of the Broadway Christian Church of Lexington, KY, 1947 | 8

List of Tables

Table 1.1: Perceptions of Christians: Consensus Items and Sextype | 13
Table 1.2: Gender Labels of Values Sought in Pastors | 14
Table 1.3: Percentage of Laity Selecting Each Value in Pastors | 14
Table 2.1: Color-Coded Gender and Generation Attendance Data Sheet | 25
Table 2.2: Jehosephat Church Average Participation by Gender and Age | 27
Table 4.1: Feminine Register Vocabulary Card | 71
Table 4.2: Simplified Empty Adjectives and Overstatements Data Card | 72
Table 4.3: Detailed Empty Adjectives and Overstatements Data Card | 73
Table 4.4: Alternatives to Empty Adjectives | 74
Table 4.5: Alternatives to Romantic Emotions | 77
Table 4.6: Alternatives to s'Mothering | 78
Table 4.7: Alternatives to Enmeshment | 80
Table 6.1: Feminine Christian Theme Card | 109
Table 6.2: Masculine Christian Theme Card | 110
Table 6.3: Feminine Christian Themes in Sample Sermon One | 115
Table 6.4: Masculine Christian Themes in Sample Sermon One | 116
Table 6.5: Masculine/Feminine Christian Theme Summary Form | 117–18
Table 6.6: Feminine Christian Theme in Sample Sermon Two | 133
Table 6.7: Masculine Christian Themes in Sample Sermon Two | 133
Table 7.1: Gender and the Particularity-Generality Dichotomy | 141
Table 8.1: Powerless Language Data Sheet | 164

Table 8.2: Powerless Language Indicators in Sermon | 169
Table 8.3: Feminine Christian Themes in Sermon | 169–70
Table 8.4: Feminine Register Vocabulary in Sermon | 170
Table 8.5: Powerless Language Data Example | 173–74

Table B.1: Q Deck Items by Gender and Valence | 216
Table B.2: Subject Assignments with Factor Weights by Type | 218
Table B.3: Correlations between Types | 218
Table B.4: Forty-three Consensus Items and Average Z-Scores across All Types | 219–20
Table B.5: Defining Consensus Items and Average Z-Scores across All Types | 222
Table B.6: Items Distinguishing between Types One and Three | 224
Table B.7: Items Distinguishing between Types One and Two | 224
Table B.8: Items Distinguishing between Types Two and Three | 225
Table C.1: Factor Analysis of the Bem Sex Role Inventory | 232–33
Table C.2: Items and Descending Array of Z-Scores for Gender Schema | 235–36
Table C.3: Correlations between Self-Schema Types | 237
Table C.4: Thirty-four Self-schema Consensus Items | 238–39
Table C.5: Items Distinguishing between Self-schema Types One and Two | 240
Table C.6: Items Distinguishing between Self-schema Types One and Three | 241
Table C.7: Items Distinguishing between Self-schema Types Two and Three | 242
Table C.8: Classification Function Coefficients for Self-Schema Types (Fisher's Linear Discriminant Functions) | 244
Table E.1: "Cross-Sex-Typed" Messages | 254
Table E.2: Factor Analysis of Bem Sex Role Inventory | 256–57
Table E.3: Factor Analysis of Cross-Sex-Typed Message Characteristics | 257–58
Table E.4: Usage: Mean Ratings and Difference Scores | 260
Table E.5: Message Characteristic Mean Ratings | 261
Table E.6: Message Usage Cell Means by Gender Schematicity and Churchedness | 261–62
Table E.7: Multiple Comparisons of Usage and Assertiveness Ratings | 262
Table F.1: "Masculine" Themed Christian Worldview Statements | 267
Table F.2: Usage Ratings for Feminine and Masculine Christian Statements by Churched and Unchurched Men and Women | 269

List of Figures

Figure 1.1: Values Most Sought in Pastors by Laity | 15

Figure 1.2: Values Sought in Leaders of Business and Industry | 16

Figure 2.1: Color-Coded Gender and Generation Attendance Photo | 25

Figure 2.2: Jehosephat Church Participation by Males, Birth to Age 34 (Percent Males within Each Age Group) | 29

Figure 2.3: Jehosephat Church Total Men and Women in Contemporary Worship (Percentages) | 30

Figure 2.4: Jehosephat Church Total Men and Women in Traditional Worship (Percentages) | 31

Figure 2.5: Jehosephat Church Contemporary Worship Generational Attendance (Percentages within Age Groups) | 31

Figure 2.6: Jehosephat Church Traditional Worship Generational Attendance (Percentages within Age Groups) | 32

Figure 2.7: Men's Participation in External Ministries (Percent Males within Each Age Group) | 33

Figure 3.1: Gender Schematicity in Men, Non-Church vs. Church | 44

Figure 3.2: Gender Schematicity in Non-Church Men | 44

Figure 3.3: Gender Schematicity in Church Men | 45

Figure 5.1: Likelihood of "Feminine" Message Use by Non-Church vs. Church Men | 88

Figure 5.2: Gender Schematicity in Church Sample | 89

Figure 5.3: Gender Schematicity in Non-Church Sample | 89

LIST OF FIGURES

Figure 5.4: Likelihood of "Feminine" Message Use by Non-Church vs. Church by Gender Schematicity | 91

Figure 5.5: Likelihood of "Masculine" Statement Use by Non-Church vs. Church Men and Women | 96

Figure 5.6: Likelihood of "Feminine" Message Use by Church vs. Non-Church Men and Women | 96

Figure 7.1: The Focus of Men's Attention | 141

Figure 7.2: The Focus of Women's Concern | 142

Figure 7.3: Frequency of Word Usage On Facebook by Gender | 150

Figure 7.4: Ted Talks vs. Sermons, Powerless Language Indicators per Minute | 156

Figure 7.5: Ted Talks vs. Staff Welcome/Announcements, Powerless Language Indicators per Minute | 157

Figure 8.1: Powerless Language Indicator Card | 163

Figure 8.2: Galilee Church Staff Members' Powerless Language Indicators per Minute (PLIpm) in Worship, 10 Week Average | 175

Figure 8.3: Galilee Church Campus Pastors' Powerless Language Indicators per Minute (PLIpm) in Pre-Sermon Set-Up | 176

Figure 8.4: Galilee Church Lead vs. Campus Pastor's Powerless Language Indicators per Minute (PLIpm) in Sermon | 176

Figure 9.1: The Pulled Back Pendulum | 208

Figure D.1: Values Most Sought in Pastors by Laity | 250

Figure D.2: Values Sought in Leaders of Business and Industry | 250

Permissions

All Scripture quotations, unless otherwise indicated, are taken from the Holy Bible, New International Version®, NIV®. Copyright ©1973, 1978, 1984, 2011 by Biblica, Inc.™ Used by permission of Zondervan. All rights reserved worldwide. www.zondervan.com. The "NIV" and "New International Version" are trademarks registered in the United States Patent and Trademark Office by Biblica, Inc.™

Photo of Billy Sunday preaching from the Billy and Ma Sunday Archive at Grace College and Seminary. Used by permission.

Photos of the Men's Bible Classes of the First Methodist Episcopal Church of Vandalia, IL (1911), the First Christian Church, Canton, OH (1912), and the First Methodist Episcopal Church of Lancaster, OH (1915) published by The Library of Congress. Used by permission.

Photo of the Men's Bible Class of the First Methodist Episcopal Church of Westbrook, ME (1917) published by Dr. Hugh Blackmer. Used by permission.

Photo of the Men's Bible Class, First Baptist Church, Charleston, WV (1923) published by The West Virginia Division of Culture and History. Used by permission.

Photo of the Men's Bible Class, Broadway Christian Church, Lexington, KY (1947) published by The University of Kentucky Special Collections Research Center. Used by permission.

Portions of *Why Men Hate Going to Church* by David Murrow © 2005, 2011, published by Thomas Nelson. Used by permission.

Song "Falling In Love With Jesus" Words and Music by Jonathan Butler © 2002 Universal Music Brentwood Benson Songs (BMI) (adm. at CapitolCMGPublishing.com) / Warner-Tamerlane Publishing Corp. And Ranjo Music. All Rights

Administered by Warner-Tamerlane Publishing Corp. All Rights Reserved. Used By Permission of Alfred Music. All rights reserved. Used by permission.

Portions of "Women Told to Speak Their Minds to Get On in Boardrooms" © 2011, published by The Guardian News and Media, Ltd. Used by permission.

Portions of *The Church Impotent* by Leon Podles, © 1999, published by Spence. Used by permission.

Portions of "How Do You Get Rejected by eHarmony? Start By Telling the Truth" by Susan Isaacs. Used by permission.

Portions of *Just Lead* by Sherry Surratt and Jenni Catron © 2013, published by Jossey-Bass. Used by permission.

Foreword

THE NET LOSSES IN the membership strength of all of the mainline denominations in the USA appears to be, largely, a significant loss in the numbers of men who now join churches, and a very significant loss in the numbers of men who attend and are otherwise involved.

We do not have enough statistical data to fully characterize these losses. (No denomination's churches, for instance, record and report how many men and how many women attended church last Sunday.) But, a generation ago, Lyle Schaller discerned that, in the 1950's, the ratio of men to women in a great many churches was approximately 46 or 47 men to every 53 or 54 women; by the mid-1980's, the ratio was approximately 40 to 60. We had partly lost, or never had, a whole generation of men. Today, as one can often count 35 to 65 in many congregations, or even 30 to 70, we can make that two generations.

A foreword lacks the space to sufficiently account for this tragic trend, or to unpack the many interventions that church leaders could engage in to reverse this downward trend. That, of course, is what this fine book will do for a generation of church leaders.

Woody Davis has undoubtedly been tracking, researching, and reflecting upon this issue longer than anyone else. This book's time has come!

George G. Hunter III
Dean and Distinguished Professor, Emeritus
Asbury Theological Seminary

Preface

WHAT MAKES THIS BOOK SO DIFFERENT?

It's not your daddy's "Men's Ministry" book, nor your mommy's "Inclusive Language" book.

FOR ONE THING, THE appeal of existing books on the missing men has been limited primarily to evangelical church laymen, their pastors, and leaders of parachurch and denominational men's ministries. But this book isn't really about men's ministry. It's about the church's ministry as a whole and how different types of men and women respond to it. For another, it is the only book that discusses the church's gender gap in the context of inclusive language—a topic whose appeal has been largely limited to progressive academic faculty, clergy, and university educated laywomen. *Church Talk Makes Men Walk* seeks to bring the men's ministry audience and the inclusive language audience together. Third, it is the only book on the subject that is a multi-disciplinary work that stands on solid communication research and draws on the fields of linguistics, psychology, church history, theology, and biblical exegesis. Because of this breadth and depth it is able to demonstrate that the same factors that have driven most men from the church have driven like-minded women away as well.

Finally, the purpose of this book is to move the gender gap from the margins to the center of the church's awareness and efforts. Therefore, it is written for the full leadership of the church—for leaders from all denominations and across the full theological spectrum; for both lay and clergy; and for men and women. And that includes the men and women who train those leaders, i.e. the faculty, leaders, and students of Christian colleges, universities, and parachurch ministries, as well as seminaries, and graduate schools of theology. A breakthrough to the gatekeepers in each context—local church, denominational, and educational—is critical if the church as a whole is to reverse its gender gap. To that end, *Church Talk Makes Men Walk* uniquely provides both the research documentation necessary for credibility in the academy, and the practical application necessary for usefulness in the local church.

I got by with a little help from my friends—especially those who disagreed with me. The process that resulted in *Church Talk Makes Men Walk* started thirty years ago. It has been a long and arduous journey that I never would have completed without the support and encouragement and challenge of my family, mentors, and friends. Chief among them have been my wife, Linda—without whom the journey would never have begun and would have stalled several times along the way—and our daughter, Leah, and son, Jeremy, both of whom put up with being guinea pigs as they grew up and became ardent supporters and helpful critics as adults. Dr. George Hunter, III at Asbury Theological Seminary and the late Dr. Robert Bostrom at the University of Kentucky helped set the trajectory of the research and raised critical questions that tightened its focus. Finally there are those too numerous to name—fellow professors and pastors, doctoral students, laymen and laywomen, and those outside the church, both "nones" and "dones." They have read developing drafts, raised questions, identified holes, pushed and challenged, criticized and cajoled, been royal pains and heaven-sent gifts. I pray God will gift you in similar ways. The pages that follow are a result of a team effort, including that of Wipf and Stock, whom I want to thank for finding a way to publish a book as risky as this. Please honor all who have contributed to it by *acting* on what you read.

1

The Missing Men

HOW TO READ THIS BOOK

You have picked up this book because you are concerned about the church's gender gap—that is, the problem of its missing men. You should know that this is not your typical book on the subject. Because of that, this book calls for the following suggestions for how to read it:

Assume the "Most . . . " There are a number of what appear to be "allness" statements throughout the book—things like, "Men are. . . ." You will be tempted to think, "Well not all men are like that." And then you will begin thinking of all the different men who prove your point. Instead of doing that, assume that there is a "Most" or "Many" or some other qualifier at the beginning or end of that statement. If I were to include one of those with every statement that could have one we would have to add twenty to thirty pages to the length of the book. As you read such statements remind yourself that they are descriptive, not evaluative. A major portion of the emotional heat in discussions of gender issues is from the value judgments people place on factual data. Even worse are those that they wrongly attribute to others in the discussion.

Forget nature vs. nurture. It is a false dichotomy. Both of these forces contribute to everything human. And even if there were something that was attributable solely to nurture, it wouldn't matter. As followers of Christ we are called to deal with people as they are, not as we think they should have been. We cannot go back and change their nurture. Neither can we enter all the families of the world and make them nurture the next generations according to our assumptions and priorities. Besides, the nature/nurture debate is a red herring. It is a means of sidestepping the issue at hand and arguing something that can never be proven one way or the other. Let it go, and ask the Holy Spirit, "What do you want to teach me today?"

Don't sweat the research. There is a lot of it in this book. It is there to provide the evidence that led to the conclusions and recommendations I make. If you are not a social science researcher you could get bogged down in the details. I have tried to translate and summarize the research as much as possible. If research is not your thing, you can get the gist of it from the body of the text and the graphs and charts, photos, and figures. On the other hand if you just love reading research or you need additional evidence, the footnotes and appendices should give you all you desire.

Read it with a friend—or five. This book is going to make you think, and thinking is hard work. Hard work is always more fun when you're not alone, when you have someone to share the load. So, if you are not reading this book as part of a class in seminary or college or your church, get some friends to join you. You will laugh together at the funny stuff. You will help each other through the tough stuff. And each of you will see applications and implications that the others, nor I, have seen.

Suspend judgment. If you read something that makes you want to shout, "Yesss!" and pump your fist, back off on your enthusiasm. I would be glad for your agreement, but there is a danger lurking beneath the surface. When we have repeated thoughts, they wear a neural pathway that sets them ever deeper in our worldview. The more emotion we attach to them, the deeper they are set. The unseen danger is this: that depth and that emotion make it more difficult for us to hear what others are saying, even when the "other" is the Holy Spirit. Conversely, if you read something that makes you want to shout, "What?!!!" and start thinking of counter-arguments, shut down your criticism. I was dragged kicking and screaming to some of the conclusions in this book. When I complained to God about this the Holy Spirit said, "Read *my* Book. Most of the people in there didn't want to hear what I was saying either. My thoughts are not your thoughts." Rather than arguing against the thought you want to criticize, think of ways and circumstances where it might be true. If you are like me, you might just hear a still, small voice.

THE DAY THE LIGHTS CAME ON

It had been an amazing few weeks. Sunday after Sunday the altar railing had been filled with people coming to faith, or coming back to faith, or taking a new step of faith.

> "It's been quite a month, hasn't it?" said one of the church leaders as we stood in the warm, North Carolina sun. "I've never seen so many people at the altar week after week."
> "Yeah, it's been great," I said, basking in the glow of pastoral success.
> "One thing bothers me, though," she said.
> "What's that," I asked.
> "Why are they all women?"

That question cast a light brighter than the sun on that spring day in 1984. It brought into sharp relief a contrast I had not noticed either in my years as a YoungLife leader or as a pastor. In the years since I have found few pastors or laypersons who had noticed that their congregations were made up of more women than men. Even with the publication of a number of books on the subject, most notably David Murrow's *Why Men Hate Going to Church*, people still seem either unaware or unconcerned about the congregational gender gap.

I recently visited a church whose pastor is a friend. This church has shown remarkable growth, expanding to four campuses and multiple ministries that impact thousands of people. The pastor is in high demand as a conference speaker across the country. As we talked before the service, he told me that he had spoken at a conference in New England the previous week.

> He said he asked the man who picked him up at the airport, "What is the biggest problem you face in the church in New England?"
> "A lack of men," the man said. "You have a lot of men in your church, don't you?"
> "A lot of men," my friend told me he had said. "In all areas—worship, children's ministry . . . "

When I took the count at two of his campuses' worship services that morning, the results were 37 percent men vs. 63 percent women at one, and 38 percent men vs. 62 percent women at the other. My friend's misperception is not unusual. If there are enough people present, the imbalance isn't immediately obvious. Yet it is present almost everywhere.

THE 50-YEAR SLIDE

Perhaps we don't notice the gender gap because it has snuck up on us gradually over time. Now, this is a book about communication. "Church Talk" is the topics we choose, the words we use, and the way we put them together. More importantly, it's about how our talk not only *reflects* the realities with which we in the church currently cope, but also has *helped to create* them. But to understand that, we must first understand the flow of history that has brought us to this point.

According to Lyle Schaller, in the 1950s church participation by women and men mirrored the ratio of women to men in America.[1] It was a different era in that day. In the years following World War II church participation reached its highest point in well over 100 years. Religious sentiment was so strong that the phrase "under God" was inserted into the Pledge of Allegiance at the urging of the then recently-baptized President Eisenhower[2] with hardly a whisper of protest.[3] The church and synagogue were thought of as the third leg of the three-legged stool of public institutions that supported American society: government, education, and religion.

No one seemed to remember that, just seventy-three years before, the church was in such decline that Robert Ingersoll, known in the late

---

1. Schaller, *It's a Different World*, 61–62.

2. Though raised in a highly religious family, Eisenhower had no formal religious affiliation until he became president. Following a visit with Rev. Billy Graham, the President undertook catechetical instruction with Rev. Edward Elson, pastor of the National Presbyterian Church and was baptized there less than a year before the amendment to the pledge was made. See David Eisenhower's *Going Home to Glory* for a discussion of the spiritual aspects of President Eisenhower's character.

3. "Prior to February 1954, no endeavor to get the Pledge officially amended succeeded. The final successful push came from George MacPherson Docherty. Some American presidents honored Lincoln's birthday by attending services at the church Lincoln attended, New York Avenue Presbyterian Church by sitting in Lincoln's pew on the Sunday nearest February 12. On February 7, 1954, with President Eisenhower sitting in Lincoln's pew, the church's pastor, George MacPherson Docherty, delivered a sermon based on the Gettysburg Address titled 'A New Birth of Freedom.' He argued that the nation's might lay not in arms but its spirit and higher purpose. He noted that the Pledge's sentiments could be those of any nation, that 'there was something missing in the pledge, and that which was missing was the characteristic and definitive factor in the American way of life.' He cited Lincoln's words 'under God' as defining words that set the United States apart from other nations. President Eisenhower had been baptized a Presbyterian very recently, just a year before. He responded enthusiastically to Docherty in a conversation following the service. Eisenhower acted on his suggestion the next day and on February 8, 1954, Rep. Charles Oakman (R-Mich.), introduced a bill to that effect. Congress passed the necessary legislation and Eisenhower signed the bill into law on Flag Day, June 14, 1954." http://en.wikipedia.org/wiki/Pledge_of_Allegiance, (accessed September 20, 2012).

nineteenth century as "The Great Agnostic," was able to say, "The churches are dying out all over the land. They are struck with death. By the dawn of the twentieth century, churches will be but relics of a bygone age."[4] Neither did anyone in the 1950s seem to remember that some sixty years earlier the church had woken up to the reality that it needed to address its increasing loss of men. For example, in the 1890s Billy Sunday left a promising professional baseball career to become an evangelist.

Billy Sunday preparing to preach to a men's meeting
in his Princeton, Illinois campaign in 1906.[5]

At that time he stated that one of his prime motives was to reach men with a man's gospel. Sunday became the Billy Graham of the early twentieth century. He included both men's-only and women's-only gatherings in his missions. His audiences in these sessions numbered in the thousands. Commenting on why men had vacated the church, the evangelist said, "The Lord save us from off-handed, flabby-cheeked, brittle-boned, weak-kneed, thin-skinned, pliable, plastic, spineless, effeminate, ossified, three-carat Christianity."

No one in the 1950s seemed to remember that Billy Sunday's (and others') preaching missions, together with The Men's Bible Study Movement, The Institutional Church Movement,[6] and The Men and Religion Forward

---

4. Keynote address at The American Society of Freethinkers, 1881.

5. Photo of Billy Sunday reprinted and used by permission of the Archives and Special Collections of Morgan Library, Grace College & Seminary, Winona Lake, IN.

6. The origin of the phrase "the institutional church" is from this movement that sought "to cover the entire life of man" by operating like an institution—organizing

Movement had helped turn churches where men had been conspicuous by their absence into churches with double and triple digit men's classes and ministries that reached men on the streets, in the bars, and in the pool halls.

Today no one seems to remember those days, even though many church members' fathers and grandfathers were among those triple-digit classes. In a focus group during a consultation with a church, one of the church leaders said, "The men aren't very involved. But, you know, men aren't as religious as women." Yet in the hallway outside that room were pictures like these:

The Men's Bible Class of the First Methodist Episcopal Church of Vandalia, IL, May 7, 1911[7]

Men's Class, First Christian Church Sunday School, Canton, OH, June 7, 1912[8]

---

committees, departments, experts, ministries, and services. Abell, *Urban Impact*, 137. Services included providing meals, athletics, gymnastics, kindergarten and day nurseries, legal training, coffee houses, libraries, health and first-aid instructions, and more.

7. Reprinted and used by permission of First United Methodist Church, Vandalia, IL. Source: The Library of Congress, https://www.loc.gov/item/2007661805/ (accessed April 5, 2015).

8. Reprinted and used by permission of the Library of Congress. Source: http://www.loc.gov/pictures/resource/pan.6a26395/ (accessed April 5, 2015).

"Largest Bible class in the world, 1316," Men's Bible Class, First Methodist Episcopal Church, Lancaster, OH, April 18th, 1915[9]

The Men's Bible Class of the First Methodist Episcopal Church of Westbrook, ME, Feb. 15, 1917[10]

9. Reprinted and used by permission of First United Methodist Church, Lancaster, OH. Source: The Library of Congress, https://www.loc.gov/item/2007661753/ (accessed April 5, 2015).

10. Reprinted and used by permission of Dr. Hugh Blackmer. Source: https://www.flickr.com/photos/blackmerh/83479264/ (accessed August 20, 1916).

Men's Bible Class, First Baptist Church, Charleston, WV, 1923[11]

The Men's Bible Class of the Broadway Christian Church of Lexington, KY, 1947[12]

    11. Reprinted and used by permission of First Baptist Church, Charleston, WV. Source: The West Virginia Division of Culture and History, http://www.wvculture.org/archives/images/celebrating%20lives/bhm10.jpg (accessed April 5, 2015).

    12. Reprinted and used by permission of the University of Kentucky Special

I see these photos dating from the 1910s to the 1950s in churches across the country. But they have become part of the wallpaper, unnoticed and forgotten. The gradual slide from the 1960s to today has brought us back to where men's participation in the church stood at the turn of the twentieth century. By 2008 the U.S. Congregational Life Survey reported that men's participation in worship had dropped to 39 percent of the congregation.[13] By 2011 the Barna Group reported that the percentage of men in the general population who attended church had fallen from 42 percent in 1991 to 36 percent in 2011,[14] and we had returned to the belief that "it has always been this way." One man commented on the Flikr.com posting of the Westbrook M.E. Church photo above, "Yeah, yeah. As though you'd get that many in a bible [sic] class. All done with mirrors."[15]

Why the Slide?

I believe we must look at the general population's changing perceptions of Christians to find an answer. From the 1940s through the early 1960s the vast majority of North Americans held Christians in positive regard. Films such as "The Robe" (1953), "The Ten Commandments" (1955), and "King of Kings" (1961) that drew from the Judeo-Christian tradition were highly popular. Perhaps influenced by stories of the heroism and integrity of WWII chaplains,[16] the clergy were highly respected. So much so, in fact, that it was considered possible and profitable to make positive biographical films about high profile pastors, such as "A Man Called Peter" (Rev. Peter Marshall)

Collections Research Center. Source: https://exploreuk.uky.edu/catalog/xt7z348g-g9oh_8_576 (accessed April 5, 2015).

13. Bruce, "Wave II," 2009.
14. Barna, *Futurecast*, 201–218.
15. Reprinted and used by permission. Source: https://www.flickr.com/photos/blackmerh/83479264/ (accessed August 5, 2016).
16. For example, newsreel footage showed Medal of Honor recipient Lieutenant Commander Joseph T. O'Callahan, the USS Franklin chaplain, who administered the last rites, organized and directed firefighting and rescue parties, and led men below to wet down ammunition magazines that threatened to explode. Or this example: Time Magazine ran the an article on February 12, 1951 telling the story four U.S. Army chaplains aboard the troop ship, USS Dorchester who brought order to the torpedoed ships decks. They got the men into life preservers and when there were no more, they took theirs off and gave them to four young G.I.s. The story concluded, "... some 600 men were lost, but the heroic chaplains had helped save over 200. The last anyone saw of them, they were standing on the slanting deck, their arms linked, in prayer." http://www.time.com/time/magazine/article/0,9171,820639,00.html#ixzz10NwLzwRU (accessed September 23, 2010).

and "The Norman Vincent Peale Story." Portrayals of priests and pastors in film and television were positive and consistent with traditional masculine stereotypes. For example, in the 1944 film, "Going My Way," Father Chuck O'Malley as played by Bing Crosby plays golf, stickball, and jazz piano. In the 1962–63 television series Gene Kelly adds baseball and basketball to Father O'Malley's resume. According to Richard Wolff, the series was

> unwaveringly set on portraying the priest as a positive, iconic social force in American life . . . this involves social activism on the part of the priest, who must battle and overcome racism, poverty, the sources of juvenile delinquency, family crises or indifference to those in need. . . . The emphasis is on the religious figure's role in transforming the secular world.

Then, right on time, according to William Strauss and Neil Howe's generational theory, there came an Awakening. The Boomers came of age in a time of spiritual reflection, a turning from an outward focus on the world to an inward focus on the spirit. Like the Idealist generations before us, we Boomers grew up closer to our mothers than our fathers, with an anti-institutional, anti-authority bias that set us at odds with those who had built, managed, and led the major organizations of society. We followed in the footsteps of our Idealist forebears, who "in every generational cycle have given spiritual awakenings an anti-masculine flavor."[17] Beginning with the Jesus People and increasing until today the primary Christian defense phrase became, "It's not a religion, it's a relationship!" Pastoral training began to be heavily influenced by psychology, to the point that sermon series in many churches could be (and often are) chapters in the latest self-help book. The pastor's role gradually shifted to that of primary care-giver for the congregation and pastoral visitation became psycho-social support rather than the "cure of souls." This had become so true by the early 80s that my parishioners were shocked when I asked them about their spiritual journey or the story of their faith. More than a few said, "We've never had a pastor ask about this stuff before." When I have recommended the practice to pastors in recent years, several have said something like, "Oh I couldn't do that.

---

17. Strauss and Howe, *Generations*, 102. Strauss and Howe's work is vital for understanding the ebb and flow of men's participation in the church. The cycle is driven by the pendulum swing of parenting styles from over-protective to under-protective in response to a secular crisis at one end and a spiritual awakening at the other. Accompanying that swing is a societal shift in mindset from one that is outwardly directed to one that is inwardly directed. This shift has a profound impact on churches' ministries, which in turn affects the gender mix of the church.

My people would think I was prying." It makes me think of Father Mulcahy on the old TV series, M.A.S.H.—weak, bumbling, wimpish.[18]

I said above that I believe we must look at the people's perceptions of Christians if we are to understand the 50-year slide. But you need more than a few references to films and televisions shows. So did I. We are about to begin a journey that will dig into those perceptions. Put on your boots; it's going to get deep.

Perceptions of Christians

In 1986 I began studying the missing men in earnest. I started by interviewing fifty-four men, age twenty to sixty-four, both unchurched and those who had come to faith and church membership within the previous two years. Nine churches (six growing, two declining, and one static), representing four denominations (United Methodist, Southern Baptist, Christian, and Free Methodist) and located in five states (Indiana, Ohio, Kentucky, Georgia, and North Carolina) were included in the sample. I was looking for what kept some men out of the church, and what brought others in. Several themes emerged from what the men said kept them outside the church—materialism, hypocrisy, irrelevance, etc. These are all common to other studies of the unchurched, both men and women.[19] But the one over-riding theme that was mentioned by every man and is mentioned only by men among the unchurched is, "It's unmanly." This is expressed in different ways. One says, "That stuff's for women and kids." Another says, "They can't make it, so they hide behind God." Another says, "All the Christians I know are wimps."[20]

Since these men appeared to be perceiving Christians along a gender continuum,[21] I decided to see how strong this perception was. I constructed a follow-up study[22] in which I selected sixty adjectives and descriptive phrases out of some 250 used in the studies of sex role and sex stereotyping. Research conducted across forty years has demonstrated that thirty of

---

18. In case you're wondering, yes, there were a couple families who left the church after that. But for most, the floodgates opened as if they had been dying for someone with the courage to "ask about this stuff."

19. See Hale, *The Unchurched*, 1980. Kunjufu, *Adam!*, 1994.

20. Davis, "Men and the Church," 50.

21. See Appendix A: Research on Gender Across the Cultures for a representative list of research and writing from the fields of anthropology, psychology, sociology, linguistics, and communication documenting the widespread existence of gender associations that are held in common. It is this set of common associations that is referred to here as a gender continuum.

22. See Appendix B: Perceptions of Christians for a detailed description of this study.

the descriptions are associated with "feminine" in North American culture, while the other thirty are associated with "masculine."[23] However, when the descriptions are presented in random order without reference to gender, their gender relationship is not evident. The participants sorted the sixty descriptions along a continuum from "most like a good Christian" to "least like a good Christian" without reference to gender.

My assumptions were these: 1.) If it is true that being a Christian means being perceived more in feminine terms and/or less masculine ones, it should be revealed when people rate these descriptions in terms of their perceptions of Christians. That is, if being a Christian means being more feminine, then those items rated "most Christian" should be predominantly those that are perceived as feminine when sorted on a gender continuum. 2.) If being a Christian also means being less masculine, then the items rated "least Christian" should be predominantly those perceived as masculine. 3.) If, on the other hand, gender is not an issue in people's perceptions of Christians, then there should be no consistent effect in the rating of the gender items.

When I ran the statistical analysis of the responses, a whopping forty-three out of the total sixty items emerged as consensus items.[24] These represent the perceptions of Christians shared by all the participants. Take a look at Table 1.1. What stands out about this consensus is that, with only two exceptions, all items identified as "like a good Christian" and all those identified as "*most* like a good Christian"[25] are feminine. In contrast, with only three exceptions, all items identified as "not like a good Christian" and all but one of those identified as "*least* like a good Christian"[26] are masculine. Clearly the

---

23. These associations were confirmed in both a preliminary study involving separate participants and a post-test involving the participants of the Perceptions of Christians study (See Appendix C: Gender Schemas and Self-Schemas). In both studies the participants sorted the descriptions from "most feminine to least feminine" and then in "most masculine to least masculine." In the Perceptions of Christians study these sorts were performed after the "like/not like a good Christian" sort so that gender associations would not be raised in their consciousness in their perceptions of Christians.

24. Consensus items are those for which the average z-scores in each type are within one standard deviation of the average z-scores in the other two types. A z-score shows where an item lies along a continuum. The closer the number is to zero, the more in the middle it is. The larger the number, whether positive or negative, the more toward the end. So, a z-score of 1.743 is at the "most like" end, and z-score of -1.935 is at the "most NOT like" end of the continuum.

25. "Like a good Christian" items are those whose z-scores greater than zero and less than 1.00). Those identified as "most like a good Christian" are those whose z-scores were 1.00 or greater.

26. Items identified as "not like a good Christian" have z-scores less than zero and greater than -1.00. Items identified as "most not like a good Christian" have z-scores -1.00 or less.

stereotypical Christian (a good one at any rate) is decidedly feminine in the positive sense and is decidedly not masculine in the negative sense.

Table 1.1: Perceptions of Christians: Consensus Items and Sextype
(F and M refer to Feminine and Masculine items respectively; +, o, and - refer respectively to positive, neutral, or negative cultural valuation.)

DESCRIPTION	SEXTYPE	DESCRIPTION	SEXTYPE
MOST LIKE A GOOD CHRISTIAN		LEAST LIKE A GOOD CHRISTIAN	
Sensitive to others' needs	F+	Fickle	F-
Aware of the feelings of others	F+	Feel superior	M-
Trusting	F+	Lack tact	M-
Devote myself to others	F+	Forceful	M+
Understanding	F+	Mischievous	M-
Sincere	F+	Cynical	M-
Devout	F+	Selfish	M-
Helpful	F+	Use harsh language	M-
Gentle	F+	NOT LIKE A GOOD CHRISTIAN	
Express tender feelings	Fo	Logical	M+
LIKE A GOOD CHRISTIAN		Know the ways of the world	M+
Cooperative	F+	Ambitious	Mo
Warm	F+	Dynamic	M+
Polite	F+	Cautious	Fo
Sentimental	Fo	Assertive	M+
Home-oriented	F+	Skilled in business	M+
Modest	F+	Like math and science	Mo
Sociable	F+	Competitive	Mo
Meditative	Fo	Manly	M+
Active	F+	Adventurous	M+
		Wimpy	F-
		Stern	M-
		Dominant	M-
		Aggressive	M-

WHAT THE CHURCH WANTS

Yet that realization is not clear to everyone. In 1993 the Office of Research of the United Methodist Church published a study of values or characteristics lay leaders wanted in their pastors.[27] It was modeled on a study of leadership characteristics by James Kouzes and Barry Posner, published in their book *Credibility: How Leaders Gain It and Lose It, Why It Matters*. Here is the list of characteristics generated by United Methodist lay leaders as those they most valued in pastors: Imaginative, Dependable, Loyal, Ambitious, Mature, Fair-minded, Courageous, Honest, Supportive, Straight-forward, Competent, Spiritual, Determined, Intelligent, Cooperative, Forward-looking, Inspiring, Self-controlled, Independent, Broad-minded, and Caring.

What they did not see is that these adjectives and descriptive phrases also appear in the studies of sex roles and sex stereotyping. Table 1.2 shows how they have broken down in those studies:

Table 1.2: Gender Labels of Values Sought in Pastors

FEMININE	NEUTRAL	MASCULINE
Caring	Fair-minded	Independent
Cooperative	Broad-minded	Determined
Spiritual	Inspiring	Courageous
Self-controlled	Intelligent	Straight-forward
Loyal	Competent	Forward-looking
Supportive	Mature	Imaginative
Fair-minded	Dependable	Ambitious

Most telling are the percentages of the lay leaders who selected each of these characteristics. Look at Table 1.3.

Table 1.3: Percentage of Laity Selecting Each Value in Pastors

FEMININE	NEUTRAL	MASCULINE
Caring 44%	Fair-minded 42%	Independent 3%

---

27. Office of Research, *Pastoral Leadership*, 1993.

FEMININE	NEUTRAL	MASCULINE
Cooperative 42%	Broad-minded 19%	Determined 3%
Spiritual 24%	Inspiring 16%	Courageous 3%
Self-controlled 12%	Intelligent 10%	Straight-forward 2%
Loyal 11%	Competent 3%	Forward-looking 2%
Supportive 9%	Mature 2%	Imaginative 0.9%
Fair-minded 2%	Dependable 1%	Ambitious 0.5%

No masculine item was chosen by more than 3 percent of the lay leaders! Now look at the composite of those percentages in the same categories in graphic form in Figure 1.1.

Figure 1.1: Values Most Sought in Pastors by Laity

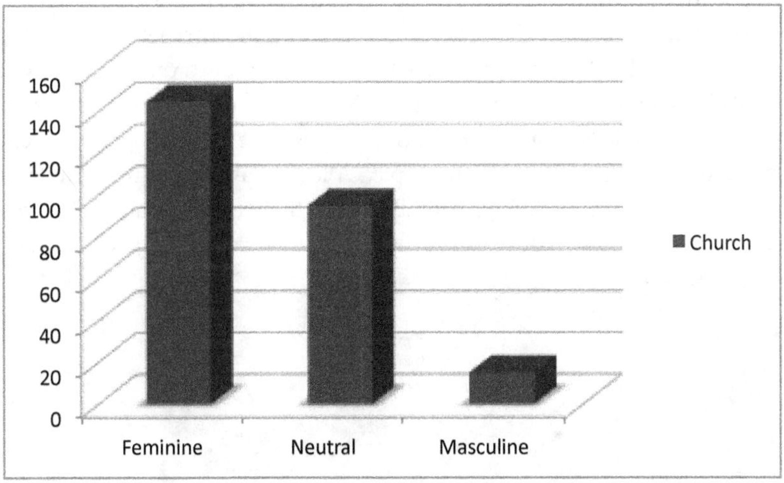

Notice the pattern. The underlying gender continuum reveals a clear preference for characteristics that most cultures around the world consider feminine.[28] In contrast, look at the pattern for the same items in Kouzes and

28. John Williams and Deborah Best conducted a study of gender perceptions in twenty countries representing each of the major cultural regions of the world. In it

Posner's study for what values are sought in leaders of business and industry in Figure 1.2.[29]

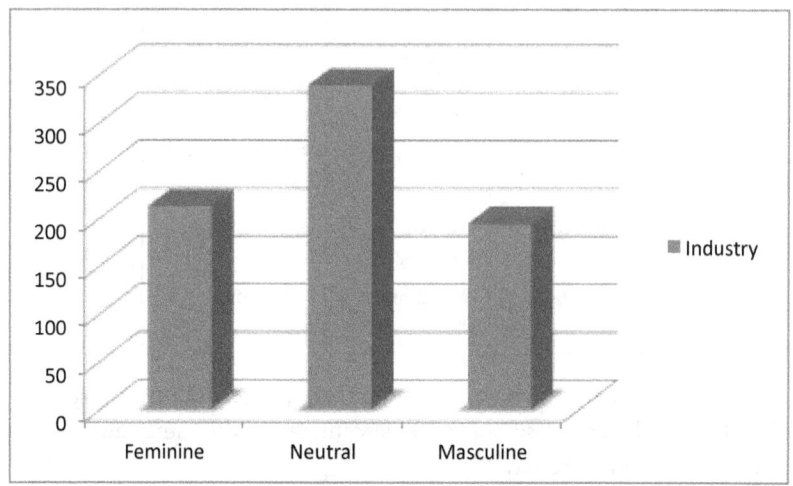

Figure 1.2: Values Sought in Leaders of Business and Industry

Compare the pattern in this chart to the previous one. The influence of a gender continuum that is so evident in the values preferred for pastors is completely lacking with regard to business and industry leaders. What is significant is that the church, unlike business and industry, is saying that it wants leaders (or rather, caregivers) who have feminine characteristics almost to the exclusion of masculine ones. As one Methodist superintendent told me during a seminar on this topic, "A lot of pastor-parish committees say they won't take a woman pastor. But when they tell me what kind of pastor they want, I say, "Look, you really want a woman pastor, just one that's in a man's skin."

---

they identified forty-nine characteristics considered masculine and twenty-five considered feminine in at least nineteen of the countries, with twenty-three of the forty-nine masculine items and fourteen of the twenty-five feminine items being found in twenty-two of the twenty-five countries. (See Williams and Best, *Sex and Psyche*, 152–57.) The majority of the masculine and feminine items in the United Methodist study are either identical, similar to, or synonyms of items in the Williams & Best study.

29. For more detailed comparisons, see Appendix D: Detailed Comparison Of Values Sought In Pastors vs. Industry Leaders.

The Result of What the Church Wants

The result? What the church wants, the church gets. In 2001 two separate studies, one of over 1,300 British Methodist ministers[30] and one of 900 Anglican ministers[31] found that the male clergy in both studies in several ways displayed characteristically feminine personality traits. For example, they were "more deferential, emotionally sensitive, more rule-conscious, and more in need of others' approval." In another study male ministers were shown to have the lowest testosterone levels compared to men of other occupations. Their testosterone levels were significantly lower than every other occupation tested.[32] All this is reminiscent of the notion of clergy as "a kind of third sex" in latter half of nineteenth century.[33]

Significantly, the studies of the British Methodist and Anglican clergy also found that that the female clergy displayed a number of characteristically male personality traits. Robbins, Leslie, Haley, and Kay concluded that while "ministry may appeal particularly to men who value and display the tender-minded personality characteristics associated with femininity . . . ministry may appeal particularly to women who value and display the stable personality characteristics associated with masculinity."[34] The laymen I have interviewed who have "trail-blazing" women pastors would support this view. These are women who have been the first female pastor or first female senior pastor a church has had. They also have stuck it out over the long haul. The men in these pastors' churches have said things like, "I wasn't too sure about a woman pastor, but she's tough," or "She's a straight shooter," or "She doesn't pull any punches," or "She get's things done." The respect they have for their female pastor is obvious. But notice the things that stand out to these men. It appears that these women do tend to identify more with

---

30. Robbins, "Personality Characteristics," 2001.

31. Musson, "Male and Female Anglican Clergy," 2001.

32. Dabbs, et al., "Testosterone and Occupational Choice."

33. For example, "Religion is always the consecration of the past; never the spirit of the future working in the present; and the clergy, who, as Sidney Smith said, are a third sex—neither male nor female, but effeminate—are instinctively conservative, thoroughly enamored of what is, and obstinately averse to all radical changes. Their timidity would be quite phenomenal, if they were *not* the third sex; and, like all timid people, they can shriek and yell and curse and foam at the mouth when they are well frightened. Were it otherwise, were Christianity a real agency for social improvement, and the clergy the moral leaders of the people, we should have seen by this time a tremendous alteration in the condition, and the relations, of all classes of society. There might still be differences, but they would be on a higher plane, and less grievous and exasperating. As the case stands, all the best of the clergy can do is to preach harmless platitudes once a week."

34. Robbins, "Personality Characteristics," 128.

"masculine" values and characteristics. The fact that trail-blazing, long-term women pastors[35] frequently have more male congregants in their churches than male pastors do suggests that the content and style of their talk affect male participation in church more than gender.

WHERE ARE WE HEADED?

We began this chapter with a question: "Why are they all women?" The answer to that question, from the mouths of men who had voted with their feet, turned out to be that they perceived the church as a place for women and wimps. When we asked why that was the case, we found that the scale used in perceiving Christians and pastors was a gender continuum with all the weight on the feminine end. The church has lost its balance. It is as if most of the men (and women) who identify with the masculine end of the spectrum have gotten off the see-saw and left the rest of the church squatting on their haunches, unable to get off the ground. People outside and inside the church, both men and women, have almost exclusively feminine perceptions of the church because we are in the midst of at least a 40-year growth in communication styles and substance that, outside the church, women use and men avoid.

We (you and I) are the church. So you and I must ask ourselves, "What is it about our church talk that makes men walk?" Much of this chapter has focused on pastors. Certainly pastors have a large influence on the church's culture. But as the "women & wimps" comment shows, it is the church as a whole that puts men off. And, as we will see in chapter 3, the same things put off many women as well.

In 1987 Nancy Hardesty wrote in her well-balanced and helpful book, *Inclusive Language,* that non-inclusive language "offers a distorted gospel to Christians and those wanting to become Christians. It conveys the message that the Christian faith is for men only or at least for men primarily."[36] Ironically, she states this immediately after noting that the ratio of women to men in most churches is two to one. "Thus," she says, "the use of male language excludes roughly two thirds of any given congregation from the

---

35. I emphasize both "trail-blazing" and long-term women pastors in this discussion because this set of women pastors have a different personality and "presence" than those who have followed in their footsteps or do not stick it out. The extent to which many women pastors continue to be more effective in reaching men may change as the ministry opens up to more and more women who have different characteristics from these pioneers.

36. Hardesty, *Inclusive Language,* 92.

most meaningful participation."[37] This raises the question, if women are the ones who are feeling excluded, why are men largely absent from the pews? If our message is slanted toward men, why do mostly women respond? The common answer is that women are universally more religious than men.[38] But the data do not support that assumption. In 2006 a study of the World Values survey found " . . . the female advantage in religiousness is not universal. Distinguishing affective (personal piety) from active (organizational participation) religiousness, in a third of nations (World Values Survey) women are no higher than men in active religiousness."[39] And in 2015 an analysis of data from the General Social Survey in the United States found that "'Universal' gender differences seem to be a primarily Christian phenomenon. American women are generally more religious than men, but this does not extend to non-Christian groups. Furthermore, there is variation even among Christian groups, with women not revealing higher levels of religiosity for all measures."[40]

As we will see, it is indeed about language. But for men it is about far more than male-referent nouns and pronouns. For men it is about everything from the words we use to the topics we choose, from the sentence structures we employ to the vocal tones we enjoy. We will see that the church has been down this road before, and that there is hope for the future.

---

37. Ibid., 92.

38. The belief has become so widespread that sociologist Rodney Stark noted, "By now it is so taken for granted that women are more religious than men that every competent quantitative study of religiousness routinely includes sex as a control variable." Stark, "Physiology and Faith," 496.

39. See Sullins, "Gender and Religion," 838.

40. Schnabel, "How Religious," 621.

2

So What Should We Do?

THAT IS WHAT EVERYONE asks at this point. And it's great, as long as we're serious about doing something, and as long as we are willing to do what it takes for as long as it takes to see it through. There is no magic bullet. The quick and easy fix everyone wants does not exist. Just doing worship in a gymnasium and using the scoreboard clock to count down the sermon will not fix it. Decking out the speaker's platform at the men's retreat with motorcycles and footballs and fishing tackle will not fix it. Adding a couple small groups for men or starting a men's prayer breakfast will not fix it. Even building a killer men's ministry will not fix it. The issues are too deeply imbedded and broadly distributed in church culture for such things to have much effect. The race that lies before us is a marathon on the order of Pheidippides' legendary first one—run not over today's smooth, paved, gently graded roadways but over rocky mountainous terrain. It will not be quick, or easy, or comfortable.

A year and a half into my first appointment as associate pastor at a large county seat church, the district superintendent invited me to his office. There was a church in trouble, it seemed, and I was "the ideal person to go in and right the ship." Why? Because it was a new church start that had struggled for two years and I had come from the epicenter of the church growth movement. I had sat at the feet both of its founder, Donald McGavran, and his successor, C. Peter Wagner. I was a graduate of the Robert H. Schuller Institute for Successful Church Leadership. If anyone could turn this fledgling church into a soaring success, he said, it would be me. Two weeks later we arrived in our new home with an air of confidence and anticipation. Two years later we closed the church.

What went wrong? There were a number of contributing factors, of course, but one in particular is important for our discussion in this chapter. Apart from the way my jaundiced view of Robert Schuller and his ministry was changed during my experience at his institute,[1] two things stood out. The first was Dr. Schuller's little mantra, "Find a need and fill it, find a hurt and heal it." This, he said, was the secret to reaching people outside the church.[2] The second was his statement that he had knocked on over 3,000 doors in Orange County in the founding of Garden Grove Community Church. I loved the first. I hated the second.

Schuller knocked on 3,000 doors so he could ask people what their greatest need was. The people behind the doors most often said, "I don't know how to potty train my child." So he brought in a child psychologist to give a potty training seminar. Then he built relationships with those who attended and, over time, earned the right to share the gospel with them. Sharing the gospel didn't bother me. Knocking on doors did. Unlike Robert Schuller, but like many other clergy persons, I am an introvert. My Myers-Briggs Personality Profile is INTJ (or P—I'm right on the borderline between Judging and Perceiving). The shorthand version of that is I'm a Scientist/Thinker. I love figuring things out—"Oh, there's a need? Let's find its root and figure how we can fill it! There's a hurt? Let's find the best way to heal it!" However, I love doing that in the lab or the study, not on the street or in the community. Unlike an extravert, I am fed by time alone whereas meeting or being with a number of people drains me. So instead of knocking on 3,000 doors, I knocked on 300. And for every one of those, I walked up to the front porch praying that no one would be home so I could write a nice note on my business card, leave it in the door, and call it done. Instead of knocking on the other 2700 doors and talking with the actual people behind them, I studied the market research for the church's target neighborhoods. I developed needs profiles and analyzed which needs were likely to be shared by different segments of the population. We planned a series of helpful events—parenting training, marriage enrichment, divorce recovery, singles gatherings, etc. We promoted and prayed. Then we wondered why all those people, people with whom we had never connected, didn't come.

---

1. I know, you are wondering why I went if I felt that way. I went because it was a requirement for one of my courses at Fuller Theological Seminary.

2. Part of what changed my jaundiced view was learning that, like McGavran and Wagner, Schuller was adamant about connecting the gospel with those filled needs and healed hurts. This is the missing link that has jaundiced the church growth movement in many eyes. Without this, church growth *is* just about numbers. With it, it becomes about transformed lives that impact the world.

I tell that story because I'm about to ask you to do some things you won't want to do—things that don't fit your personality or that make you feel uncomfortable or that seem tedious or that take more time than you think you can spend. In the process of earning my PhD, I learned that those are the things that enable you to fulfill your call. As I have worked with churches across the country I have seen many pastors and lay leaders making the same mistake I did. They are staying within their comfort zone, hoping that God will do something miraculous on the outside to bring people in. But if we want our people to have faith, *we* must have faith. And you don't need faith if you stay where it is comfortable. I think Peter, the Church's first pastor would say, "Get out of the boat! You may get a little wet. You may sink a bit. But our Lord will lift you up!" (Matthew 14:22–33) Your first task, then, is this:

STOP READING AND PRAY

Invest the time to allow the Holy Spirit to align your thoughts with God's thoughts, your will with God's will. Ask God to enable you to make, and keep, the commitment to see this journey through. Ask the Holy Spirit to show you the men and women God is calling to join you on the journey. Who has God set apart to be the leadership team for this task? Ask God for those who will also seek and commit to God's will. Wait patiently. Listen intently. Write the names of those who come to mind on the Team Candidates page at the end of this chapter. As you pray, prioritize the list in terms of which God would have you speak with first, second, and so on. Then make appointments with each to explore whether he/she is truly God's choice. (Yes, "she"—you will not affect the church's culture as a whole without the involvement of some key women leaders. Without this, efforts to reach and involve men end up encapsulated and outside the rest of the system, merely a colostomy bag on the body of Christ.) Ask each person to read this and the previous chapter and to pray with you about being part of the team. Be clear that this is matter for mutual discernment. In other words, neither of you should assume that a desire on their part to be on the team is automatic confirmation of God's call. Too often we accept anyone who will say yes, or can't say no, and then wonder why we end up with poor or burned out leadership. Remember that, as with the sons of Jesse, the obvious choice is not always the right choice. Samuel must have been listening carefully to the Spirit's voice to have chosen David to anoint as king of Israel instead of one of his brothers (1 Samuel 16:1–16). As you start building your team begin your next task, which is:

THE FIRST BABY STEP: TRACK MEN'S PARTICIPATION IN YOUR CHURCH

Also too often in church life, we go off half-cocked. We realize we have a problem and we look around for solutions before we have a clear picture of our condition. We fan through the latest books and conduct internet searches and run off to conferences to find the things that "successful" churches are doing. Then we cherry-pick the activities that catch our fancy and try to pull them off in our church. In most cases there may be an initial period of excitement with a promising start that rapidly fades into disappointment and disillusionment. One reason this happens is that our conditions are different in key ways from those where the ministries we've chosen were developed. As the saying goes, there are three ways to be lost: you don't know where you are going, you don't know how to get there, or you don't know where you are. Even if you know where you want to go, if you don't know where you are, it's impossible to figure out how to get there.

So, the first step you need to take is to get accurate information on where you stand. When you don't feel well but can't put your finger on what it is or why, what does your doctor do? Gather as much information as possible in order to get an accurate and complete picture of your condition. You may be asked to keep a log of what you eat, when you eat, and how much you eat. You may be asked to keep a log of your symptoms, or your exercise. And you'll hate doing it. But you will gain critical information that will lead to an improvement in your health. The same is true regarding men's participation in your church. In fact you need to know this about all your people's participation, men and women, adults and children. What are the *actual* numbers of men and of women in each expression of spiritual life and ministry in the church and across the generations? To date, the difference between men's and women's participation has only been inferred from polls by Gallup, Barna etc., and has only dealt with worship attendance. We need to be looking at actual, verifiable participation by men and women, girls and boys, across the whole life of the church.[3]

As your leadership team reviews the totals and percentages that are revealed, it will lead you to ask important questions—questions that should lead to an improvement of your church's ministry. For example, in many churches we are finding a natural biological gender mix in their children's ministry up until about the fourth to fifth grade. Then it begins an

---

3. My research team is engaged in an on-going national project on men's and women's involvement in spiritual and religious life. You can be a part of this project by simply tracking that information in your church and emailing the completed Excel file to research@teaministries.com.

accelerating decline until their middle school youth ministry settles into a reflection of the adult church gender mix—in these churches about the same 61/39 mix we see nationally. That kind of information should lead your team to dig deeper to uncover the factors contributing to that shift—factors in the families, in the community, and especially in the church. Having that additional information will enable you to develop creative ways to address those factors. If on the other hand you find no falloff, or even an increase in boys' participation, you will want to find out why—for three reasons. First, so that you don't accidentally upset the apple cart by changing something critical to your church's effectiveness. Second, once you identify the principles that are at work, you will be able to adapt as circumstances inevitably change over time. And third, you can share the wealth—that is, help other churches learn and apply those principles to their situations.

How to Gather the Information

STEP ONE: Simply have your ushers or other volunteers accurately record and report the number of men and boys, and the number of women and girls in every worship service. To get the most useful information, have your team estimate each person's age bracket as well. A simple way to do the count is to take photos of the congregation from the front corners and several along the sides of your worship area. You can do this easily and unobtrusively with today's digital cameras and phones. Then enlarge them on a computer to make your counts. As you see in the sample photo below (see Figure 2.1), I have tracked each age category as well as gender by placing a color-coded dot on each person.[4] This procedure allows for the thorough analysis provided in the next section,[5] but is not essential if you just want to do a simple gender count. At this stage in your journey doing the simple gender count is fine. It will give you enough information to start but not overwhelm you with TMI (Too Much Information).

---

4. Due to printing limitations, the color-coding is in gray scale. You would use easily distinguished colors for each gender and generation.

5. It also protects the identity of the individuals in this photo.

SO WHAT SHOULD WE DO?

Figure 2.1: Color-Coded Gender and Generation Attendance Photo

STEP TWO: Then record the numbers of each on a form like that in Table 2.1 (if you're doing the detailed count):

Table 2.1: Color-Coded Gender and Generation Attendance Data Sheet[6]

Date_____ Time _____		
Worship Service Style_____		
Leaders (Ushers, Singers, Musicians, Speakers, etc.)		
Age	Males	Females
65+	●	●
50–64	●	●
35–49	●	●
18–34	●	●
13–17	○	○
3–12	◎	◎

---

6. The circle in each cell should be the color used for that age and gender in color-coding the photo.

	Congregation Participants	
65+	●	●
50–64	●	●
35–49	●	●
18–34	●	●
13–17	○	○
3–12	○	○
0–2	○	○

STEP THREE: Have the leader of every class, group, committee, and ministry team do the same for their group.

STEP FOUR: Then have a secretary or volunteer who understands spreadsheets accurately enter the totals for each category in the appropriate column on a spreadsheet. If you are doing a simple gender count, have them enter totals for worship, Sunday School/Small Groups, and committees/teams.[7] If you don't have someone who can do this, consider recruiting several candidates and pay the fees for the local adult education or online classes in Excel.

Complete this process for six consecutive weeks during a high attendance season and again during a low attendance season. Here is an example of one church's results:[8]

---

7. You can download both the detailed and the simplified pre-formatted Excel worksheets from www.TEAMinistries.com/research.

8. The percentages in Table 2.2 are calculated by formulas incorporated into the Excel data sheet.

Table 2.2:
Jehosephat Church[9] Average Participation by Gender and Age (Percentages)

	Cont Worship	Trad Worship	Sun Sch	Sm. Grp	Intrnl Min	Extrnl Min
Men 18–34	28.6	25.9	0	0	33.3	44.4
Women 18–34	71.4	74.1	100	100	66.7	55.6
Men 35–49	38.3	34.3	37.8	21.7	39.1	50.7
Women 35–49	61.7	65.6	62.2	78.3	60.9	49.3
Men 50–64	42.9	46.6	49.5	18.4	37.3	33.6
Women 50–64	57.1	53.4	50.5	81.6	62.7	66.4
Men 65+	40.5	33.1	31.8	13	38.9	45.2
Women 65+	59.5	66.9	68.2	87	61.1	54.8
Adult Men	37.4	38.6	34.3	18.4	37.6	41.7
Adult Women	62.6	61.4	65.6	81.6	62.4	58.3
Boys 15–17	33.2	25	31.2	28.2	34.3	36.8
Girls 15–17	66.8	75	68.8	71.8	65.7	63.2
Boys 12–14	40.3	39.9	40.8	37	0	43.3
Girls 12–14	59.7	60.1	59.2	63	100	56.7
Total Boys (12–17)	38.3	33.8	38.2	33.6	26.9	40
Total Girls (12–17)	61.7	66.2	61.8	66.4	73.1	60
Boys 6–11	47.8	56.7	50.5	44.4	0	0
Girls 6–11	52.3	43.3	49.5	55.6	0	0
Boys 0–5	48.9	60.3	55.5	55.5	0	0
Girls 0–5	51.1	39.7	44.4	44.4	0	0

I know—it's a mass of numbers, and numbers are not your strong suit. They're not mine either. I hated having to take advanced statistics and quantitative research methods courses. But then one day I had a vision in which

> I saw heaven opened and something like a large sheet being let down to earth by its four corners. It contained all kinds of

---

9. Not it's real name

mathematical tools and formulas—abacuses and calculators and computers, as well as analysis of variance and multiple-regression formulas. Then a voice told me, "Get up, Woody. Enter data and analyze."

"Surely not, Lord!" I replied. "I have never used anything from the ungodly realm of numbers."

But the voice spoke to me a second time, saying, "Do not call anything ungodly that God has made useful."

This happened three times, and immediately the sheet was taken back to heaven.

I'm just kidding, sort of. "Sort of" because I regularly encounter church folks who are suspicious of numbers and think that counting their participants is wrong. All of those folks have been in dying churches. It strikes me that refusing to analyze the numbers is like refusing to go to the doctor when you're not feeling well because you're afraid of what you might find out. Here are some issues that the numbers raise in this church:

How to Use the Information

First, this is one of the churches where participation in worship, Sunday school, and small group starts as children at about the normal biological gender mix. Then, some time between ages six and eleven, male participation begins a steep parallel decline in all three, followed by a precipitous drop to zero in Sunday school and small groups at age eighteen (see Figure 2.2). The decline in worship begins to level off at that point, but only among the men between ages eighteen and thirty-five.

Figure 2.2: Jehosephat Church Participation by Males, Birth to Age 34 (Percent Males within Each Age Group)

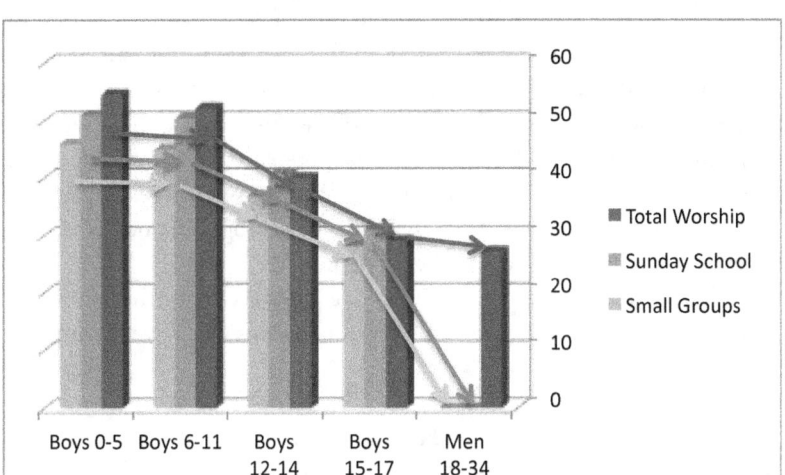

If you see this pattern in your church, you need to do three things: 1) Search the content, activities, and culture of your children's ministry for things that say, "Church (or Christianity, faith, or religion) is not for boys and men." 2) Identify which boys and men are regularly missing, analyze the relationship between the two groups. (To what extent are non-participating dads influencing their sons, and what factors might be influencing the others?) And 3) *go talk to them!* Tell them you want their help in making the church do a better job with boys and men. Ask questions like this:

1. What was the best thing that ever happened to you at church? What is your best memory? What was the worst thing?
2. When boys get to be about your age (or your son's age) a lot of them stop going to church. Why do you think that is?
3. What would our church need to do (or be like) for you and your friends to want to be part of it?
4. Let's say you think I'm asking the wrong questions. What questions should I be asking?

Second, among those thirty-five and up the gender mix in Sunday School participation mirrors that of worship (see Table 2.2). However, there is a huge drop in the men's small group participation in all age groups. Most churches celebrate if they can get even a few men's small groups going. They need to be asking their men (the ones voting with their feet, not the active ones) what makes small groups distasteful to them. Their church's men undoubtedly gather in small groups at work, club, and pub. Ask what makes those groups worthwhile and the church's not? Notice also that the difference is also evident among boys in the mid-week program. Whereas boys make up almost 51 percent of the elementary (ages 6–11) Sunday school, they are only about 44 percent of the mid-week group (see Table 2.2). Similarly, the almost 41 percent male population of the middle school (ages 12–14) Sunday school drops to 37 percent in mid-week. Again, this church, and yours if it is similar, needs to be asking these boys and their parents what is missing, competing, or turning them away.

Third, the contemporary service averaged six times the number of men as the traditional service, but the gender mix is virtually the same (see Figures 2.3 and 2.4).

Figure 2.3:
Jehosephat Church Total Men and Women in Contemporary Worship (Percentages)

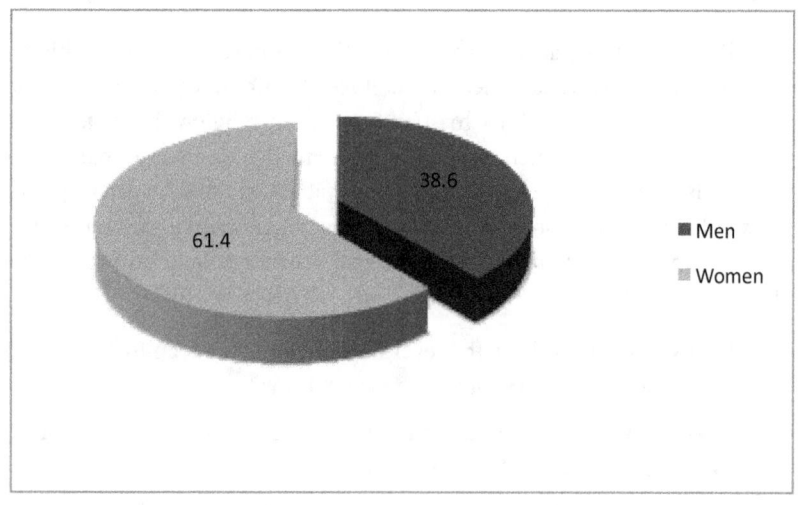

Figure 2.4:
Jehosephat Church Total Men and Women in Traditional Worship (Percentages)

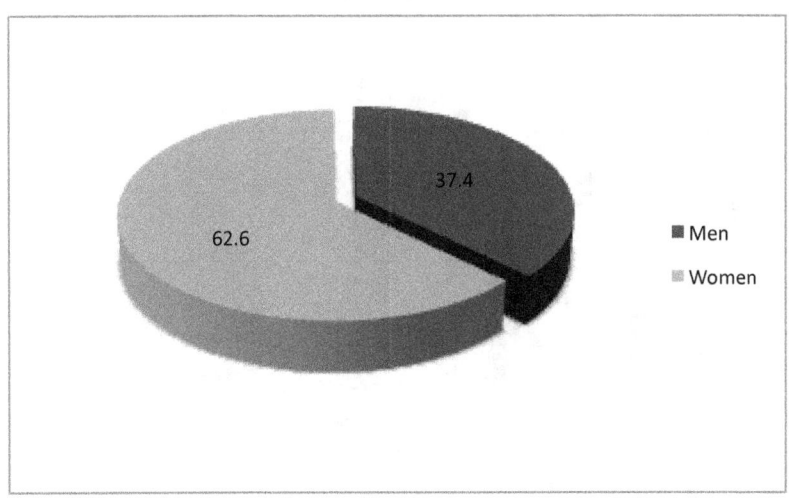

This was true in every age bracket (see Figures 2.5 and 2.6). Most churches are surprised when they see this, because they assume that contemporary services will reach more men. As we will see in the coming chapters, there is good reason they do not.

Figure 2.5: Jehosephat Church Contemporary Worship Generational Attendance (Percentages Within Age Groups)

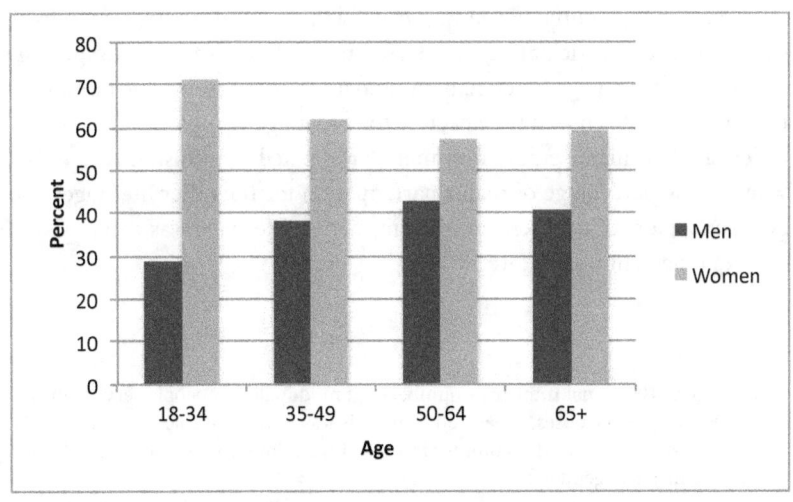

Figure 2.6: Jehosephat Church Traditional Worship Generational Attendance (Percentages Within Age Groups)

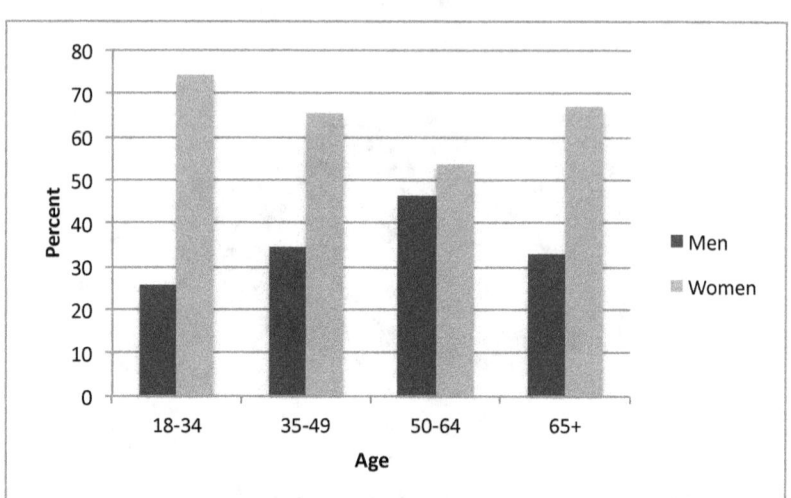

Notice also that, in both services, below age 65 the gap between men's and women's participation in worship gets larger as the age decreases (see Figures 2.5 and 2.6). So much for the common explanation that the gender gap in church is the result of women outliving their husbands! In this church, like most, widowhood was a significant factor only among those over age 65 and helped explain the gender gap in that group only for those in the traditional service.

Finally, this church had almost exactly the same *number*[10] of men from each age group participating in external ministries.[11] This was despite the fact that the 50–64 age group had one and a half to two times the number of men active in the church than each of the other age groups. In other words, fewer of the available empty nest men participated in ministry. As a result, whereas the percentage of male's participation for the other life stages was between 44.4 and 50.7 percent, the empty nest life stage was composed of only 33.6 percent (see Figure 2.7).

---

10. Internal/External ministries numbers are muddy due to people serving in several roles. For our purposes, repetition of roles is less important than the gender mix. Greater imbalance slants the communication climate and content/activity selection toward the majority gender.

11. This church had between two and three times as many people doing internal versus external ministry in every almost gender/age category. That's better than most churches but still shows an inward ministry orientation.

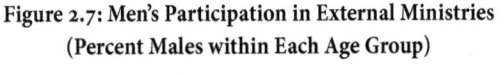

Figure 2.7: Men's Participation in External Ministries (Percent Males within Each Age Group)

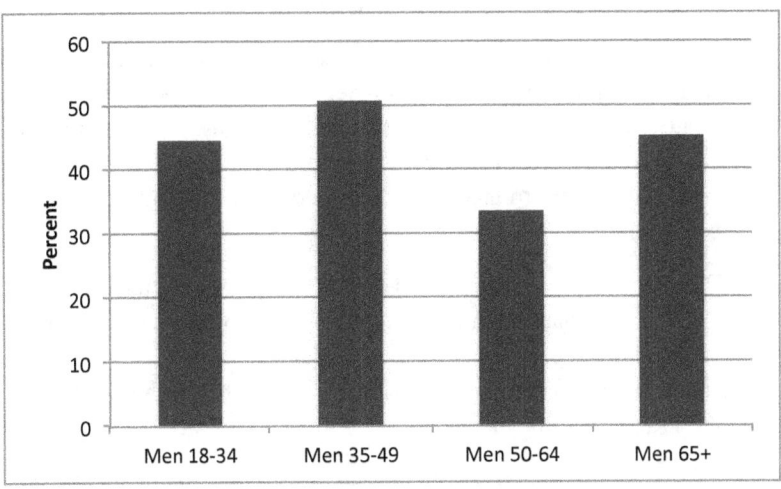

The question for this church is, why are the empty nest men not maintaining their level of participation in ministry to the same degree as the empty nest women?[12] If your church is like this, meet these men individually or get two to three of them together at a local guy place and talk with them about it. Target the guys who do attend worship but are not involved in a ministry. Tell them you want to get their perspective on how the church can better help their families and the community. Tell them you want them to give it to you straight—no pulled punches. Have one of the guys who is a ministry leader join you. One of you should take detailed notes. For both of you, your job is to listen, not talk them into joining up or defend what the church is doing. You will learn a lot about your church's ministry, and a lot about how to reach the men you talk with. Here are some questions to ask:

1. What four to six words or phrases describe your experience with the church over the past three years?

2. What words or phrases describe a church that is faithful to God for you? To what extant does that describe our church. Where are we falling short?

---

12. The variation in *percentages* (see Table 2.2) was due to greater or lesser numbers of women in each life stage. In internal ministries the empty nest women outnumbered the women from every other age category by one and a half times. In external ministries they outnumbered the other age categories by two times.

3. What words or phrases describe a spiritual leader for you? Thinking of all our church leaders, lay and staff, in which of those characteristics are we strong and in which are we weak.

4. Think of a time when God was more than a name to you: Give me four to six words or phrases that describe it. (This question is intended to create the opportunity to take their spiritual pulse. Don't pounce on the opportunity. Tell them you'd like to hear more about it at a later time. If they want to talk about it immediately, fine. Otherwise make an appointment for a later date—and keep it!)

Think about the key words and phrases they name in terms of those words' gender associations in your culture. What do they say about these men's perceptions of your church and its leaders?

Make sure you get to their involvement in ministry, or the lack thereof. You might say something like this:

> We want everyone in our church to be part of making a real difference for both our people and the people in the community. We're clearly missing the mark with you. Either what we're doing or how we're doing it doesn't float your boat enough for you to want to be part of it. How are we blowing it? What would make you say, "Yeah, let me in on that!"?

Be prepared for non-committal or deflective responses like, "Oh, the church isn't doing anything wrong—I just don't have the time," or "I'm just not into the church thing—never have been," etc. You will have to convince them that you will take what they say seriously, and non-judgmentally.

The Principle of the Thing

The above is an example of how to learn the most from the detailed information you can glean from your counts. The principle is this: You must ask questions about your current practices, and you must ask them of the people those practices affect (or fail to). Without this, the numbers are meaningless and the questions are useless. So, in summary, this is your first task: Gather the information, ask what unexpected and/or undesired results have surfaced, AND go talk with the pertinent people to uncover what attitudes, actions, and/or inactions are producing those results. Your next task is to:

GO FIND OUT WHAT MEN (AND WOMEN) OUTSIDE CHURCH CIRCLES ARE LIKE!

Why? Because when we insulate ourselves from the world around us we condemn ourselves to disintegration. David Boyd was a military strategist who developed the "OODA Loop." OODA stands for Observe-Orient-Decide-Act, and is a process for individual and organizational decision making in an ever-changing environment. It applies not only to the military but also to business and, yes, even the church. Boyd argues, "Living Systems are open systems; closed systems are non-living systems. Point: If we don't communicate with the outside world—to gain information for knowledge and understanding as well as matter and energy for sustenance—we die out to be come a non-discerning and uninteresting part of that world."[13]

When I completed the masters degree in missiology at Asbury Seminary and moved on to the communication program at the University of Kentucky to complete the two schools' cooperative PhD, I was shocked at how insulated from the secular world I had become in twelve years of seminary and local church ministry. Not only was I studying and teaching on a secular university campus, I was also taking temp jobs—on the assembly line in an auto parts factory, delivering Coca Cola products to the state prison system, cleaning and dis-assembling abandoned warehouses, etc. I found myself surrounded by people with very different assumptions, values, and language, especially when the crew was mostly men.

If you are a pastor I urge you, re-enter the world of men. If you are like most pastors, most of your time is spent in the company of women, whether in worship, or classes, or meetings, or even funerals. For most this is merely a function of the current make-up of the church. For others it is an unconscious choice. David Murrow says for some, church is a place to hide from men:

> Some pastors are uncomfortable in the presence of men. I once heard a minister tell this brutally honest story about his struggle to love his men. Here's my paraphrased version:
>
> *I was a bookish kid with skinny arms and thick glasses. When I entered junior high, the big, athletic boys started picking on me—calling me "faggot" and "mama's boy" and slamming me into lockers. I hated this bullying and learned to avoid the jocks through high school.*
>
> *In college, I heard a call to ministry. I discovered a deep love for the Scriptures. I went on to seminary and became a pastor.*

13. Osinga, *Science, Strategy and War*, 95.

My first church was a small, rural congregation full of old people. I took to my role with gusto. Life was good as my bride and I settled into our roles.

One Sunday, something unexpected happened: a power couple in their late twenties walked into the church. She was petite and beautiful, and he was . . . a jock. Broad shoulders. Prominent brow. Large fists.

I could hardly get through my sermon that day. By the time I delivered the benediction I was an emotional wreck—but I had no idea why.

The following week, the power couple showed up in the adult Sunday school class, which I led. I stammered through my lesson, and then opened it up for discussion. The jock opened his mouth and offered a brash opinion that contradicted Scripture. I felt a rush of pleasure as I corrected his theology. My tone was harsh and condescending. We never saw the couple again.

Years later, I was hired by a larger church. It had a men's ministry program. The guys always invited me to participate, but I was so busy in my new job I never seemed to have the time.

One day Elmer, one of our elders and a leader in the men's ministry, made an offhand comment that brought me to my knees. He said to me, "Pastor, why don't we see you at our men's gatherings? Are you afraid of men?"

Elmer had hit the bull's-eye. In a moment of shining clarity, I saw myself slammed against a locker. My survival strategy since junior high was to avoid men—particularly masculine ones. In fact, by going into the ministry, I had chosen a career that kept me away from manly things altogether. Eighty percent of my daily interactions were with women—and I liked it that way. In those rare instances when I had to deal with men, there was usually a woman present, which kept me safe.

When I was a boy, I was powerless against the jocks. But now the tables were turned. As a pastor, I had the power. My weapon was my doctor of theology, and I used it like a club to bludgeon my adversaries and have my revenge.

I prayed and asked God's forgiveness. I asked him to give me a real love for men—even the big, scary ones.

So I attended my first men's breakfast. I started mentoring a group of young men. I told my story to other pastors. One Sunday I even wore shoulder pads and a football jersey in the pulpit as an illustration.

To my delight, when I began investing in my men, my heart changed. And so did my church. We started growing. A lot of the *gossip and backbiting went away. Even the youth group grew. Young men started sitting in the front row.*

I entered the pastorate to protect myself from men, but now I can't imagine doing ministry without them. They are no longer my adversaries—they are my brothers.[14]

So how can you re-enter the world of men, particularly those outside the church? By literally entering the world. We in the church have turned Jesus's prayer for the church on its head.

> I am coming to you now, but I say these things while I am still in the world, so that they may have the full measure of my joy within them. I have given them your word and the world has hated them, for they are not of the world any more than I am of the world. *My prayer is not that you take them out of the world but that you protect them from the evil one. They are not of the world, even as I am not of it.* Sanctify them by the truth; your word is truth. As you sent me into the world, I have sent them into the world. For them I sanctify myself, that they too may be truly sanctified (John 17:13-19).

In a misguided attempt to sanctify ourselves we have taken ourselves out of the world. If you are a layperson this applies to you as well. Most church folks have few if any friends outside of church circles. Even when they are in the working world their friends are among the other church folks. It's time to let God do the sanctifying as we soak in God's word and get ourselves back in the world where Jesus sent us.

How? Regularly have lunch at a sports bar and grill. Become part of the community at the local bar/tavern/pub. Join a gym or health club and get to know the guys there. Get on a weight-training program and talk with the guys in the weight room. The weight room is more conducive to conversation than the rows of treadmills, stair-masters, and elliptical machines. Make sure you spend time in the locker room. It is one of the last expressions in Euro-American culture of "the men's house" prevalent throughout history in cultures around the world. I've had a number of meaningful conversations with non-church men in the modern "sweat lodge"—the health club's sauna and steam rooms.

Across the country I have found one of the best times and places to find and get to know non-church men is Sunday morning, nine to noon, in coffee shops and fast food joints. At the largest Starbucks in my area the

---

14. Murrow, *Why Men Hate Going to Church*, 149-51. Taken from *Why Men Hate Going to Church* by David Murrow Copyright © 2005, 2011 by David Murrow. Used by permission of Thomas Nelson. www.thomasnelson.com.

Sunday morning gender mix is at least five men to one woman and has been as high as twelve to one for as long as thirty minutes. It has been easy to start conversations with them. My University of Kentucky cap during basketball season always gets a rise out of somebody.

If you are a pastor, devote a day or two a month to working a temp job. And if you are a layperson, defend your pastor's doing so—and keeping the pay with no reduction in his/her church salary. S/he will be in ministry as much in that setting as in the church. Consider the hourly wage s/he will get to be "overtime pay." S/he will more than earn it. After all, both Jesus (Luke 10:7) and Paul (1 Timothy 5:18) said workers are worthy of their wages, and besides, most pastors are woefully underpaid.

In all these settings, observe the clientele. Keep a journal of your conversations as you become a regular and get to know the guys (copy the "Insights From The World Of Men" journal page below). What are these men like? How do they talk? What do they talk about? How are they similar and different from the men who are active in your church? As you read the upcoming chapters listen for the elements discussed in each and compare that with what you hear in your church. Track the similarities and differences between the talk in the church and non-church settings. Work hard at suspending judgment. Listen and think beyond the surface level. Avoid the temptation to "fix" your new friends. Your role is to listen, observe, and learn.

TEAM CANDIDATES			
Name	Phone & Email	Contact Priority	Appointment Date/ Time
1.			
Notes:			
2.			
Notes:			
3.			
Notes:			
4.			
Notes:			
5.			
Notes:			
6.			
Notes:			
7.			
Notes:			

INSIGHTS FROM THE WORLD OF MEN		
Make blank copies for your journal. Record impressions and reflections immediately after experience.		
Date and Time	Setting/Location	Teammates Present
Names of the Guys	Common Words/Phrases	Topics of Talk
Similarities with Your Church's Men's Talk		Differences from Your Church's Men's Talk

3

The Words We Use

During a break in one of my "How To Reach and Involve Men" seminars, a pastor told this story:

> When I was in seminary I worked on road crews during the summer. The guys were standing around talking one day and I said, "Hey guys, let me share something with you."
> They all started laughing and one of them tiptoed, limp-wristed through the group saying, "Ooo, we're going to shaaare!"
> The pastor commented, "I never realized until then how much our church language is feminine. These guys don't 'share.' They tell!

That pastor was fortunate. Most pastors and church members are so immersed in church culture that they don't realize they are in a different environment from the rest of the world. They are like fish in an aquarium. They don't realize they are surrounded by water (or that they are walled off from the rest of the world) until they are taken out of that environment. Guy, the pastor who told the story, had the experience of being outside the church fish bowl early in his ministry. He was fortunate to have a group of guys show him he was out of the tank. Once that happened, the contrast between church language and non-church language became obvious.

Go into a men's locker room. Sit down near a table full of guys at a sports bar restaurant. Listen to the group of old guys that gather at the local burger joint or coffee house to solve the world's problems. Join a four-some of guys on the golf course or fill in on a construction crew. Wherever there is a group of guys, the talk will be different from the talk in the church. The content, the character, even the cadence will be different. For pre-Christian men who come into the church, the contrast is obvious. They might not be able to put their finger on it, but they know they are in different waters.[1] One man said, "It took a while, but after I'd been to church a few times it hit me. I felt like I was swimming in estrogen."

SWIMMING IN A SEA OF VERBAL ESTROGEN

What is it? What makes a man feel like he's been immersed in a pink sea of perfume? At its most basic and pervasive level, it's the language we use. The words we say both create and reinforce the culture in which we live. From the earliest age we learn to associate words with different experiences, objects, actions, emotions, and people. Over time we make unconscious connections between sets of words and particular settings, situations, kinds of people, etc. Those connections carry the assumptions, beliefs, attitudes, and feelings of those who are important to us. That is what the statement, "Culture is more caught than taught" means. We catch our culture from our families, from our communities, from our countries.

One of the first components of culture we begin to catch is gender.[2] Certain words and patterns of speech become associated with boys and others with girls. Those associations continue to develop and deepen on into adult life between men and women. They can be changed, but it takes a conscious, concerted effort to do so. And there has been such an effort—centered in the higher education systems of America and Europe. Yet nearly forty years of teaching and writing in Euro-American universities aimed at eliminating gender stereotypes has barely dented them in American society as a whole, especially when it comes to men. In their 2016 analysis of a decade of studies using the Bem Sex Role Inventory,[3] Kristen Donnelly, and Jean Twenge found

---

1. Newman, et al, found significant differences between women's and men's language in both writing and conversations. Women's language focused on their thoughts, emotions, senses, other people. In contrast, men talked about external events, objects and activities or processes. In doing so they used more long words, articles, and swear words whereas women used more social words and pronouns. Their concluding comment was this: "*Gender differences in written and spoken language appear to be subtle, but reliable. The fact that we are confronted with these differences every day yet fail to notice them highlights the degree to which they are a part of everyday life.*" Newman, et al., "Gender Differences" 230.

2. The three stages in the development of conscious gender identity—gender awareness, gender orientation, and gender identity—begin between fourteen and eighteen months and proceed through age six or seven. (Condry, "Gender Identity.")

3. The instruments used to measure psychological sex-type or gender schematicity are still providing valid results. For example, Patricia A. Oswald wrote of the Bem Sex-Role Inventory, "The results of this study suggest that, almost thirty years after it was developed, the categories can still be used to categorize men and women of various

that while women's scores on the femininity scale decreased significantly, there were no significant changes among men on either the masculinity or the femininity scales.[4] When they expanded the analysis to include data from 1974 to 2012,[5] they found that while women's masculinity and androgyny scores rose significantly, neither men's masculinity nor their femininity scores budged. Similarly, the women's androgyny scores showed a significant increase since 1974 (though not since 1993), whereas men's androgyny remained unchanged. This is great news for women. Perceptions have changed somewhat and possibilities are expanding. But that should not make us think that men have changed in how they think of themselves and other men.

GENDER ASSOCIATIONS AND CHURCH CULTURE

Researchers across several disciplines (psychology, sociology, anthropology, and communication[6]) have documented across decades and across cultures that most people associate femaleness with a relational or communal orientation whereas they associate maleness with what has been variously called an "instrumental," "agenic," or "action[7] orientation."[8] So, while current scholarly

---

ages." Oswalt, "Examination." 1336.

4. Donnelly and Twenge, "Masculine and Feminine Traits," 2016. This analysis included thirty-four samples involving 8,027 participants.

5. Ibid. The expanded analysis included ninety-four samples involving 24,801 participants.

6. See Appendix A: "Research on Gender Across the Cultures" for a representative list of references.

7. The meaning of relational and communal is obvious. Instrumental and agenic refer to the ability to affect situations or people, i.e. to have influence. Action is frequently required if one is to have an effect or impact, hence the reference to an "action orientation."

8. In one of the original works on this issue, Dr. Sandra Lipsitz Bem studied commonly-held gender associations and developed the Bem Sex-Role Inventory to measure the degree to which a person identified with those associations—what she called at the time "psychological sex-type." The give and take of social science research and review helped her refine her thinking into what is now known as gender schema theory. Other key players engaged in the debate/discussion were Spence, Helmreich, & Stapp, who developed a competing measure called the Personal Attributes Questionnaire, and Gough & Heilbrun, who developed The Adjective Checklist. The process of developing each of these instruments involved participants rating a pool of personal characteristics, including non-relational and non-instrumental items, in terms of how much each was true of women and of men. The results of this process were then factor-analyzed—a statistical procedure that identifies the number and nature of factors that produce the correlations in the data. Across a decade of research the findings were refined down to the essentials of what were both necessary and sufficient to explain the data. Bem's conclusion was that the gender schema was composed of two factors, relational characteristics and instrumental characteristics, which correlated in participants responses with the feminine and the

practice is to emphasize the *differences* in cultural definitions of masculinity and femininity, there is actually *widespread consistency* in perceptions of female and male characteristics as being relational/communal and instrumental/agenic, respectively.[9]

There is, of course, a caveat to all of this. Some of you are saying to yourself "but not all men are like that, or not all women are like that." And you are right. I am not like that. I am what used to be called "androgynous," and is now generally called "gender aschematic." That is, my way of relating to the world is an almost equal combination of instrumental and relational characteristics. (Don't you love how scholarly types—like me—replace one non-understandable word with another one? Let's just say I'm a "Combination Man"). Some men are primarily relational and some women are primarily instrumental in how they relate to the world around them. These folks are said to be "gender cross-schematic." We'll call these men "Relation Men," and these women "Action Women." Men who are instrumental and women who are relational are "gender schematic." We'll call these men "Action Men," and these women "Relation Women."

Those of us who are aschematic or cross-schematic need to remind ourselves of this fact: we are in the minority, at least in the general population. This is especially the case when it comes to men. In surveys I have conducted periodically since 1990 involving respondents ages 17–72, in the general population 69 percent of males were Action Men, 20 percent were Combination Men, and 11 percent were Relation Men. In contrast, among the men in the churches I have studied since 1990, only 35 percent were Action Men, 41 percent were Combination Men, and 24 percent were Relation Men (see Figure 3.1).

---

masculine respectively. Spence, et al's conclusion also identified two factors, which they called communal and agenic. See Appendix C: Gender-Schemas and Self-Schemas for an example my research updating this work, which informs the rest of the book.

9. In the most comprehensive cross-cultural study of gender perceptions to date, John E. Williams and Deborah L. Best (Williams and Best, *Sex and Psyche*) asked people in 25 countries representing the major cultural regions around the world to identify masculine and feminine characteristics from The Adjective Checklist (Gough and Heilbrun, *Adjective* Checklist), one of the instruments used to measure gender perceptions. A review of Williams and Best's data reveals 49 masculine and 25 feminine perceptions shared in at least 19 and up to all 25 of the countries. Significantly, 92 percent of the positive masculine items were directly instrumental/agenic and 92 percent of the feminine ones were directly relational/communal. Participants were students in universities in Europe, Asia, the Pacific Rim, Latin America, North America, Africa, and the Middle East. The fact that these were university students is significant in that they would be those most likely to be exposed to the philosophy of de-genderization that is valued in western higher education and being exported to universities around the world. Even with this pool of participants, the perception that women are relational/communal and men are instrumental/agenic is virtually universal.

Figure 3.1: Gender Schematicity in Men, Non-Church vs. Church

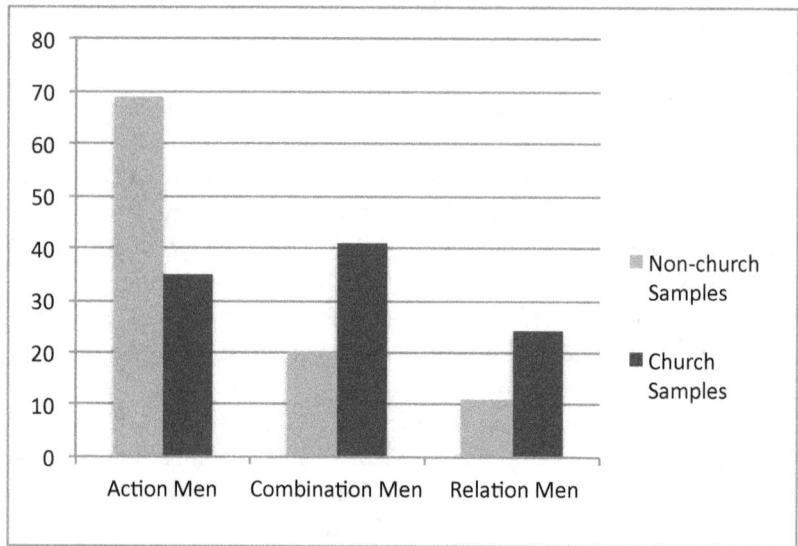

Or to look at it another way, here is what is out there on the American male landscape (see Figures 3.2):

Figure 3.2: Gender Schematicity in Non-Church Men

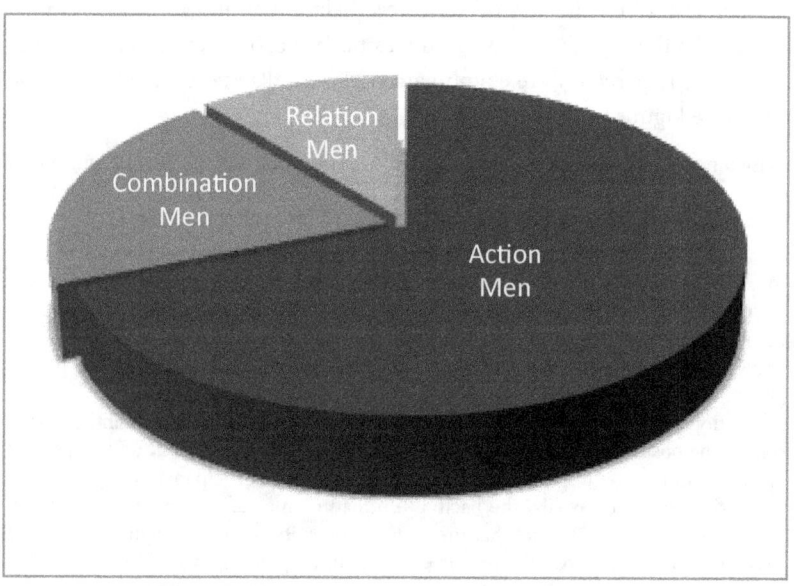

And here is whom we are reaching in the American church (see Figure 3.3):

Figure 3.3: Gender Schematicity in Church Men

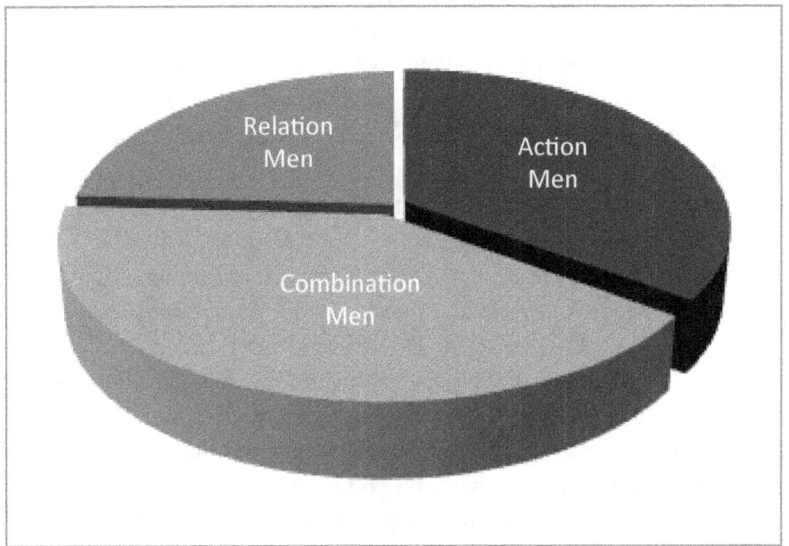

I want to be clear here. It is not that Action Men (and Action Women) do not want relationships, nor value relationships, nor have relationships. They do. It is just that relationships and relational issues are not their primary focus. The relationships they have are often the *reason* for their efforts to affect the world around them and/or the means by which they do so, but they are not their primary way of relating to the world around them. Anthropologist David Gilmore says there are three purposes common to the traditional view of men's roles around the world: 1) to ensure the reproduction of the next generation, 2) to provide for their family and community, and 3) to ensure the safety of their family and the community.[10] For short we'll say, to procreate, provide, and protect. Relationships are integral to all three of these. But for the Action Man or Woman they are a *part* of their attention, experiences, and memories rather than their focus. That difference shows up both in the talk they use and the talk they seek.[11]

---

10. Gilmore, *Manhood*. 223–225.

11. There is evidence that there is a hormonal reason for this. Pennebaker, et al studied "Two participants, a man receiving treatment for loss of upper-body strength and a female-to-male transgendered individual, supplied records of injections over 1–2 years along with e-mails or journal entries as writing samples. Results showed that *higher testosterone levels correlated with reduced use of words related to social connections. Language relating to anger, sexuality, and achievement was unrelated to testosterone levels.* It appears

Your Kind Isn't Welcome Here

Over the past forty years the church has gotten increasingly out of balance. Go back half a century and you will find that the church had communicated both the need for action, and our need for relationships. Now we have become almost completely focused on relationships. Our language is saturated with words and phrases like "personal relationship," "intimacy," "small group," "commuuuunity,"[12] "share," "open up" "draw close," "hug," "embrace,"[13] etc. How do Action Men or Women respond when they hear so much of this relational talk that it drowns out what action-oriented talk does occur? They say to themselves, "These people are so wrapped up in each other—I don't belong here." Nor would he or she want to. It is an indication of how out of balance we have become that many people in the church think that it is just fine for those folks to feel that way. Don't believe me? Read on.

Dr. Adair Lummis of the Hartford Institute for Religious Research did the church an invaluable service in leading the U.S. Congregational Life project. In one instance, however, she illustrated the difference between a research finding and the conclusion you draw from that research. When she presented that project's finding of the church's current 61 percent female—39 percent male gender mix to the 2003 annual meeting of the Society for the Scientific Study of Religion, Dr. Lummis concluded:

> The findings in this paper suggest that mainline congregations may increase the number of men involved in worship services and programs, by offering events, projects with a concrete task focus which will appeal more to men's agenic interests in the world outside the church. However, even assiduous attention to these approaches is unlikely to greatly expand the proportion of men active in congregations.
>
> Denominations and congregations have survived long without a balance of men to women in the pews. If *real men* [emphasis in original] support the church financially and approve of their family members attending, why be concerned that men are not present? Solution: let the jocks be and let the *more*

---

that testosterone steers attention away from social connections but not necessarily toward concerns with aggression or sexual activity. (Pennebaker, "Testosterone," 172.)

12. No, that's not a typo. That is how it's said. And when it's said it means, not the town or neighborhood in which we live and serve, but a particular kind of shared experience.

13. There has been a sudden explosion of new churches naming themselves "Embrace Church." How many Action Men and Women do you think are going to say, "THAT'S where I want to go!"?

spiritually advanced [emphasis added] women and men both people and manage the congregations![14]

Dr. Lummis's conclusion reflects an assumption that men, or at least agenic ones (Action Men, remember?) are less spiritual or less spiritually advanced. For some unexplained reason, maleness or jockness or sportsness or actionness or testosteroneness is assumed to be hazardous to one's spiritual health.[15] Theologically this makes no sense. It would mean that God created the human animal, but made the male of the species such that a key component in his make-up would prevent or inhibit his connection with God (and that of the females who share this characteristic). If I were, say, a female chauvinist Calvinist I might be able to swallow that. But I believe God loves all God's children, including the agenic jock.

Dr. Lummis' concluding remark troubles me. It reminds me of a question one of my dissertation mentors once asked me. Dr. Rush was a militant feminist, an atheist, and a friend. She said, "I love your work because it shows how tight the cultural straight-jacket is for men. But I have to ask you, why you do care about the men who are not in church? Sounds to me like you've got things pretty nice in the church. You've gotten rid of all the Bozos."[16]

My answer to Dr. Rush was, because God loves the "Bozos." Some of the men Jesus called to become apostles were Bozos. He died for the "Bozos." My dad is a "Bozo." He's an action-oriented, agenic, ex-jock, coach and athletic director. My Brother is a "Bozo." He's a balls-to-the wall, instrumental, ex-fighter pilot, flight instructor, and air-combat commander. Neither of them could come to faith apart from the gospel expressed in agenic/instrumental/action-oriented terms.

If you think the church is nothing more than a spiritual club of like-minded people who care for each other and do kind, so-called "paternal" (but actually maternal) things for people who are less fortunate, the good

---

14. Lummis, "Men's Commitment," §4.

15. Dr. Lummis also assumes that it has always and everywhere been true that the church has lacked gender balance. She and others cite complaints made about the gender imbalance in the pews at different moments in American history as evidence for this belief. What this ignores is the historical context of those moments. Each of them occurs at a time when the Idealist generation that came of age during a spiritual awakening has matured and come to power in society (See Strauss and Howe's *Generations*). That is, it is a cyclical rather than a perennial phenomenon. It also ignores the effect of the efforts in each case to remedy the situation, such as those discussed in chapter 1.

16. Dr. Lummis would agree. One of the survey questions in her study of Episcopal pastors and lay leaders was, "3. How can we get men with masculine interests (who are in good health, *and not arrogant, lazy or grouchy*) to be involved in our congregations?" (Ibid., emphasis added.)

Drs. Lummis and Rush make sense. But I believe the church is a movement through which God intends to transform (influence/impact/affect) individuals and communities into what God originally intended when we were created. And if that is true, then the church not only is called to reach Action Men and Women; the church also NEEDS Action Men and Women to fulfill its mission.

What It's Like for the "Bozos"

Suppose one of these men or women sits down in church on a Sunday morning. What does he hear? Here is a sample:

> Let's all sing together,
> Falling in love with Jesus
> Falling in love with Jesus
> Falling in love with Jesus
> Was the best thing I ever, ever done [sic]
> (Repeat)
> (Verse 2)
> In His arms I feel protected
> In His arms never disconnected (no, no)
> In His arms I feel protected
> There's no place I'd rather, rather be[17]

Or suppose he reads a pastor's blog from a church website or a Facebook post or watches a church video series such as these:

> "Its about being in community: . . . Every week, people will walk through the doors of our churches who need love, encouragement, support, a word of comfort or counsel or just simple, uncomplicated friendship. And you can be there for that person. So many churchgoers think, 'Oh, there is nothing special going on this week. I won't miss much. And I don't really have a job there so I can skip this time.' But it's not a matter of what you will miss. It's a matter of who will miss you."(Pastor's blog, Jan. 1, 2012)

---

17. On "Falling In Love With Jesus," CD, by Jonathan Butler. Copyright © 2002 Universal Music—Brentwood Benson songs (BMI) (adm. at CapitolCMGPublishing.com / Warner Tamerlane Music (BMI) All rights reserved. Reprinted and used by permission of ALFRED MUSIC.

"I found a wonderful post for Valentine's Day from a marvelous blog for young mothers. I hope it blesses you as it did me." (Pastor's post on Facebook, Feb. 10, 2012)

"The problem is today many Christians are lethargic, they're burned out and they're living lives no different than those of unbelievers. They need to fall in love with Jesus all over again. That's what Awakening is all about—getting close to Jesus Christ." (Pastor Rick Warren in a video greeting to Awakening participants)

"Today we will have the opportunity to give our Estimate of Giving cards, we will hear our wonderful Bell Choir play, and we will hear [our lay leader] share her vision and hope for our church.... God's extravagant love has made such a difference in the life of this church. God is doing such wonderful things and we can celebrate all of this TOGETHER [emphasis in original] as we bring our song and our gifts to God." (Church web page, Nov. 24, 2011)

"The problem is today many Christians are lethargic, they're burned out and they're living lives no different than those of unbelievers. They need to fall in love with Jesus all over again. That's what awakening is all about—getting close to Jesus Christ." (Pastor Rick Warren in a video greeting to Awakening participants)

"Seedbed has produced a marvelous series with our very own Dr. Craig Keener on the topic of Miracles. Don't miss this!" (Asbury Theological Seminary "Seedbed" on Facebook, Jan. 12, 2012)

Now if you've been involved church life for a while, you're probably saying, "Yeah, so? And your point is . . . ?" But take a look at those again with italics:

Let's all sing *together*,
"Falling in love with Jesus
Falling in love with Jesus
Falling in love with Jesus
Was the best thing I ever, ever done [sic]
(Verse 2)
In His arms I feel *protected*
In His arms never disconnected (no, no)
In His arms I feel *protected*
There's no place I'd rather, rather be."

"Its about *being in community*:... Every week, people will walk through the doors of our churches who *need love, encouragement, support*, a word of *comfort* or counsel or *just* simple, uncomplicated friendship. And you can *be there for that person. So* many churchgoers think, 'Oh, there is nothing special going on this week. I won't miss much. And I don't really have a job there so I can skip this time.' But it's not a matter of what you will miss. It's a matter of *who will miss you*." (Pastor's blog, Jan. 1, 2012)

"I found a *wonderful* post for Valentine's Day from a *marvelous* blog for young mothers. I *hope* it blesses you as it did me." (Pastor's post on Facebook, Feb. 10, 2012)

"The problem is today many Christians are lethargic, they're burned out and they're living lives no different than those of unbelievers. They need to *fall in love with Jesus* all over again. That's what awakening is all about—getting close to Jesus Christ." (Pastor Rick Warren in a video greeting to Awakening participants)

"Today we will have the opportunity to give our Estimate of Giving cards, we will hear our *wonderful* Bell Choir play, and we will hear [our lay leader] *share* her vision and *hope* for our church.... God's *extravagant* love has made *such* a difference in the life of this church. God is doing *such wonderful* things and we can celebrate all of this *TOGETHER* [all CAPS in original] as we bring our song and our gifts to God." (Church web page, Nov. 24, 2011)

"Seedbed has produced a *marvelous* series with our *very own* Dr. Craig Keener on the topic of Miracles. Don't miss this!" (Asbury Theological Seminary "Seedbed" on Facebook, Jan. 12, 2012)

LESSONS FROM THE LINGUISTS

All those italics above reflect words and phrases that your Average Joe associates with women, especially when they are piled up on top of one another. Linguists have long noted that such associations existed.[18] In the 1970s feminist linguists Mary Ritchie-Key[19] and Robin Tolmach Lakoff[20] began cataloguing them in detail. Lakoff called them at the time "the Feminine Register." Build-

---

18. See, for example Jespersen, *Language*, 1922.
19. Key, *Male / Female Language*, 1975/1996.
20. Lakoff, *Language and Women's Place*, 2004.

ing on their work and using it to analyze North American church culture, I have identified five categories that characterize our church vocabulary.

Overstatements and Empty Adjectives

Dr. Ritchie-Key noted women's tendency to use hyperbole or overstatements to a much greater extent than men. Dr. Lakoff called some of those overstatements "empty adjectives." This meant that the words were such overstatements that they had become disconnected from their original meaning. She included in this category words like wonderful, marvelous, fantastic, incredible, beautiful, divine, etc. If you think about the root word of any of these, you will realize each should refer to things that would be rare rather than commonplace. A wonderful experience should actually fill you with wonder. A fantastic one should be so unusual that you would have thought it could only occur in a fantasy. Something incredible should be beyond your ability to believe. And something divine? Well, we could count God's stroll in the Garden of Eden, the burning bush, another stroll on the Sea of Galilee, but few things in this life are "simply divine." Yet all of these words have become commonplace in church talk. In today's church talk we could add to Lakoff's list such popular words as excited or exciting, awesome, extravagant, and lavish.

Like overstatements in general, what all these words do is increase the emotional content of the talk. They focus on the feeling—of wonder or awe, excitement, or having been lavished upon. Perhaps that is why they are used so much when church leaders move into promotion mode. Listen to the announcements in most churches and you will hear things like, "We're really excited about our annual Family Camp that's coming up in two weeks. We had such a marvelous time at last year's camp. If you weren't there you missed something really special . . . " This Sunday during announcements or when you get the next church email or newsletter, count the number of empty adjectives in the descriptions of upcoming events. You might be surprised. Why is that important? Because this heightened emotional component of empty adjectives is yet another gender difference. Communication scholar and best-selling author Deborah Tannen called this difference "rapport talk vs. report talk." "Women speak and hear a language of connection and intimacy, while men speak and hear a language of status and independence."[21] Men use "report talk," with its focus on information and action, to establish position and get things done. Women use "rapport talk," with its focus on emotions and relationships, to establish connection and

---

21. Tannen, *You Just Don't Understand*, 42.

build community.[22] So, Average Joe sits in your worship service and hears, "We have this wonderful opportunity coming up—I'm super-excited about it. It's our fall retreat, 'Getting Closer with Jesus.' It'll be really awesome—I hope you'll come." What do you think he's thinking? Here's how one man responded in a consultation focus group about his church's worship service: "I thought the guy doing announcements was going to hop up and down on his toes and clap his hands like a little girl."

Romantic Emotions:

If the focus on emotions in empty adjectives is a problem, how much more is the prevalence of words and phrases that, outside of church, are associated with romance? On any given Sunday you are likely to hear some combination of adore, fall in love, in love with Jesus, and multiple "heart phrases" (God touched hearts, open your heart, give your heart, etc.). There is a place for *some* of that language in the church. It is, in fact, present in both the Hebrew and Christian scriptures and has a long history in the church. Yet at times it comes into fashion in church life to a far greater proportion than it is found in the scriptures. That is one reason men go missing during certain periods of church history. But contrary to common belief, it has not always and everywhere been so. Author Leon Podles uncovered a major turning point in the expression of western Christianity in Bernard of Clairveaux's twelfth century development of Bridal Mysticism.

> Bernard claimed that "if a love relationship is the special and outstanding characteristic of bride and groom it is not unfitting to call the soul that loves God a bride." Realizing that this application needed defense, Bernard explained that "although none of us will dare arrogate for his own soul the title of bride of the Lord, nevertheless we are members of the Church which rightly boasts of this title and of the reality that it signifies, and hence may justifiably assume a share in this honor. For what all of us simultaneously possess in full and perfect manner, that each single one of us undoubtedly possesses by participation. Thank you, Lord Jesus, for your kindness in uniting us to the Church you so dearly love, not merely that we may be endowed with the gift of faith, but that like brides we may be one with you in an embrace that is sweet, chaste, and eternal."
>
> Having established the principle for the use of such language, Bernard then elaborated. He referred to himself as "a

---

22. Ibid., 74–75.

woman" and advised his monks to be "mothers"—to "let your bosoms expand with milk, not swell with passion"—to emphasize their paradoxical status and worldly weakness."[23]

If this sounds over the top and not likely to be repeated in our day, a passage from popular speaker and author Beth Moore takes on the feel of a romance novel in her Bible study "Breaking Free." She describes an imaginary scene that takes place after the rape of King David's daughter, Tamar, by her half-brother, Amnon (2 Samuel 13).[24] Knowing that the context of this imaginary scene is the devastating aftermath of a rape might cause one to dismiss the notion that there's anything romantic in this passage. And in fact, some have responded with indignation at the thought that Beth Moore "would ever advocate anything romantic in our relationship with Jesus." Yet in her preface to this story, Moore describes what Christ does in the story as his "tender— and if I may say, romantic—ministry."[25] With that in mind, the passage reads as if Jesus were taking the place of a romantic partner for Tamar.

Ms. Moore stands squarely in the stream that has flowed from St. Bernard. She places the emphasis on the individual as the bride of Christ rather than the church as the bride of Christ. She writes: "Our union with Christ is common to all believers, and but the intimacy of this relationship is expressed between Christ and *individual* believers. Whether we are male or female, we are the bride of Christ.[26]

That theological stance, while consistent with the hyper-individualism of Western culture, is antithetical to the male spirit. It provides a wider door for women's entry into the church, while placing a barrier in the path of men. But that wider door for women is actually not beneficial for them either. It leads to a false path toward an inappropriate relationship. It leads to emotions, connections, and connotations that find their origins in the fertility religions against which Judeo-Christian people have had to contend throughout their history. Don't believe me? Podles shows how far some of the women of Bernard's day went:

> "Hildegard of Bingen carries the erotic imagery a little farther in her song "O dulcissime amator," in which she addresses Christ: "O sweetest lover, sweetest embracer.... In your blood, we are joined to you, with nuptial rites, scorning men, and choosing you."
>
> For Hildegard, and many others, the bridal union of the soul and Christ is not simply higher than earthly marriage; it

---

23. Podles, *The Church Impotent*, 103–104.
24. Moore, *Breaking Free*, 145–46.
25. Ibid., 144.
26. Ibid., 146–47 (emphasis added).

replaces it and takes on some of the physical eroticism of the missing sexual union. Margaret Ebner feels Jesus pierce her "with a swift shot (*sagitta acuta*) from His spear of love." She feels her spouse's "wondrous powerful thrusts against my heart," and she complains that "[s]ometimes I could not endure it when the strong thrusts came against me for they harmed my insides so that I became greatly swollen like a woman great with child." Jesus spoke to her these words: "Your sweet love finds me, your inner desire compels me, your burning love binds me, your pure truth holds me, your fiery love keeps me near. . . . I want to give you the kiss of love which is the delight of your soul, a sweet inner movement, a loving attachment." She had learned of this kiss from Bernard: "I longed for and greatly desired to receive the kiss just as my lord St. Bernard had received it."[27]

A perfect example of the modern western church's journey down this path is its current infatuation with the words intimate and intimacy. Week after week in church after church, in vision statements, mission statements, sermons, blogs, newsletters, podcasts, I hear and see references to "our need for intimacy with God." I understand what they are saying. Yes, we need to be close to God. Yes, God wants us to have a close relationship. But the choice of the word "intimate" shows how far the church is out of touch with the culture in which it operates. Do a Google search on the word intimacy and what you find is that most of the references, especially the images, have sexual connotations.[28] This confusion shows up on the Merriam-Webster website in responses to the question, "What made you look up *intimacy*?" A contributor named "Mary Ann" responded, "I am writing a book on intimacy with the Holy Spirit in his chambers." To which another contributor, "Santasha," responded, "Some people have the wrong interpretation of intimacy."

Unfortunately, for close to twenty years Christian authors have been using that wrong interpretation with regard to God, right up to the edge of sexual connotation. Brent Curtis and John Eldredge, for example, go beyond Jesus's references to the wedding feast and focus instead on "the unique intimacy of the wedding *night*." In this discussion of intimacy they refer to Jesus as "our Lover," and conclude it with, "In the *consummation* of love, we shall know him and be known."[29]

27. Podles, *The Church Impotent*, 103.

28. This, despite the fact that the synonyms for intimacy according to the Merriam-Webster website are belonging, chumminess, closeness, inseparability, familiarity, and nearness. I don't think those synonyms are what Christians are trying to communicate either.

29. Curtis and Eldredge, *The Sacred Romance*, 183 [emphasis added].

We live in a highly sexualized culture, and we must choose our words with care. Do a Google search for "funny church signs" and here are some of the photos you will find:

"You can't enter heaven unless Jesus enters you."

"Bored? Try a missionary position."

"Easter comes once a year. How often do you?"

"Staying in bed and shouting, 'Oh God!' does not constitute going to church."

Someone clearly did not think through the connotations of their language. (Well, maybe the last one was intentional. If so, I like it.)

Apart from the assumed sexual connotations, it is hard to justify the use of "intimate" or "intimacy" on biblical grounds. A review of the various versions of the Bible currently in use finds few instances of these words. "Intimate" and "intimacy" appear in the New International Version three times, never in either the old or new King James Versions, once in the Good News Translation, four times in the New Living Translation, twice in the English Standard Version, nine times in the New American Standard Version, never in the Contemporary English Version, and three times in The Message. When used, it is mostly in reference to sexual relations, though sometimes it refers to a close friendship. In only three instances, among all the aforementioned versions combined, is it used to describe our relationship with God.

So how did we get here? As with most major changes, by small incremental steps, the first of which were greatly needed. I remember well the discussions in the 1970s about the need to translate the scriptures from the "antiquated" language of the Revised Standard Version. One phrase in particular stands out, "Be reconciled to God" (Romans 5:10). What did that mean? We didn't use that kind of language. So it became, "Be put right with God." But what does that mean? Well, it means "to have a right relationship with God"—which morphed in sermons and Bible studies and conversations into "have a personal relationship with God"—which has now morphed into "have intimacy with God." That may seem innocent enough, but notice the subtle yet monumental shift that occurs between the beginning and end points. "Be reconciled to God" is something that *happens to* us—"God was in Christ reconciling the world (us) to himself" (2 Corinthians 5:19). In contrast, having "intimacy with God" is something *we do*. We tell people they need to be intimate with God, intimating that they need to move closer to God. And so, by small steps we have been seduced from the freeing power of grace to the enslaving treadmill of works. More than that, the former phrase preserves an awareness of God's holiness, that God is greater and "wholly other" than we. The latter phrase eliminates that sense, bringing God to our level or us to God's. It reminds me of the words in the Garden, "For God knows that when you eat of it your eyes will be opened, and you will be like God" (Genesis 3:4). It is a dangerous thing to bring the language of romance into spirituality.

Enmeshment

Related, but broader in scope than romantic emotions, is the language of enmeshment. On any given Sunday one is likely to hear, "life is all about relationships," or "relationships are the most important thing in life," or "Christianity is a relationship not a religion," or "you have to have a personal relationship with Jesus." All of this is true, and it *is* important. BUT, church culture is so awash with it that it conveys the message that Christianity is exclusively about relationships.

The interesting thing is, there is no word for "relationship" in the Greek or Hebrew biblical lexicons—only words for types of relationships, like kinsman or sister, etc. As a result, "relationship" appears 0 times in the KJV, 0 in the Revised Standard Version, 0 times in the English Standard Version, 0 times in the Good News Translation, 0 times in Contemporary English Version. Relationship also appears zero times in Young's Literal Translation, the Darby Translation, the Douay-Rheims 1899 American Edition, the Easy-To-Read Version, the New International Readers Version, the NKJV, 21st Century KJV, New Life Version, Worldwide English New Testament, and the Wycliffe Bible. It appears once in the New Century Version not in the actual translated text, but in a heading, "*Laws and Relationships*."

So how did it become so prevalent today? In the late 1950s and early 1960s "religion" again began taking on negative connotations, as something one did for personal gain or for show. Some Christians began emphasizing the relational nature of the faith over its religious elements. At the same time, new translations of the scriptures began to be produced. As time went on these proliferated, including the addition of paraphrased versions. As church culture began to change, "relationship" began to show up: 4 times in the 1984 NIV, yet with only one in reference to God, 6 times in the 2005 NIV (only two of which are in reference to God); 4 times in the NASB only one of which is the actual text, with the other 3 in a heading and all 4 are in regard to relationships between people, 3 of which refer to family relationships, and none of which refer to a relationship with God. But the latest versions and paraphrases have virtually exploded with "relationship: the Message—27 times, New Living—15 times, and Amplified Bible—19 times.

You may be saying, "So what? What's the problem?" There are two problems, one related to scripture and the other related to gender. As with the case of "intimacy," "relationship" has taken us far afield from the original intent of some of the scriptures in which the word is now found. Take for example the New Living Translation's version of Colossians 1:28:

> So we tell others about Christ, warning everyone and teaching everyone with all the wisdom God has given us. We want to present them to God, perfect in their relationship to Christ.

We will focus on the last sentence (which is, significantly, a subordinate clause in the Greek[30]). There are two phrases in this sentence that are not present in the Greek manuscripts, "to God" and "their relationship to." It is possible that Paul was thinking in terms of presenting those under his charge to God. However, the context suggests other audiences. In verses 25–27 Paul writes:

> I have become its servant by the commission God gave me to present to you the word of God in its fullness—the mystery that has been kept hidden for ages and generations, but is now disclosed to the saints. To them God has chosen to make known among the Gentiles the glorious riches of this mystery, which is Christ in you, the hope of glory. (NIV)

God has "disclosed to the saints" and "chosen to make known among the Gentiles" that "the mystery that has been kept hidden" is "Christ in you" (the Colossians). So, Paul says in vs. 28, he "proclaims Christ to everyone and admonishes and teaches everyone in all wisdom in order to present them" (including the Colossians) to the saints and the Gentiles. In other words, the audience is the Jewish Christians[31] (amongst whom Paul frequently had to defend his ministry) and the Gentiles (to whom Paul was

---

30. This translation breaks one strongly connected sentence into two weakly related ones. The Greek construction ἵνα παραστήσωμεν (the conjunction "*hina*" with the present subjunctive verb form "*—sōmen*") expresses purpose, not desire or hope, or even intention. It is much stronger than "We want to . . . " As we will see in later chapters, the strength of a statement is an important issue when communicating with men.

31. Ben Witherington makes the case for "the saints" as a reference to Jewish Christians in his commentary on Romans: "If we compare 1.7, where the letter is addressed to 'the beloved of God' and 'those called to be saints,' it is possible to believe that this refers to Gentiles and Jews in Christ respectively. Since Paul is primarily addressing Gentiles, he mentions them first. Again, if the letter is primarily addressed to Gentiles, with Jewish Christians listening in, then this portion of the letter becomes an exhortation for one part of the body of Christ, the larger Gentile part, to do a better job of helping and being understanding of the Jewish Christian minority. It becomes a word on target, which comports with the rest of the unitive rhetoric of the letter." Witherington, *Romans*, 294.

sent as a missionary). Gentile Christians in general and the Colossian Christians in particular are thus God's evidence of "the glorious riches of this mystery . . . the hope of glory." That makes the meaning of the final phrase very important. The Greek is τέλειον ἐν Χριστῷ (teleion en Christō). Τέλειος (telios), when used of persons, in both classical and New Testament Greek means "fully grown," "having attained adulthood" or mature. Paul is not saying he wants to present them "perfect in their relationship to Christ," whatever that means. He is saying he proclaims, admonishes and teaches in order to present them as "completed"—i.e. fully mature Christians. This is precisely parallel to Ephesians 4:11–13:

> It was he who gave some to be apostles, some to be prophets, some to be evangelists, and some to be pastors and teachers, to prepare God's people for works of service, so that the body of Christ may be built up until we all reach unity in the faith and in the knowledge of the Son of God *and become mature, attaining to the whole measure of the fullness of Christ.* (NIV)

Colossians 1:28 isn't about relationships, not even our relationship with Christ. It is about becoming completely like Jesus the Christ in every way. Inserting relationships into any-and-everything Christian prevents us from seeing all God wants us to see, and becoming all God wants us to be.

s'Mothering

Another component in the church's current relational culture is language that takes men back to their teenage years when they were first trying to figure out how to make their way in the adult male world. It reminds them of those times that they felt smothered by their mother. On any given Sunday in your church experience you will likely hear the language of the nursery. Words like "precious" and "sweet" appear regularly, sometimes in reference to Jesus other times in reference to events or experiences. We are told "nurture your children's faith" instead of "bring up your child in the discipline and teaching of the Lord" (Ephesians 6:4). Both phrases deal with the same topic, but the first says "Mom" and the second says "Dad." We hear a lot about the need to care and comfort one another, but not much about the need to challenge and strengthen one another. Even when we are trying to be bold, the nursery creeps in. Look, for example, at this promotional graphic from a church that boldly decided to address hard issues in a sermon series titled, "Elephants" (as in "in the room").

Not only that, there were 18-foot pastel papier-mâché sculptures of these in the major common areas and sanctuary in the church on 3 campuses. Do you know many Action Men who are going to be attracted by pastel pachyderms? The sermon series dealt with Abuse, Homosexuality, Porn, and Poverty. These are mean, bull elephant issues. What's with the cutsie herd? And is that a pink pastor pachyderm preaching in the glasses and tie? Yes, it was. It turned out the staff was afraid someone would be upset that they were talking about abuse, homosexuality, porn, and poverty. So they tried to lessen the shock by using nursery school images to promote it. Ironically, three women I interviewed at this church were upset because the images said to them that the series was going to be for children but the topics were anything but. The fear that someone will be upset is rampant in the church. It is an expression of over-protectiveness, aka, s'mothering. In many churches you'll hear frequent references to concern about someone getting or having been hurt. One pastor said, "I'm sick of hearing the word 'hurt.' I've sometimes wondered if I needed to carry around a box of Band-Aids to take care of everybody's emotional boo-boos."

That brings me to the biggest expression of s'mothering in the church: the inordinate concern about safety. Safety seems to have become the primary concern for church people, so much so that the national Christian radio syndicate, "The Fish," has taken this as their theme. At regular intervals throughout the day as you listen to these stations you will hear something like, "95.5, The Fish: Safe for the whole family." They know their market well. In fact, this concern for safety is so prevalent in the church that some researchers have said that the concern for safety, or the fear of risk, is the single factor that best explains the absence of men from the church. Alan Miller and John Hoffman found a high correlation between risk aversion and religiosity.[32] In other words, the more a person wanted to avoid risk, the more highly religious that person was likely to be.

Miller and Hoffman found this to be a paradox, since "there is scant reason to believe that becoming more religious makes one more risk aversive. Religious doctrines do not typically promote risk aversion; indeed,

---

32. Miller and Hoffmann, "Risk and Religion," 63–75.

they often encourage risk-taking behavior in the form of missionary work, proselytizing, or a number of other beliefs and behaviors at odds with secular norms. One can even argue that religiosity might increase risk taking rather than risk-averse behavior not only by promoting these acts but also by decreasing the individual's fear of death."[33] Yet with few exceptions churches seem to be reaching and/or retaining only those men and women who want to avoid risk.[34]

Once that becomes a noticeable characteristic of a church, it's hard to reach the person who enjoys risk. Steve, a friend at church was telling me that he had been trying to get another friend of his to come to church without much success. He asked what approach I would take. I asked him what his interests were:

> "We go off-shore fishing. He really likes to get out on the water—he's a diver," he said.
>
> "So get some your friends from church," I said, "and invite him to go fishing or diving with all of you. He needs to know more Christians than just you. How about Tim over there? He's a diver, isn't he?"
>
> "You gotta be kidding me," Steve snorted. "Look at him. Look at the way he walks. The way he moves, you can tell who runs things in his house—and it ain't him. The guy I'm talking about—last week a hammerhead shark starts swimming around the boat and he jumps in to swim with it! And you want me to put him with Tim? He wouldn't want anything to do with Tim."

Steve's friend is obviously on the high-end of risk-takers, but the fact remains that men in general value and seek risk more than women do, whereas women in general value and seek safety more than men do. Which is the higher value in your church—playing it safe to protect the church and its people, or taking whatever risks necessary to fulfill the mission God is calling you to?

Several years ago, I was speaking at an international conference held at Cliff College in Sheffield England. As I was speaking, the Bishop of the Wesleyan Methodist Church in Pakistan came in and sat down in the front row. After a while, he raised his hand and asked,

---

33. Ibid., 72.

34. You may be wondering if this is just in the church or across religions. There were participants representing other religions in Miller and Hoffman's original study, though the great majority claimed a Christian background. A follow-up study by Miller found that the correlation between fear of risk and religiousness was not present in Asian culture. (Miller, "Going to hell in Asia," 5–18.) Another study found the same among Muslims in Turkey. So there is evidence to suggest that the connection between fear of risk and religious involvement is strongest in the church.

"Are you saying that you have a problem in your country reaching men?"

"Yes," I replied.

"And is this true in most of the rest of your countries?" he asked of the other participants.

There was widespread affirmation from the other people in the conference hall.

He then said, "This is not true in my country. In my country we have more men than women in the church."

"Why do you think that is?" I asked.

The Bishop stood up and addressed the audience.

"In Pakistan, it is illegal to be a Christian. To become a Christian is to take a death sentence on your head. Men know—if there is little risk, there is little worth. If you have to risk your life . . . " he said as he spread open his hands, and then sat down.

We have become inordinately comfortable in the established churches of Christendom. The biggest risk many churches are willing to take is a building program and funding campaign. When we do ministry in risky places, it is at arms length. We will raise the money, but we want someone else to take the risks. We think we are safe and secure inside our walls. It is time we realize that the Church was not created for that. Jesus implied that the church was created to storm the gates of hell. Doesn't sound safe and secure to me. We need to take the words of Helen Keller to heart and apply them to our churches: "Security is mostly a superstition. It does not exist in nature, nor do the children of men as a whole experience it. . . . Avoiding danger is no safer in the long run than outright exposure. . . . Life is either a daring adventure, or nothing."[35] We need to follow the example of Rev. Phyllis Sortor, 71, a missionary with the Free Methodist Church, who was kidnapped by armed men in Nigeria in February 2015 and released several weeks later.

"Phyllis was aware there were risks associated with her ministry, but also knew there are very few places in the world without risks and dangers," a statement by the Free Methodist Church said. . . . [A spokesperson for the partnering mission project] didn't know if Sortor planned to return to Nigeria, but told NBC News, "I know her heart is there."[36]

---

35. Keller, *Let Us*, 50–51.

36. http://www.nbcnews.com/news/us-news/american-missionary-captured-nigeria-rev-phyllis-sortor-released-n319006 (accessed March 7, 2015).

If we follow her example—if we begin to again value risk—and if our language reflects that value, Action Men and Action Women will once again join us in the adventure.

Weakness/Brokenness

On December 27, 2011 the Facebook page, Jesus Daily, was named the most engaging site on Facebook. Jesus daily had almost 4.8 million interactions on its page for the year, over twice the number of its nearest competitor.[37] So on New Year's Day 2012 I went to the Jesus daily page and reviewed what the posts had been. Here's what I found (notice the words in italics):[38]

> JESUS......*please*......*carry*......*me*!!! December 26 122,017 people like this.
>
> LIKE if CHRIST is your *PROTECTOR*. LIKE if CHRIST *watches over YOU*. LIKE if CHRIST *takes care of your FAMILY*. LIKE if CHRIST *takes care of your HEART*. LIKE if CHRIST is *your SECURITY*. LIKE if CHRIST is your SAVIOR! CLICK SHARE NOW IF WANT OTHERS TO KNOW CHRIST! ♥♥♥ December 27 148,409 people like this.
>
> JESUS, thanks for *handling our problems* today. We love You!!! December 28 111,466 people like this.
>
> SHARE JESUS......if He loves us. SHARE JESUS......if He *calms us*. SHARE JESUS......if He *repairs us*. SHARE JESUS......if He pardons us. SHARE JESUS......if He answers us. SHARE JESUS......if He *understands us*. Has JESUS done all of this for you??? December 28 99,101 people like this.

Notice a theme in those italics? I certainly did. So I kept watching:

> LIKE if JESUS *comforts* you! January 4 89,667 people like this.
>
> JESUS......*carry*......*me*......*over*......*my*......*troubles*!!! January 9 122,701 people like this.
>
> JESUS...I...*desperately*...*need*...You!!! January 10 142,125 people like this.
>
> ††† Dear CHRIST, I really *need you desperately*. I know you hear my cries even though *I have failed you*... have mercy and PUT

---

37. http://allfacebook.com/jesus-daily-ends-2011-as-facebooks-top-engager_b72001 (accessed January 12, 2012).

38. Italics added, all CAPS in original.

MY BROKEN PIECES BACK TOGETHER. I'm *begging* You to *repair me*. I only have my love to give you in return. February 4 145,295 like this.

And on it goes, not just on Facebook but also in church worship services, Sunday school classes, Bible studies, etc. Words like "needs," "needy," "hurt," "wounded," "broken," and "desperate" show up again and again. Yes, we do need to come to a realization of our need for God. Yes, we need to help people admit their brokenness, so that they can allow God to heal their wounds. But, again, we have gotten out of balance. It is part of what I call the social-psychological captivity of the church. What I mean by that is that over the last forty years, the goals of ministry have become identified with the goals of social psychology. I say this as a person who majored in psychology and attended a seminary with a school of psychology whose courses are integrated into their ministry training classes. I value all that I gained from my psychological training. However, it has reached the point that the goals of social psychology have come to define ministry rather than simply inform it. And this is reflected in our language.

A perfect example is "small group ministry." Small groups, or "smá-grp" as the technical term is pronounced, have become a goal in many churches' ministries. A number of lead pastors have said to me, "My small group ministry pastor seems to think his (or her) job is just to get people into small groups." In other words the means has become the end. And even when the end is acknowledged, it has become confused with psychological rather than spiritual goals. For example, a friend was describing their new church to me.

> "I like it much more than our church in our previous community," she said. "Our previous church was huge, you know, a megachurch with all kinds of things going on. And that was great. But they were all the time after you to be in a small group. I didn't want to be in a small group and I got tired of hearing about it."

As she talked about her new church, she mentioned that she was in two Bible studies and a prayer group.

> "You do realize," I said, "that you are in three small groups." She paused for a moment, and said, "Well . . . yeah . . . But that's different."
>
> "How?" I asked her.
>
> "Well, small groups are, like, for support and stuff. You know, sharing hurts and talking out problems. I'm just not into that," she said.

Now if this woman feels that way (and this is not an Action Woman), how do you think your Average Joe Action Man feels about the references to small groups? Have you noticed that most men are not enamored of psychology? If a couple is having marital problems, it is most often the man who resists counseling or group therapy. It is difficult to get most men to participate in a support group, or self-help group, or encounter group. Why is this? It is not, as is commonly assumed, that men do not like to be in groups. Men gather in groups all the time. At the sports bar, the coffee shop, during breaks at work, on the golf course, at the fishing tournament, and on and on you'll find small groups of men talking, sometimes laughing, sometimes arguing, sometimes even in deep discussion. It is because the connotations associated with "small groups" are those mentioned by my female friend that they want no part of the church's small groups. They smack of brokenness, weakness, and neediness. Men don't talk about getting together with "my small group." They get together with "the guys," "my buddies," "the team," "the band," "the brew crew," and so on.

The church has always had small group ministries, but only in the last forty years has it been calling them that. In the 18th century Methodist revival in England, for example, it was a comprehensive system of small groups that enabled people to be transformed into mature Christians, which eventually led to the transformation of English society as a whole. Every Methodist was required to meet weekly with their "class meeting," a group of ten to twelve fellow seekers.[39] In that class they examined their lives in light of the Scriptures and sought to help one another "be transformed by the renewal of their minds" (Romans 12:1–2). The focus was on discipline, commitment, and obedience.[40] Yet in that context they experienced nurture, care, forgiveness, and encouragement.

The difference between those small groups and the small groups of the church of today is that there was an expectation of personal growth and real

---

39. One did not have to have become a Christian to be a Methodist. The classes were seekers groups where people explored and tried to live the Christian life.

40. Beginning with the leader, class members examine their lives with a series of questions: 1) When did you last commune (i.e. attend worship)? 2) What good have you done for which you could expect no return?; 3) Wherein have you been tempted? 4) How were you delivered? 5) Wherein may we assist you in overcoming? Generally within 4 to 6 months people would discover their inability to fulfill these expectations (i.e. the law). At this point they either dropped out, or realize that the Christian life is possible only by the grace of God, and became conscious Christians. They would then move into a "band," a group of 6 to 8 fellow Christians who helped one another grow to maturity in Christ. When the desire to "go onto perfection" awakened within them, they would move into a "select society." This was a group of highly committed Christians who agreed to examine their lives with one another to the closest degree, and seek the ongoing grace of God that is Christian perfection.

life change. In the early Methodist system, the small groups were a means of grace to achieve the acknowledged goal of being "made perfect in love." In today's small groups there is an expectation of support and care, but an acknowledged "reality" that "nobody's perfect."

One young man I interviewed expressed frustration with his accountability group about this:

> "I was able to tell my group that God completely set me free from addiction to porn and lust. After seventeen years of lust and porn addiction I'm finally free; the temptation is no longer tempting" he said. "But then the leader of the group responded, 'That's great; just know that you're going to still struggle. I meet with my accountability partner each week and more often than not, I have to tell him that I have not been as free from lust as I should have been that week. There will still be times when you'll fall.' My reaction was 'Who do you think you are?' I felt the chains fall off. I didn't do that. God's power did. Why is failure inevitable? I don't have to fight that temptation anymore. God does. And you know what, seven months later—I'm still free."

It is as if today's church people think that when Paul wrote that God's "grace is sufficient for you, for my power is made perfect in weakness" (2 Corinthians 12:9), he meant we were supposed to remain weak, perhaps even to welcome weakness.[41] My son, Jeremy, noticed church folks' assumption of weakness in their responses to one of his posts on Facebook:

> As my first child's arrival approaches, virtually all of my conversations with churchgoers (primarily male—because I have not had many conversations with female churchgoers) have had a common theme. These conversations have gone something like this: Churchgoer—"You ready to be a dad?" Me—"Oh, yeah."

---

41. Yes, I know that the passage ends with Paul saying, "Therefore I will boast all the more gladly about my weaknesses, so that Christ's power may rest on me. That is why, for Christ's sake, I delight in weaknesses, in insults, in hardships, in persecutions, in difficulties. For when I am weak, then I am strong." (vs. 9b–10) But to take this at face value is to ignore the immediate context of the passage and the greater context of Paul's writings. The passage begins in chapter 10 where Paul begins to answer his critics who have claimed he is overly boastful of his authority. It is filled with irony, sarcasm, and hyperbole. Just as Paul said, "What, shall I sin all the more that grace may abound?" (Romans 6:1) he would here say, "What, shall I be as weak as possible so that God's strength may abound?" Throughout his writings Paul urged people to persevere, to fight the good fight, to "Be on the alert, stand firm in the faith, be courageous (ἀνδρίζομαι—andrizomai—literally 'act like men'), be strong" (1 Corinthians 16:13). He understood that at our strongest we are still weak compared to God—and that we sense that comparative weakness. He was not saying, "Seek weakness." He was saying, "When our strength runs out, God's strength completes it (τελεῖται—teleitai—to perfect or complete)."

Churchgoer—"No you aren't. No one is ever ready for it." The common theme focuses on being overwhelmed as a parent. This is in direct contrast to my non-church-going friends (both Christian and not, and again mainly male) who say things like, "It's the best thing that will ever happen to you," and "It is a great adventure," and "You are going to be a great dad." I found the contrast startling because I find the comments said by non-church-goers far more Christ-like and helpful.

When Jeremy commented on this difference in responses between church folks and non-church folks, both on Facebook and in person, their response was, "Oh, no no—you'll do well. You'll be a really good dad. Don't listen to those people." Their root assumption was still that Jeremy was uncertain or lacked confidence, even when he had expressed confidence about becoming a father. In other words, in their minds, if you are a Christian you must think of yourself as weak.

That attitude is evident in over 122,000 people clicking "Like" on the Jesus Daily Facebook post, "JESUS. . . . . .please. . . . . .carry. . . . . .me!!!" It stands in stark contrast to Paul's statement, "Therefore put on the full armor of God, so that when the day of evil comes, you may be able to stand your ground, and after you have done everything, to stand" (Ephesians 6:13—NIV). We need to heed the message in this parody of the popular poem, "Footprints in the Sand:"

> One night I had a wondrous dream,
> One set of footprints there was seen,
> The footprints of my precious lord,
> But mine were not along the shore.
>
> But then some stranger prints appeared.
> I asked the Lord, "What have we here?
> Those prints are large and round and meet;
> But Lord, they are too big for feet."
>
> "My child," he said in somber tones,
> "For miles I carried you alone.
> I challenged you to walk in faith,
> But you refused and made me wait."
>
> "You disobeyed, you would not grow;
> The walk of faith you would not know . . .
> So I got tired, I got fed up,
> And there I dropped you on your butt."

"Because in life there comes a time
When one must fight and one must climb,
When one must rise and take a stand
Or leave their buttprints in the sand."[42]

SO WHAT?

That may be what you are saying: "So what? I hear overstatements on television all the time, even ESPN. And of course you hear about love at church. God is love, after all. And what's wrong with talking about relationships? People are dying for positive relationships. And don't we all want to be cared for? Why call it smothering? And don't we all experience weakness and need to acknowledge our brokenness?" My answer is, you are right. None of these things taken by themselves are major problems. In fact, most of them are important parts of Christian faith and life. However, when taken in concert and given play in the majority of our time, they do become a major problem for Action Men and Action Women. These men and women probably could not put their finger on why, but their response has been "This isn't for me," and they have voted with their feet. I propose a different question. Rather than "So what," let's ask that more important question, "So what should we do?"

My answer is, recover our balance. We do not need to be swimming in a sea of testosterone any more than a sea of estrogen. We should think of the church as a coastal estuary where saltwater and freshwater mix to form one of the most fertile environments on the planet. If the estuary gets either too salty or too fresh it becomes less fertile, less capable of doing what it was designed for. It is to that question that we turn next.

---

42. Every citation of this Christianized version of "Buttprints In The Sand" lists the author "unknown." The earliest version I have been able to find is on a pagan website: (http://cern.proboards.com/index.cgi?board=Misc&action=display&thread=118, accessed June 13, 2011). It lists the author as Ray Brumback. In this version it is "the Goddess" who walks along the beach and speaks. (This may explain why the Christian who originally adapted the poem "lost" the author's name.) The fact that many of the consciously pagan folks on this discussion site are former Christians makes this an interesting comment on how they perceive Christians—as whiny wusses who want to be carried.

4

What Should We Do about the Words We Use?

BASEBALL AND BALANCE

MY SOPHOMORE YEAR IN college was one of the most frustrating years of my life. From seventh grade on I had planned to play four years of college baseball and then become a major league pitcher. All had gone according to plan—all-state honors, a scholarship—but then in fall practices at Ohio University I blew out my elbow. Ulnar nerve relocation surgery over Thanksgiving break, rehab with the OU athletic trainers for six months, light throwing over the next summer, and I was supposedly ready to go. Only I'd lost both my fastball and curveball and, worst of all, I couldn't find the plate. From the beginning of that fall's practice through winter workouts to the middle of that spring's season I watched myself go from promising to doubtful to done.

Fast-forward forty years. I discover the old fart baseball leagues, Roy Hobbs Baseball and the Men's Senior Baseball League (MSBL), and start to play again. I decide to try pitching, but I still can't find the plate. It's so bad, for three years none of the managers will let me go near the mound. Then one day through the wonders of 21st century video technology I discover that during my windup I have been leaning back toward second base as I gather for the pitch. As a result, my center of gravity had gotten outside my pivot leg. My top half was lagging behind my bottom half, robbing the delivery of its power. The imbalance also caused me to fall off toward first base in my delivery and forced my arm to rush through the release point for the pitch, destroying any chance for consistent control. So I decide to change where my front foot lands on the stride to deliver the pitch. My foot comes down about ten inches to the right, and everything clicks. I do it again, and again, and again. The "feel" is back. The motion is tight. The curveball snaps, and this 61-year-old man's fastball hits 80 mph on the radar gun. And best of all, the pitches are on target.

Here's the point. When I moved my foot-plant to the right, it made me keep my torso over the inside of my pivot leg. I was balanced. With balance restored "the whole body, joined and held together by every joint with which it is supplied, [had] each part working properly and made the body [throw]"[1] the way God intended. (You do know that baseball is the first thing mentioned in the Bible, right? It starts, "In the big inning . . . " Not only that but did you know there are baseball references throughout the Bible?)

> Jesus said, "Listen then to what the parable of the [thrower] means. . . . The thrower is the church, whose pitches are so wild that two thirds of them are landing in the batters box and even the dugout. When the thrower throws strikes they are like seeds landing in fertile soil. But he can't throw strikes because his motion is off-balance. So the church has been sent down to the minor leagues until it regains its balance (Matthew 13:18–23, slightly paraphrased).

To begin to recover our balance, we need to move our foot-plant to the middle of the gender spectrum. We need to cut back on the use of "feminine" linguistic markers and increase our use of "masculine" ones. This means the use of fewer overstatements and the inclusion of masculine forms in the ones we do make. For example, men use words like great, strong, excellent, outstanding, first-class, etc. more than wonderful, marvelous, or lovely (unless you're a Brit). It means eliminating references to romantic emotions such as being or falling in love with Jesus or God, and referring instead to familial love. There can be great warmth, closeness, and strength between blood brothers and sisters, whether that blood bond is formed in the womb, in adoption, in the tree-house, or on the battlefield. In the truest sense Jesus is our blood brother. We need to re-learn and recover the strength of that brotherly love. It means that our language should not only be about relationships, but also about what we are called to accomplish because of those relationships. It means we should not only be caring for one another, but also challenging one another to take the risks necessary to be and do what God intends. And it means we should help people experience not only forgiveness and emotional support, but also the full healing of God that results in a greater strength and a higher purpose than they ever thought possible.

---

1. Ephesians 4:16, paraphrased.

We will look at each of those in detail shortly. But first, you need to look at your church in detail. Just as I was unaware of how I had changed my pitching motion,[2] you are probably not aware of how the language in your church has changed subtly over the past 40 years. So your first task is to assess communication climate of your church. But before you do:

STOP READING AND PRAY

It is no easy thing to change one's language. It is ingrained in us. We begin learning it while still in the womb. In fact, researchers at Pacific Lutheran University found that prenatal infants begin distinguishing between and remembering vowel sounds by English and Swedish speakers as early as ten weeks before birth.[3] When we become part of a group we adopt their speech patterns. Their talk becomes our talk. We don't have to think about it. It is comfortable. It feels right—to us and to them.

With this chapter you are beginning the process of changing not only your own language but also your whole church's language. That is a task that is beyond us. There will be apathy. There will be resistance. There will be distractions. There will be weariness. So what else is new? The church is, or should be, in the business of doing the impossible because we serve the God who makes all things possible.

So, right now, ask the Holy Spirit to take charge, to stay in charge, and to provide the charge for this task. Ask God to make you, your team, and your church open to change. Ask for eyes to see and ears to hear. Ask God to shield you from any temptation to self-promotion or self-protection. Ask Jesus to enable you to pray as he did in the garden, to trade your will for God's will. Ask God for the strength of will to see the task through to the end.

THE NEXT BABY STEP: A LOOK AT LAST WEEK

Before you can start doing this live in worship, classes, meetings, or conversations you need to get familiar with the process. That will be easier if you review written rather than spoken forms first. So, you and your team should divvy up the past week's publications to review using Lakoff's "Feminine Register."

---

2. It was probably over 40 years ago in response to the oblique abdominal muscle strain that produced the elbow injury.

3. "The ambient language to which foetuses are exposed in the womb starts to affect their perception of their native language at a phonetic level. This can be measured shortly after birth by differences in responding to familiar vs. unfamiliar vowels." Moon, "Language," 160.

This should include the sermon, bulletin, presentation slides, welcome/information packet, newsletter, blogs, social media posts, etc. Each team member will sit down with whatever piece of communication they are reviewing, five different colored highlighters or pens, and the following card:

Table 4.1: Feminine Register Vocabulary Card

FEMININE REGISTER VOCABULARY
Empty adjectives/overstatements [Highlight in yellow]: *wonderful, marvelous, fantastic, incredible, beautiful, excited, exciting, extravagant, awesome*
Romantic emotions [Highlight in fuchsia]: *adore, fall in love, in love with Jesus, heart (touches/open your heart)*
s'Mothering [Highlight in aqua]: *nurture, care, comfort, safe, safety, feeling, precious, sweet, cute, be there for you*
Enmeshment [Highlight in mint] *personal relationship, intimacy, drawing close, dear (dear hearts), embrace, hug, community, share, sma'gr'p (small group)*
Weakness/Brokenness [Highlight in khaki] *need, needy, hurt, neglect, wounded, broken, despair/desperate, help, small group (i.e. support group)*

Highlight each of the above words you find with the appropriate highlighter. (By the way, you can choose whatever colors you like, though it would be good for the whole team to use the same ones.) Here's an example from one church's review of the lead pastor's article in their weekly e-newsletter (Imagine each italicized word in the color named in brackets): When I went over this article with the staff I said, "This one has me stumped. You caught how gushy the first paragraph is. Look at all that yellow. But look at the second paragraph. Look at what I've highlighted in red. See how strong and challenging that is? I don't see how these two paragraphs could come from the same person." The lead pastor stopped me and said,

"That's because they didn't. I wrote the second one, but I was in a time crunch so I asked my assistant, ["Beth'], to write the first one." Going through the process of analyzing your church's publications can lead to epiphanies like this. Give your team several days to complete their reviews and then get together at a coffee shop or restaurant to discuss their findings. Do this for two or three weeks to get a feel for your church's communication culture. Once your team has done this a few times you will be ready to go on to doing it live. At that point, you can begin to:

TRACK THE TALK IN YOUR CHURCH

On the surface of it, this task seems simple. All you have to do is listen and count, right? But when my research team began doing this in the live settings of the church rather than the controlled conditions of the study we found things moving so fast it was hard to keep up. For example, when we compared our tracking during live worship services with that done of recordings of those same services, we found that we had missed up to 40% of the instances in the live setting. The problem was, there were too many words and phrases to keep in mind and find on the data sheet. Look again at Table 4.1 to see what I mean. You can imagine the complexity of the data sheet that produced. The answer was to assign a category to each team member to track on a data sheet dedicated to that category. To start your tracking we recommend doing likewise and having each team member simply track hits in their category as a whole, rather than counting the instances of the specific words and phrases in that category. Table 4.2 shows an example of a completed data card using this approach:

Table 4.2: Simplified Empty Adjectives And Overstatements Data Card

EMPTY ADJECTIVES AND OVERSTATEMENTS				
Date: 12/21/14		Service or Meeting: Contemporary Service announcements		
Speaker: Kris Christian		Approximate Speaking Time: 2 minutes		
Highlight, check, or circle words used:				
✓			✓	✓
wonderful	marvelous	fantastic	incredible	awesome
	✓			
beautiful	excited	exciting	extravagant	
Add others used that would fit this category: *Super-cool*				
Mark each time one of the words above is used: 卌 卌				

As your team gets accustomed to the process, you can make your tracking more detailed as in Table 4.3.

Table 4.3: Detailed Empty Adjectives and Overstatements Data Card

EMPTY ADJECTIVES AND OVERSTATEMENTS					
Date: 12/21/14		Service or Meeting: Contemporary Service announcements			
Speaker: Jill Christian		Approximate Speaking Time: 2 minutes			
Each time a word is used, place a mark in its box. Add other words used that would fit this category in the blank boxes.					
Wonderful |||	Marvelous	Fantastic	Incredible ||	Extravagant
Beautiful ||	Excited |||	Exciting	Awesome |||	*Super-cool*	

This detailed tracking enables you to identify each speaker's tendencies so they can work to overcome them. When you put them all together you will begin to get a feel for your church's overall communication culture. As you and your team become more able to hear the chimes of the Feminine Register, you will begin to recognize them in Bible study and prayer groups, planning meetings, and more. You can document how pervasive it is in your church by having a team member keep a running tally in each group or meeting.

During the time you are tracking the talk in your church you will, of course, continue going to the gym or the pub or the sports bar or wherever you are getting to know men outside the church. Remember from chapter 2: "If we don't communicate with the outside world—to gain information for knowledge and understanding—we die out to become a non-discerning and uninteresting part of that world."[4] By now you should be getting to know who the regulars are. For example, I take my dad to lunch at one of the sports bars in town every Wednesday. Apart from the wait-staff, the men out-number the women by about five to one. Most weeks we see the four seniors who play doubles tennis nearby, a trio who ride in on their Harleys, a half dozen guys in their thirties who work for a local contractor, and the management team from the Pro Football Hall of Fame. The patterns and topics of each group's talk differ only slightly from one another but differ significantly from church talk. Keep a mental tally of the number of times you hear the chimes of the Feminine Register. Record

---

4. Osinga, *Science*, 95.

it in the journal you began in chapter 2. Listen for any words or phrases that the men use but the women don't and visa versa. Compare them with of your church's talk. Think about how you could you use what you are hearing to help your church's vocabulary become more balanced. Here are some examples to get you started.

ALTERNATIVE EXPRESSIONS

Once you have a handle on both your own and your church's tendencies, you can begin recovering your verbal gender balance. Here are a few suggestions to get you started:

Empty adjectives/overstatements

First, use fewer of these. Men do use overstatements, just not as many of them. And those they do use have more of a connection to actions, physical characteristics, or a sense of hierarchy—or profanity[5]. This makes them more concrete and thus less a sense of being empty. (See Table 4.4.)

Table 4.4: Alternatives to Empty Adjectives

wonderful, marvelous, fantastic, incredible, awesome	great, rare, impressive, outstanding, quality, choice, the top
excited, exciting	stoked, fired up, pumped, jazzed, charged, energizing, exhilarating, invigorating

---

5. Yes, "F—king" is an empty adjective—a word whose use has become separated from its original meaning. Lackoff did not discuss profanity in these terms, but she did devote an entire section to the ways in which profanity, which is more permissible for men, lends a power to their talk to which women are denied. Selnow found that not only is profanity perceived as a male prerogative, but also that weak expletives (Shoot, Gosh-darn, Oh-fudge, etc.) are restricted to female usage. Women use "such substitutions more frequently than men, and men asked to play female roles choose weak expletives over their stronger counterparts. (Selnow, "Sex Differences," 1985.) And while standards for acceptance of profanity (male-appropriate language) are changing such that its use by females is now more condoned than previously, "it appears that male use of weak expletives (female-appropriate language) is not condoned" (Arlis, *Gender Communication*, 1991). Thus, Christian men's conscious choice to substitute weak expletives for profanity would evaluated negatively, and both contribute to and confirm feminine/not-masculine Christian stereotype.

extravagant	extreme, steep, immense, limitless, quantum

How does this work out in practice, you ask? Here's an example, using one of the announcements cited in the last chapter: Instead of

> We're really excited about our annual Family Camp that's coming up in two weeks. We had such a marvelous time at last year's camp. If you weren't there you missed something really special ... [6]

you could say

> This year's Family Camp will help you take your family to the next level. We've put together a team challenge course that will show how much we're capable of working together. Plus, our leaders for the weekend have a reputation for stoking families' spiritual fires ...

Romantic emotions

Remind yourself how hard it is for many men to talk about feelings. Now remind yourself how hard it is for many men to talk about love. Now remind yourself how hard it is for many men to talk about romance. Now recognize that today's emphasis on openness and acceptance of gay men has actually increased many men's determination to prevent any possible perception that they might be gay.[7] Remind yourself that the less education persons have the more likely they are to have traditional views of masculinity/femininity and negative attitudes about homosexuality.[8] Remind yourself that even though

---

6. Please stop talking about people who "missed it." Based on our talk, churches pay less attention to the people who are there than those who are not. And please stop talking about last year or last week or yesterday.

7. Witness the rise in the use of the caveats "I'm not gay, but ... " and " ... no homo" to statements that might be remotely construed as homosexual markers, especially those dealing with feelings.

8. "In general, 'education' increases acceptance of homosexuality, that is, attitudes improve as a function of time spent in education (Eliason 1995; Herek and Capitanio 1996; Kelley 2001; Kurdek 1988; Lottes and Kuriloff 1994; Seltzer 1992; Spark Jones 2000; contra Van de Ven 1994). For example, in 2000, 65 percent of General Social Survey Respondents with a high school education believed homosexual relations were always wrong, compared with 47 percent of college graduates (American Enterprise Institute 2004). In a longitudinal study conducted by Lottes and Kuriloff between 1987 and 1991, participants scored 25% higher on measures of homosexuality tolerance (as well as other liberalism measures) in their senior college year than they had as first-year students (1994). Senior students reported majority approval of homosexuality, which contrasted sharply with

the percentage of the population that begins college is at an all-time high, over two thirds of the US working age population has not attended college. That means that over two thirds of the adults have not experienced the social liberalization process of today's secular higher education. In such a context, statements like this are unlikely to connect with the majority of men:

> Judas stopped being Jesus's disciple, not when he betrayed him, but when Judas fell out of love with Jesus.[9]

Yes, even "fell out of love" will cause many people to think in terms of romance rather than reverence.

We need alternatives to language of romance. Remember the former NFL player who was doing prison ministry? He said the hardest part of his ministry was, "Helping these guys see that they have to open up—it's all about intimacy. If they can't do that they can't know Jesus." It isn't really all about intimacy. It's about honesty. They, and we, need to "man up" or own up—to face the failings, falls and F—k-ups[10] that separate us from God and each other. It's about owning our responsibility for our actions, being honest with ourselves about the choices we made and continue to make. It's about admitting that not one of us has the strength to change those choices in the future—that only the one who had the strength to choose the cross and break the chains of death is the only one who can break the chains of our

---

national findings (approximately 75 percent disapproval in both years: American Enterprise Institute 2004). Some research has found that students studying particular subjects or taking particular courses are more tolerant of homosexuality. Humanities, social sciences and psychology students are generally less homophobic than students studying subjects such as business and science (Matchinsky and Iverson 1996; Parker and Bhugra 2000; Schellenberg et al 1999), although some studies have found no difference (Cotten-Huston and Waite 2000; Ellis et al 2002). It is unclear whether humanities and social sciences students are less prejudiced as a result of course content, or because these courses tend to be chosen by less homophobic people or people predisposed to attitude change, or because these courses are dominated by women (Corley and Pollack 1996; Schellenberg et al 1999). It is generally accepted that increased tolerance is the result of what is learnt both inside and outside the classroom. For example, education fosters liberal attitudes, gives individuals the ability to think critically, the opportunity to interact with a diverse range of people and a greater awareness of the negative effects of prejudice. (Lewis 2003; Lewis and Rogers 1999; Lottes and Kuriloff 1994; Schellenberg et al 1999)." Attitudes Towards Homosexuality: A Literature Review Gail Mason & Mischa Barr Sydney Institute of Criminology, Sydney Law School, University of Sydney January 2006 Australian Hate Crime Network.

9. Leonard Sweet, Facebook post, 2/23/15. 143 likes. 21 shares.

10. If that reference bothers you, you will have to get over it. You will be unable to reach most men, and many women, today if you have a knee-jerk reaction to such language. They will dismiss you from consideration at the first hint of it on your face.

choices. That is a far cry from "You need to be intimate with Jesus." So here are some alternatives:

Table 4.5: Alternatives to Romantic Emotions

Adore, fall in love, in love with Jesus	prize, worship, honor, love, revere, brotherhood/sisterhood, blood-brother
heart (as in "touches/open/share your heart")	soul, spirit, being, marrow, gut, self, center
intimate/intimacy, drawing close	honest, open, authentic, transparent, truthful, fidelity, constancy, getting real

And here's a practical example using Pastor Rick Warren's unwitting use of romantic emotions in a video greeting to Awakening participants, followed by a re-worked action-oriented version.

> The problem is today many Christians are lethargic, they're burned out and they're living lives no different than those of unbelievers. They need to fall in love with Jesus all over again. That's what awakening is all about—getting close to Jesus Christ.

Try this instead:

> ... They need to decide to act on their love for Jesus, like they did when they first met him. That's what awakening is all about—choosing to focus our attention and actions on Jesus Christ.

Pastor Warren's statement shows how framing our love for Jesus in romantic terms accesses a whole constellation of inappropriate connections. The notion of the rekindled romance that leads to changed behavior is a Hollywood fantasy, and a rare one even in that make-believe realm. People who drift apart in relationships don't fall in love again by magically stumbling into it or somehow working up the emotions so that they want to be together again. Rather, most often with the help of a good counselor, they choose to spend time together and work to act in ways consistent with the relationship they once had, or wish they did. Then, over time, the emotions come. Biblical love is an act of will—"You *shall* love the Lord your God." To do that you must continually *choose to do so* "with all your heart and with all your soul and with all your strength and with all your mind." Action-oriented men and women are more likely to respond positively to the language of decision and action than to the magic moment of the chick flick.

s'Mothering

We have a special tie to our mothers. Have you ever noticed how dads spend years teaching their boys to play football, to the point of even being run over by them as they get bigger, and when the kid scores a touchdown in college on national TV he turns to the camera and says, "Hi Mom!" We love our mothers. But to everything there is a season—a time to be mothered, and a time to leave the nest. To most men and many women, the church is a haven for momma's boys. Take, for example, the descriptions of church men by Susan Isaacs in her blog, "How Do You Get Rejected by eHarmony? Start By Telling the Truth":

> I tried Match.com. Lots of interesting, successful, men with mojo. But none of them shared my religious faith. I already tried dating men outside my faith. At best, the guy says, "that's great for you." And doing the spiritual life alone got really lonely. So, I knew I needed a man with my faith. But all the church boys had NO mojo WHATSOEVER. I was screwed.... I tried eHarmony again. This time I lied, and said I always thought life was full of meaning. I got matched with nice Christian mojo-free men who worked in the Air Force or computer sales. Men who were never brave enough to admit that sometimes life sucks and doesn't make sense.... The others I got matched with looked into the camera but had creepy vacant eyes, like the church had stolen their spontaneity.[11]

To change that we're going to have to add the language of dads, a lot of it.

Table 4.6: Alternatives To s'Mothering

nurture	train, discipline, develop, cultivate, strengthen, fortify, enrich, foster, build up, upgrade, challenge
care, care for, comfort	protect, defend, fight for, guard, provide, uphold, assist, build up, boost, spur, galvanize
safe, safety	strong, capable, equipped, effective, potent, controlled, etc.

---

11. http://storylineblog.com/2013/08/07/how-do-you-get-rejected-by-eharmony-start-by-telling-the-truth/. Accessed 2/10/15. Used by permission of Ms. Isaacs, author of "Angry Conversations With God: A Snarky But Authentic Spiritual Memoir" ISBN-13:978-0446555449, website: thesusan.com.

feelings	acts, action, thought, will
precious, sweet, cute	invaluable, prized
be there for you (relational orientation)	count on me (actional orientation)

A special word on "safety"—place the emphasis on the characteristics of God that provide the ultimate, eternal safety rather than on our desire for immediate, earthly safety. This world is not safe and if we focus on our desire for safety we will remove ourselves from the world and the mission to which we are called. And that is what the church has done—become so concerned about safety that we hide behind walls. Recall from David Gilmore's observation that two of the three purposes common to the traditional view of men's roles around the world are to provide for and to protect the family, the community, the nation. Those roles require risk and the readiness to sacrifice self and life. The cross Jesus said we must bear is not the shiny one we wear inside our walls. It is hard and heavy, and must be carried up the rough road of sacrifice.

Enmeshment

You may be feeling like one the church leaders who commented on one of our online Church Without Balls videos:[12]

> Ok I get the whole intimacy and relationship type of thing but what other terms should I use to explain the experience between God and men through prayer life?

Here's how I responded:

> Good question. As we point out in the video, Scripture doesn't talk *about* our relationship with God—it *describes* it, using images and analogies. The Bible is full of both masculine and feminine analogies of how God relates to us. Some emphasize closeness (as father has compassion for his children or a mother who nurses her child), others protection (a hen gathers her brood), others discipline (the gardener prunes the vine), etc. Scripture has done it pretty well for 2000+ yrs. So has the Church until the last decade or so. Take, for example, St. Augustine's observation that, "One cannot know another except

[12]. "Personal Relationship and Male Intimacy Coaching Session" https://www.youtube.com/watch?v=1x6JQ8FczOs.

through friendship." Church folks today would be more apt to say (as one client pastor did), "You can't really know someone unless you invest in the relationship." See how different that feels? To a guy outside the church it sounds more like a frustrated girlfriend than your buddy.

With regard to how to talk with guys about prayer, I like the way Brother Lawrence describes prayer as an awareness of being immersed in God's presence & love, coupled with an awareness that God is in charge. He urged cultivating that awareness at all times, rather than just at specific prayer times, making the smallest action a joint venture with God. Prayer then is less about talk & more about shared action. Fishing with my dad or building a doghouse with him was like that. Not a lot of talk, but a lot of love and learning.

Table 4.7: Alternatives to Enmeshment

personal relationship	brother, sister, son, daughter, friend, confidant, ally, comrade, teammate, mentor, guide, etc.
embrace, hug	grasp, grab, clasp, grip, seize, hold
community, sma'gr'p (small group)	brotherhood, fraternity, kinship, team, crew, posse
share (BTW, there is no mention of sharing as talking *in the dictionary)*	tell, say, affirm, enlighten, bring out, fill in, admit, reveal, entrust, own/'fess/man up, get it out, come out with

Here's your practical example of getting away from the language of enmeshment. Remember this from chapter 3?

> "Its about being in community: . . . Every week, people will walk through the doors of our churches who need love, encouragement, support, a word of comfort or counsel or just simple, uncomplicated friendship. And you can be there for that person. So many churchgoers think, 'Oh, there is nothing special going on this week. I won't miss much. And I don't really have a job there so I can skip this time.' But it's not a matter of what you will miss. It's a matter of who will miss you."(Pastor's blog, Jan. 1, 2012)

Try this instead:

> It's about being a community—not just a crowd. . . . Every person who walks through the doors of our churches every week needs something—an act of love, an honest word of counsel or encouragement, the firm grip of friendship. You can provide that. A lot of churchgoers think, 'Oh, there is nothing special going on this week. I won't miss much. And I don't really have a job there so I can skip this time.' You do have a job here. It's your job to provide that special act, that word, that grip for the person who needs it. God is counting on you every week to make a difference for someone who will walk through our doors.

Weakness/Brokenness

Desperate: Don't use this, period. Don't sing songs that use it. It smacks of a rejected person lying on the ground crying, "Don't leave me, please don't leave me! I'll do anything for you!" It means acting from despair with no hope of success. I would venture to say that not one of the disciples chose to follow Jesus out of feelings of despair. That doesn't mean nobody does. It does mean that not everyone must. The woman who touched the hem of Jesus's robe is often portrayed as desperate, but nothing in the text says so. Instead it emphasizes her faith (Luke 8:40–49). Similarly, the Roman centurion who asked Jesus to heal his servant was not desperate. He was confident that Jesus could and would do so (Matthew 8:5–13).

Need, needy, hurt, weak, wounded, broken, help: Having alternatives to these is not what is necessary. Rather, these should be used sparingly and in the context of the battle that is life. Without that context we get surprised by pain. I once asked a friend from Kenya what difference he saw between parenting practices in America and in his homeland. He said

> Americans are amazing people—great power, every one of you, but no discipline. You think you must teach your children that everything can be theirs. In Kenya we understand—we must teach our children that life is pain. If we do not, when pain comes—as it must—they will think they have been betrayed by God.

So how do we talk about being wounded or broken and needing help in a way to which many of the men and women we are missing will respond? Here is an example from C. H. Spurgeon's 1916 sermon "The Battle of Life."

> When life is represented as a warfare, some peaceful minds may feel a little alarmed at the pictures; yet there are other minds with enough of gallantry in their constitutions to feel their blood pulsing the stronger at the thought that life is to be one continued contest. I do but borrow a reflection from the secular press when I say that it were ill for us if the love of peace, fostered among us as a nation, should degenerate into a fear of danger, a reluctance to bear hardships, or an indifference to the accomplishment of exploits.... For me the battlefield has no charms. With host encountering host, and carnage left behind, I have no sympathy, but spiritually my soul seems enamoured of the idea; I buckle on my armour at the very thought that life is to be a conflict and a strife, in which it behooves me to get the mastery...
>
> Do I see some young man, eager, earnest, all of a glow, ready for the crown? Let me remind thee that thou mayest be defeated. Though it is well for thee to begin life with a resolute determination to fight through the battle, still I would have thee remember that thou mayest be led captive by thy foe.... So, then, charges there will be in this life-battle. It is not to be won without pain and cost. Let us just glance at some of these charges. You will soon see how they mount up. If any man shall get up to heaven what a demand for courage he will have to meet! How many enemies he must face! How much ridicule he must endure! How frequently must he be misrepresented and maligned! How often must he be discreet enough to be silent, and anon, bold enough to speak and avow his convictions and his purpose!... It is so, and I pray you count the cost. There is no "royal road" to heaven, except that the King's highway leads there. There is no easy road skillfully leveled or scientifically macadamized. The labour is too exhaustive, the obstructions are too numerous, the difficulties are too serious, unless God himself come to our help...[13]

In my great-great-great-grandfather's Methodist hymnal the most worn, and therefore most used, section is titled, "The Warfare." The hymns in that section are full of references to being in need or broken or wounded. But the focus is not on the neediness nor the brokenness nor the woundedness. It is on the certainty of Christ's victory and the assurance that our sacrifice is integral to it. If we are to reach and retain action-oriented men and women, we must not only empathize with the pain of the wounded. We

---

13. Spurgeon, Charles H. "The Battle of Life." http://www.spurgeon.org/sermons/3511.htm (accessed 2/26/15).

must also emphasize the value of the wounds we take and the sacrifices we make in the cause of Christ:[14]

> Now I rejoice in what I am suffering for you, and I fill up in my flesh what is still lacking in regard to Christ's afflictions, for the sake of his body, which is the church (Colossians 1:24). For just as we share abundantly in the sufferings of Christ, so also our comfort abounds through Christ (2 Corinthians 1:5).

PUTTING IT ALL TOGETHER

Here is where the need for discipline and perseverance will kick in. You will be tempted to say, "Ok, I've got this. I'll just keep it in mind. That'll take care of it." If you do you may see some change in the short term, but in time you will slip back into old patterns. We are, after all, cognitive misers. We try to conserve as much mental energy as possible. But changing the way we talk consistently is like learning a new language—it takes a lot of mental energy. That means you and the others in your church, group, or class will have to be both intentional about the process of change and supportive of one another throughout.

How to Use the Information

First, have each writer/speaker summarize his/her tendencies from their data cards (see Tables 4.1 or 4.2) on a single sheet. Each can then highlight their tendencies on copies of Tables 4.4-4.7, the Feminine Register alternatives. Use this as a filter in all your writing and preparations for church events and meetings. In your word processor use Find & Replace to balance—not eliminate, balance—your use of the Feminine Register with alternative expressions. In conversations with your teammates in this process, make a game of catching each other's slips into old patterns. Consciously work at including the patterns you are noting in your research journals from the time you are spending among men at the sports bar, in the locker room, and elsewhere. As you see changes taking place in your language tracking data sheets, take time to celebrate your progress with each other. Tell others about the progress you are making and invite them into the process. In this way you will begin to change your church culture.

---

14. No, I am not talking about the so-called persecution some claim that American Christians are supposedly suffering. Such claims do nothing but confirm the stereotype of Christians as wimps.

5

The Topics We Choose

In February, 2013 Rev. Meagan Manas, co-chair of the Words Matter project of the National Council of Churches, wrote a guest blog titled, "Is God a He? And Why This Question Really Does Matter." It appeared on a number of different individuals' and denominational websites and Facebook pages.[1] In it Rev. Manas told of the beginning of the Words Matter project:

> "Dear God, are boys really better than girls? I know you are a boy. But try to be fair. (signed) Sylvia."—Taken from a child's letter to God.
>
> About three years ago around this time of year, I was lucky to get involved in a conversation between many wise women who work in denominations and their women's organizations, in seminaries and churches, who were concerned about the way words were being used. Most of them had been active in the "original" inclusive language battles in the 60s, 70s and 80s. They had worked hard to write articles opposing male-only language for God, they had passed through denominational and seminary policies that required use of gender-neutral words for God and for people: *chairperson* instead of *chairman*, *brothers and sisters* instead of simply *brothers*, and the repeated use of the word *God* instead of any pronouns at all (For *God* so loved the world that *God* gave *God's* only . . . etc.)

---

1. For example, http://manmadegirls.com/guest-post-is-god-a-he-and-why-this-question-really-does-matter-by-meagan-manus/, https://www.facebook.com/permalink.php?id=77023877889&story_fbid=308351425935304 (National Council of Churches), https://www.facebook.com/WomenoftheELCA/posts/171226246261841 (Evangelical Lutheran Church of America), http://horizons.pcusa.org/magazines/2011/hrznmyjn11/wordsmatter.pdf (Presbyterian Church, USA) (all accessed February 25, 2013).

Each of these women, about 20 of us on a conference call, were deeply troubled at the state of the usage of inclusive language in churches and seminaries today, after all these policies and regulations were in place. Instead of an improvement, they had seen a decline. Students brushed off the concern for inclusive language as the pet project of one professor, not a central justice issue for people who would become leaders of faith communities. Pastors and people in charge of denominations used inclusive language when they felt like it, or remembered to do so—which was not often.

That was the problem identified on our phone call; when folks were just handed a rule or a policy, they were not apt to understand why it was important to follow. We needed a way to not just tell people what kinds of words to use, but to help individuals understand how much was at stake in the language they chose—how the words we use can reinforce the very systems of injustice we say we want to dismantle: patriarchy, racism, ablism, heterosexism, and on and on.

The other problem we saw was the problem of neutral language. When pastors talked about God and Godself, we all found ourselves continuing to picture a male, often white, God. The neutral language did nothing to equalize or change; it only masked the systems of power rampant in Christianity. Instead of neutral language, we determined, what we needed was *more* language. *More* words, images and pictures of God. A greater diversity. Instead of simply "inclusive" language, we needed something expansive.

Out of this conversation sprang *Words Matter*, a project based in storytelling and conversation with awareness and awakening as its goal. Words Matter gathers a group together and then asks each person to tell the group a short (3 minutes or less) story about a time when they noticed the power or importance of words. Every time I lead this process, I am surprised again that *everyone* has a story. When we give the prompt, we are careful to specify that these can be stories of hurt or of healing, but the vast majority of stories I hear are those of pain. They are stories of not belonging, of being unworthy, being left out, being discriminated against.[2]

---

2. Rev. Manas struck a responsive chord. In August 2013, Audrey J. Krumbach, United Methodist GCSRW Director of Gender Justice and Education posted the following announcement: "The General Commission on the Status and Role of Women is seeking to rekindle conversations about the names and ways Christians talk about God, with a particular interest in understanding the impact of previous 'inclusive language' movements." http://umcconnections.org/2013/08/15/names-of-god-survey/ (accessed August 15, 2013).

As I read this I remembered the wistful look of sadness on my mother's face as she told me of an experience while growing up in rural southern Ohio. It was 1935 and she was ten years old. She was at the well beside the barn, pumping water to carry to the washhouse, when she heard an airplane in the distance. It came into view and flew low, right over the barn. "I just stood there and cried," she said. "I wanted to grow up to do that so bad, and I knew I never could . . . because I was a girl." Mom went on to accomplish some pretty incredible things as a professional speech pathologist. But she always felt constrained, and I felt her pain. I'm glad my violinist daughter came of age as professional orchestras stopped being bastions of male exclusivity. I don't want her to be or feel excluded from anything she wishes to pursue. Neither do I want my son to be or feel excluded from anything, particularly from life in the church. The unfortunate fact is that he and many men, young and old, are experiencing exclusion from the church because of the language we use. Rev. Manas was right, words do matter—to men as well as women. She was right; we do need a greater diversity, something more expansive. We need it for the women who have felt and been excluded by the limits our language has placed upon them. We also need it for the men—because for men the issue is less obvious than the use of masculine nouns, pronouns, and images in reference to God. For men it goes to the very topics to which we currently limit the church's message.

WHAT IS INCLUSIVE LANGUAGE?

Remember from chapter 1 my study on perceptions of Christians? All agreed, both churched and unchurched, male and female: Christian characteristics were almost exclusively feminine while un-Christian characteristics were almost exclusively masculine. Those findings led me to surmise that one source of the "feminine Christian" stereotype might be the themes Christians themselves choose to emphasize. So I held a series of focus groups with members of Sunday school classes and Bible study groups, asking them to identify and discuss the primary themes of the Christian faith. The ten most mentioned responses were these: being open or sharing feelings, submission, community, nonviolence or nonaggression, support, nurture, forgiveness, love, humility, service, and becoming (as opposed to doing); all themes from American culture's feminine set. To see if church and non-church men perceived these themes differently, I constructed ten conversational statements using those themes, based on Christian educational and sermonic material. Here they are:

"Cross-sex-typed" (for men) Messages

Each statement is followed by the church-related source from which it was adapted.

1. "Don't keep your worries, fears, and problems bottled up inside. We need to share our feelings with each other." (Adult Sunday School lesson)
2. "You come to realize at some point that you are not in charge of your life." (Senior High Sunday School lesson)
3. "Nobody can go it alone. You have to learn to lean on other people to make it in this world." (Adult Sunday School lesson)
4. "You should always refuse to get into a fight. Even if there seems to be no way to avoid it, you should always 'turn the other cheek.'" (Junior High Sunday School lesson)
5. "I'd like to support people, to nurture them so they can be all they want to be." (Sermon)
6. "We all need forgiveness. I do. You do. It's the only way we can get a fresh start." (Sermon)
7. "The greatest need we have is the need for love. You need to know you are loved and to love others." (Sermon)
8. "It's important to be humble. You should put other people first and think of them as better than you." (Philippians 2:3, NIV)
9. "Though it may mean having less money and prestige, serving others should be a person's central goal in life." (Small group Bible study guide)
10. "It's not so much what you do or accomplish that really matters. It's the kind of person you are." (Sermon)

Then I asked ninety-three church men and ninety-eight non-church men to rate them as part of a "Conversational Perceptions Survey." The men were to rate on a seven-point scale how likely they would be to use each statement in a conversation with a male friend and with a female friend. On average, the Church Men group endorsed saying these things to both men and women, and there was no real difference between saying them to men or saying them to women. The Non-church Men group were not likely to say them, but said they were far more appropriate for women than men. The difference between the Non-church Men's rating for a woman or a man was four times the Church Men's difference![3] (See Figure 5.1).[4]

Figure 5.1: Likelihood of "Feminine" Message Use by Non-Church vs. Church Men

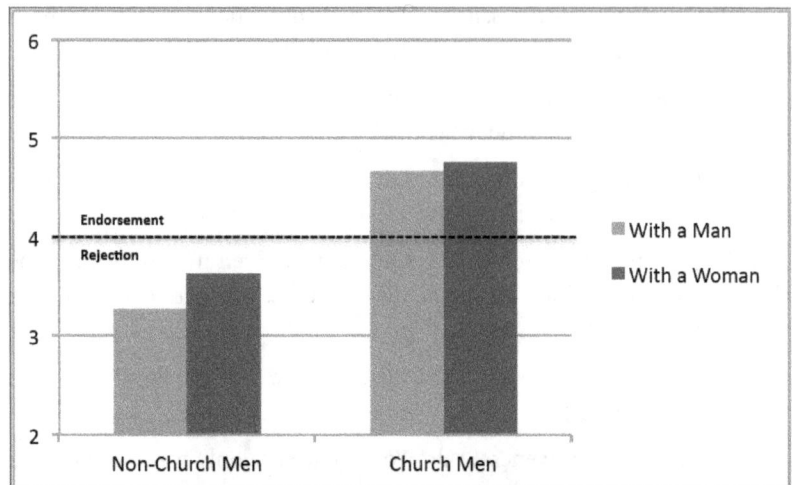

So, the Church Men thought these were fine things to say to either a man or a woman, while the Non-church Men would not use them in a conversation, especially one with a man. Let me say it one more way to be clear; Church Men would say things to another man that the Non-church Men considered entirely inappropriate for male conversation. Yes, I know these ten themes are legitimate and important elements of the Christian worldview. I am not suggesting eliminating them. What am I suggesting? Be patient. We'll get there.

This difference in perceptions becomes even more important when the men's gender schematicity—that is, the extent to which they identified with America's definitions of masculinity and femininity, as we discussed

---

3. Usage ratings were the means of the sum for statements one through ten. T-test of the data showed differences between the church and non-church samples. Means, difference scores, T scores, and statistical level of significance can be found in Appendix E.

4. They also rated how likely they thought an independent person, an assertive person, a sensitive person, and a gentle person would be to use each statement. These four personality characteristic ratings provided a validity check for how the statements were perceived in relation to the gender schema. In previous studies I had found that "independent" and "assertive" had the highest loadings on the masculine factor, while "gentle" and "sensitive" had the highest loadings on the feminine factor. Thus, these ratings indicated how masculine and how feminine each of the statements were perceived to be and were consistent with each groups usage ratings of their use with men and women. Reliability coefficients, means, difference scores, T scores, and statistical level of significance can be found in Appendix E.

in chapter 3—is taken into account. In the church sample, 37 percent were Action Men, 29.4 percent were Combination Men, and 33.6 percent were Relation Men (See Figure 5.2).

Figure 5.2: Gender Schematicity in Church Sample

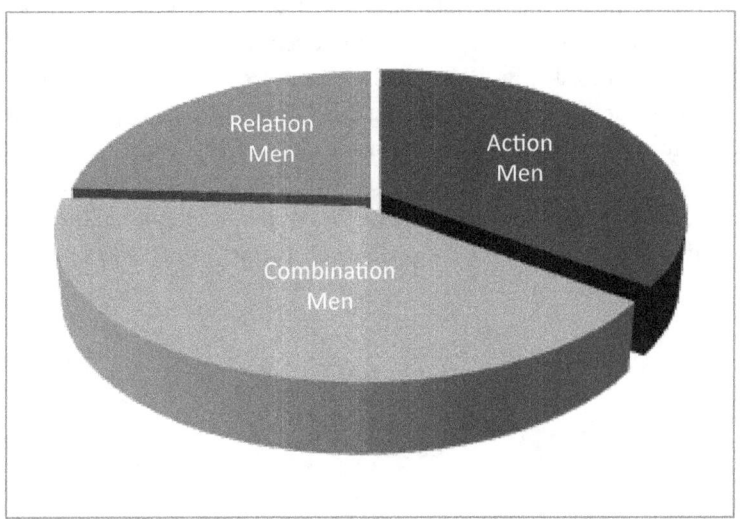

In contrast, the non-church sample was 63.4 percent Action Men, 25.5 percent Combination Men, and 11.1 percent Relation Men (See Figure 5.3).

Figure 5.3: Gender Schematicity in Non-Church Sample

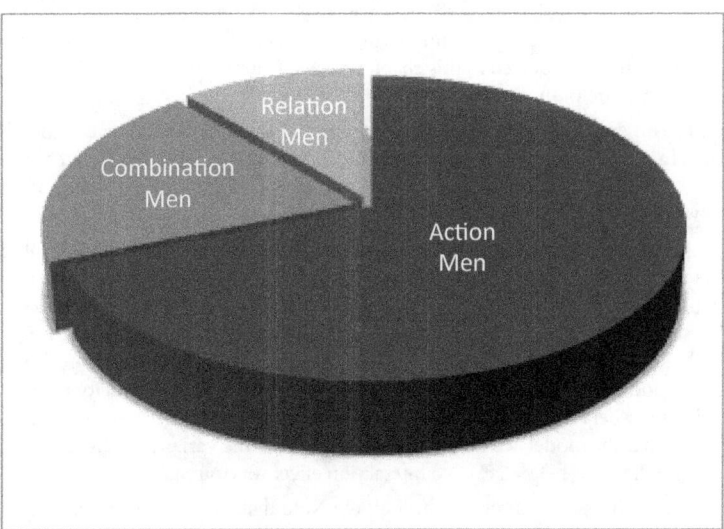

These percentages are consistent with those found in my twenty-three years of surveys referenced in chapter 3. And they are significant, both statistically[5] and in terms of importance.[6] There was almost twice the number of relationally oriented men (Relation Men + Combination Men) among the church sample compared to the non-church sample. In contrast there were almost three times the number of action-oriented men (Action Men + Combination Men) among the non-church sample compared to the church sample.

You might ask why I have included the Combination Men in those that are "relationally oriented" among the church sample, but put them with the "action-oriented" among the non-church sample. It is because of what the Church Combination Men thought of the statements compared to the Non-church Combination Men.[7] Among the church sample, all three types of men rated the statements as equally appropriate for men and women.[8]

---

5. Statistical significance refers to the likelihood that the result has occurred by chance. A .10 level of significance means we are 90 percent certain it is not by chance; .05 means we're 95 percent certain; .02 means 98 percent certainty, etc. Significance levels for the results reported in this chapter ranged from .02 to .000. The details (along with the devil) are in the Appendix E.

6. The difference in the proportion of androgynous and cross-sex-typed individuals in the sample of church men compared to the non-church sample was tested by means of cross-tabulation with chi-square test of significance. Chi-square Likelihood Ratio value was 15.108 (df = 3) and was significant at the .001 level.

7. An analysis of variance using unique sums of squares revealed significant main effects for schematicity on the male usage index (f $(3,181)$ = 8.17, $p < .000$) and on the female usage index (f $(3,181)$ = 7.64, $p < .000$), as well as for churchedness on the male usage index (f $(3,181)$ = 35.26, $p < .000$) and on the female usage index (f $(3,181)$ = 24.52, $p < .000$). Multiple classification analysis on the male usage index indicated that the model accounted for 30.3 percent of the variance (schematicity beta = .32; churchedness beta = .38). Multiple classification analysis on the female usage index indicated that the model accounted for 25.5 percent of the variance (schematicity beta = .33; churchedness beta = .32). No interaction effect was found.

8. See Figure 5.4, columns 4a through 6b: Note that the columns in each pair are almost the same height.

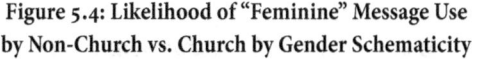

Figure 5.4: Likelihood of "Feminine" Message Use by Non-Church vs. Church by Gender Schematicity

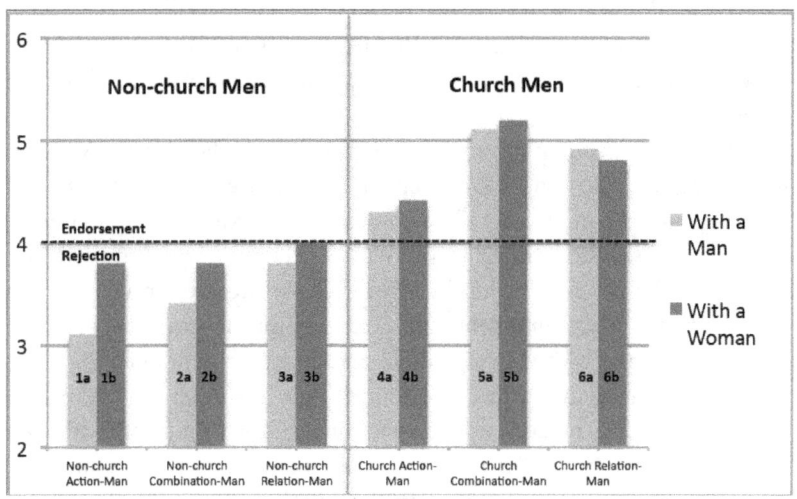

But the Church Combination Men stand in stark contrast to their Action Men brothers. While Church Action Men did cross over the line into endorsement (See Figure 5.4, column pair 4), their rating was significantly lower than either Church Combination Men or Church Relation Men. (See Figure 5.4, column pair 4ab vs. column pairs 5ab and 6ab.) These are the men who go to church, but hate it. The Church Combination Men and Church Relation Men, however, strongly endorsed using the statements for both men and women. (See Figure 5.4, column pairs 5ab and 6ab.) Finally, while the Church Combination Men differed significantly from the Church Action Men in their endorsement, they showed no statistically significant difference from the Church Relation Men. So, inside the Church Combination Men act like Relation Men.

But outside the church Combination Men do not; they act like Action Men. The evidence? The greatest difference between men of the same type was among the Non-church and Church Combination Men. (See Figure 5.4, column pairs 2ab and 5ab.) Non-church Combination Men maintained the distinction between making these statements to men or to women—better to say to a woman than a man (column 2a vs. 2b). The fact that they make this distinction suggests that they should be included among those who are "action-oriented" in the non-church sample. This means the non-church sample would be 89 percent action-oriented. Church Combination Men, however, do *not* distinguish between saying them to men vs. women (column 5a vs. 5b). Plus, they rate the statements higher than any other type for both men and women (column pair 5ab vs. all other columns). *This means that Combination Men outside the church apparently feel the need to edit their talk to fit cultural expectations, while Combination Men inside the church feel free to express themselves fully.* That freedom is something to celebrate. However, if practiced indiscriminately it simply confirms the "feminine Christian" stereotype.

In contrast, among the non-church sample only the Relation Men did not distinguish use with men or women. (See Figure 5.4, columns 3a and 3b are almost the same height.) All three types of Non-church Men were equally likely say these things to women. (See Figure 5.4, columns 1b, 2b, and 3b are almost the same height.) However, the more a non-church man identified with the cultural definition of masculinity, the lower he rated the statements for use with men. The Non-church Action Men rated the statements significantly lower for use with men than any other type of man in the study. And they made a larger distinction between using them with men vs. with women as well. (See Figure 5.4, column 1a vs. all other columns.)

So, the men who are present in the greatest numbers in the general population (the Action Men, plus Combination Men who act like them, combine for a total of 89 percent) strongly consider these statements to be sending a women's message. Yet all the men in the church consider these statements equally appropriate for use with men and women. And the men who are present in the greatest numbers in the church (the 65 percent Relation and Combination Men who act like them) say strongly that they would use them.

In sum, then, this study showed, 1) that gender appropriateness is a primary measure by which Non-church Men evaluate statements containing Christian themes, and 2) that Church Men report they would make such statements to other men, while Non-church Men consider them altogether inappropriate for use with men. These findings suggest that the decades-long quest for inclusive language has been far too limited in scope. For men outside the church, the issue of inclusive language appears to extend beyond the use of masculine nouns and pronouns to the very themes Christians choose to communicate. This would not be such an issue if the church hadn't been limiting itself to culturally defined feminine themes for decades.

OH, WE FORGOT ABOUT THAT!

Whenever I present the above material in one of my seminars someone invariably says, "But that is what the Bible teaches! Look at the fruit of the Spirit. It is mostly 'feminine.'" And they are right. Look at the list:

> But the fruit of the Spirit is love, joy, peace, forbearance, kindness, goodness, faithfulness, gentleness and self-control. (Galatians 5:22–23, NIV)

Most of those characteristics do show up on the feminine side of the gender schema in most cultures around the world. But Paul never meant this as a comprehensive list of what is to characterize God's people. The whole of Galatians 5 is actually about our being people of character who have honor and integrity. The "fruit of the Spirit" is only a subset. Many Christian themes are "masculine" in the sense of being agenic or action-oriented. James 1:22—2:26 says we are to be people of influence who take action to make a real difference, rather than just promising to pray. First Corinthians 12 says we are to be functioning parts of the Body (or members of the Team to use a modern image) who know and are satisfied with our role. Romans 8:18–39 says we are part of a plan that works to accomplish God's purposes. Matthew 11:7–15 holds up John the Baptist as an example of the courage Paul says over and over we are to have. Philippians 3:7–14 issues the challenge to respond to the high call of life in Christ. Ephesians 4:11–16 says the purpose of every leader in God's church is to enable every Christian to mature to their full potential, which is nothing less that the full character of Christ. In Luke 17:5–10 Jesus teaches that the life of faith is about fulfilling our responsibility, not about receiving rewards. First Corinthians 9:24–27 says that the Christian life takes discipline and perseverance in order to finish the race. First Thessalonians 1:2–10 shows that the Holy Spirit gives us power so that we have the strength to live a life that stands out as a witness.

"Masculine" Themes Make a Difference

To test whether men would respond more positively to "masculine" (i.e. action/agenic) themed Christian worldview statements, I constructed 10 such statements and added them into the Conversational Perceptions Survey. I selected the biblical characteristics discussed above for the statements because they were rated most strongly as masculine in my earlier gender research.[9] Here are the statements:

9. In this study I performed factor analysis on data from the standard administration of the Bem Sex Role Inventory (aka: BSRI). A minimum of four items with .60 loadings was the criterion for acceptance of a factor. A .30 loading was the minimum criteria for inclusion of additional items on a factor. Principal components analysis with Varimax rotation resulted in two factors consisting of twenty-three and twenty-four items that met the criteria. I also conducted a Q Methodology study of the BSRI for purpose of comparison with the BSRI. These results were remarkable for their almost exact match to Bem's classification of the items as masculine, feminine and neutral,

"Masculine" Themed Christian Worldview Statements

(Numbers represent each statement's order in the Conversational Perceptions Survey.)

3. "I want to be somebody who makes a difference. I want to make the world a little better than it was." (Influence—James 1:22—2:26)

6. "You've got to have somewhere to belong. You need a team you're a part of." (Belonging or Teamwork—1 Corinthians 12:1-31)

7. "There's got to be a purpose in life—a plan you fit into." (Purpose or Position—Romans 8:18-39)

9. I want to be known as a person with integrity. It's time we re-discovered the idea of honor." (Character—Galatians 5:1-26)

12. "At some point you've got to have the courage to stand up for what is right." (Courage—Matthew 11:7-15)

13. "There's something more asked of us than most of us realize. We are called to live on a higher plane than we do." (Challenge—Philippians 3:7-14)

16. "You have to try to live up to your potential. That's the only way life is worth living." (Fulfillment—Ephesians 4:11-16)

18. "Some things you just have to do because they're your responsibility. If you don't, you let people you care about down." (Responsibility or Duty—Luke 17:5-10)

19. "You have to be tough with yourself sometimes. It may hurt or it may be hard, but you just have to 'suck it up' and do it." (Discipline or Perseverance—1 Corinthians 9:24ff)

20. "I want to be somebody who can find the strength to face any challenge." (Strength or Power—1 Thessalonians 1:2-10)

I also included women in the sample to compare their responses as well.[10] Separate indices for the feminine statements' use and the masculine

---

and thus confirmed the results of the factor analysis. The ten themes chosen for the Masculine Christian Worldview Statements were those with the highest loadings on the masculine factor. See Appendix F: Responses Of Men And Women To Masculine and Feminine Christian Messages for a detailed description.

10. A balanced sample of one hundred seventy-six non-church and church men and women rated the statements as before. See Appendix E for details of the sample demographics.

statements' use, each with men and with women, were computed.[11] As with the previous study, a measure of each person's gender schematicity was also taken. Preliminary analysis showed results for schematicity's influence on the message ratings consistent with the previous study. That is, the more action-oriented the person, male or female, the lower they rated the feminine statements and the higher they rated the masculine statements. Relational orientation reversed that effect. For Combination Men & Women, church participation correlated with a preference for feminine statements while non-participation revealed a preference for masculine statements. Finer distinctions between the groupings were also evident. However, the sample is not yet of sufficient size for this more complex research design[12] to provide reliable predictive power for any of these findings. We will see where these trends lead, if anywhere, as this research continues. If the future research is consistent with these findings, it would provide one more piece to the puzzle of the church's decline over the last forty years. It would suggest that have we been losing not only the majority of men, but also those women for whom personal action and impact is a priority. The church's current awakening to its lack of missional focus would be reflective of that reality.

The results of comparing responses by church vs. non-church, and men vs. women, were robust and instructive. Only Church Men and Non-church Women differed significantly from each other in rating masculine statements for use with men.[13] The difference seems to be a function of the Non-church Women's perception of appropriate statements from a woman to a man, as evidenced they their strong endorsement of these same statements for use with other women. This is an important finding, as it suggests that the gender schema remained a factor in their response to the masculine messages. The Non-church Women strongly endorsed these statements' use with women, but were the only ones to be significantly less likely to use them with a male friend. Thus, they identified with the themes expressed, though they considered them less appropriate for a woman to say to a man.

---

11. The indices were the sum of the mean scores for the ten feminine statements and the sum of the mean scores for the ten masculine statements. Two-way analysis of variance of the scores for these indices showed main effects for both churchedness and sex of the respondents. That is, there were significant differences between the responses of churched and unchurched persons, and between men and women. See Appendix F for the specific data.

12. A three (gender schematicity) by two (churchedness) by two (sex) design results in comparisons between twelve conditions.

13. See Figure 5.5. Compare columns 1a and 4a.

Figure 5.5:
Likelihood of "Masculine" Statement Use by Non-Church vs. Church Men and Women

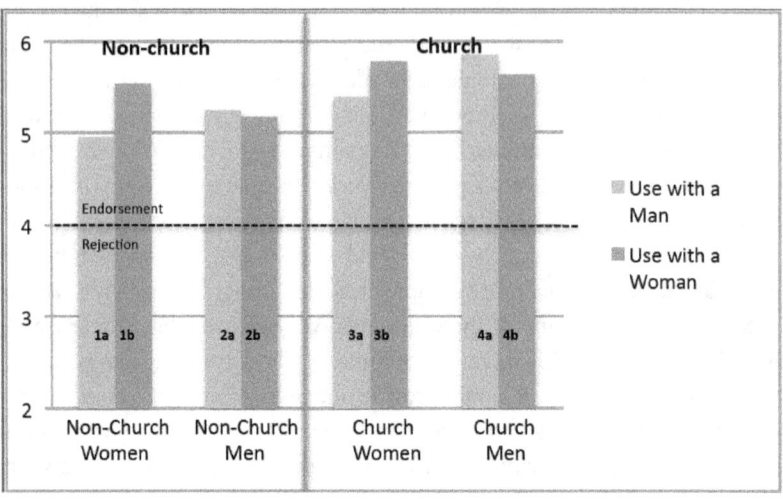

Figure 5.6:
Likelihood of "Feminine" Message Use by Church vs. Non-Church Men and Women

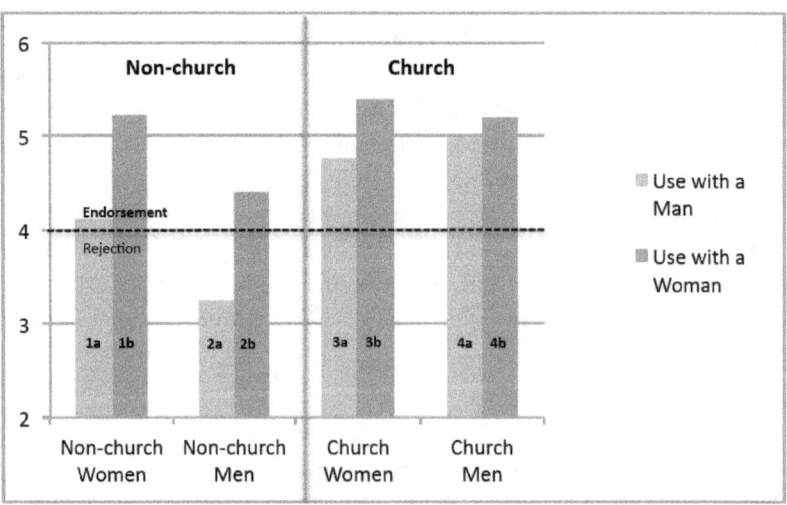

The fact that there was no significant difference between the Non-church Women's ratings for the masculine statements with a man and for the feminine statements with a woman[14] confirms that they did, in fact, identify

---

14. Compare column 1a in Figure 55. with column 1b in Figure 5.6.

with the masculine statements. Indeed, both the Non-church and Church Women's strongest endorsements were for using the masculine statements with a woman.[15] And there were *no* significant differences between any of the groups with regard to the use of the masculine statements with women.[16] All, both men and women, strongly endorsed their use.

It is also important that Non-church Men did not differ significantly from Church Men with regard to using the masculine statements with men—or women[17]—while they did differ with regard to the use of the feminine messages.[18] Non-church Men were significantly less likely than any other group to use the feminine statements, even with women. They clearly do not identify with the feminine themes. In contrast, Non-church Women strongly endorsed the feminine statements but *only* for use with women.[19] Church Men were significantly more likely than were either Non-church Men or Non-church Women to use the feminine statements with a man.[20] This finding is consistent with the earlier study.

In sum, then, this study confirmed the findings of the previous study with regard to Non-church Men's response to feminine Christian messages—messages that Church Men indicated they are equally likely to use with women and men. The addition of church and non-church women to the sample, and masculine statements to the survey enables us to see these findings in a more complete context. It reveals that non-church women also consider the feminine messages inappropriate for use with a man, but that both men and women, churched and unchurched identify strongly with the masculine statements and consider them appropriate for use with both men and women, particularly when in a conversation with a person of their own sex.

Implications

The results of the studies outlined above suggest that, while issues such as influence, power, discipline, courage, etc., are associated with men and masculinity in America and around the world,[21] both women and men (at least in America) identify with messages expressing those themes. Therefore, if

---

15. See Figures 5.5, columns 1b and 3b.
16. See Figure 5.5. Compare the four "b" columns.
17. See Figure 5.5, column pairs 2ab and 4ab.
18. Compare each column in Figure 5.5 with the corresponding column in Figure 5.6.
19. See Figure 5.6, columns 1a and 1b.
20. See Figure 5.6. Compare column 4a with columns 1a and 2a.
21. Cf. Hess and Ferree, *Analyzing Gender*, 1987; and Williams and Best, *Sex and Psyche*, 1990.

the church (again, at least in America) will emphasize these themes, we may expect both women and men to respond.

Some will say that adopting such themes amounts to baptizing secular values which are not uniquely Christian and which perpetuate patriarchy. Such would be the view of Sheila Collins, who identifies patriarchy as "the whole complex of sentiments, the patterns of cognition and behavior, and the assumptions about human nature and the nature of the cosmos that have grown out of a culture in which men have dominated women."[22] Brian Wren also cautions against using the language of power and hierarchy, saying that "we should be highly suspicious when we realize that God, theologized as beyond male and female, is overwhelmingly depicted and praised in male terms as the highest hierarch (king) at the top of every power pyramid (Almighty God).[23]

While Wren's work is generally helpful regarding inclusive language, yet it is my contention that the position described above goes too far. It comes close to saying that things commonly associated with masculinity are the *problem* and those things associated with femininity are the *solution*. Or, to put it more theologically, masculinity is sin and femininity is righteousness. The late James Dittes puts it this way:

> Though the specific indictments and recipes vary, the conventional wisdom goes something like this:
>
> Men are—and shouldn't be—controlling and dominating, preoccupied with performance and competition, over-intellectualizing and under-feeling, defensive and withholding, workaholic, narcissistic, disconnected. Men should be—and aren't—expressive of feelings, sensitive, vulnerable, caring about relationships, wanting to make commitments—and willing to stop and ask for directions.[24]

Is it not more theologically sound to consider that men and women are equally created in the image of God, that masculine characteristics—however they are defined by a given culture—may be expressions of the image of God just as the feminine characteristics are? This is certainly the witness of scripture: "So God created humankind (Hebrew: adam) in God's image; in the image of God, God created them; male and female God created them (Genesis 1:27)."

---

22. Collins, *A Different Heaven*, 51.
23. Wren, *What Language*, 82.
24. Dittes, *Driven by Hope*, vii.

What does this mean in specific terms? Let us take as an example men's need for achievement.[25] Margaret Mead notes, "in every known human society, the male's need for achievement can be recognized," regardless of the activity the culture defines as male.[26] Men's need for achievement is often interpreted as drivenness, caused by a weak ego or a demanding parent or some other demon. But suppose instead that it is an expression of the creative and sustaining image of God. Humankind is placed in the garden, not simply to "be" and enjoy its beauty and its fruits, but to participate with God in its on-going creation and care: "The Lord God took the man and put him in the garden of Eden to till it and keep it (Genesis 2:15 NRSV)." Mead goes on to observe that in many societies the need to achieve is linked to some activity that women are not allowed to practice. She explains this phenomenon as men's need to preserve their maleness, "that men do need to find reassurance in achievement, and because of this connection, cultures frequently phrase achievement as something women do not or cannot do, rather than directly as something which men do well."[27]

However, if we understand the need for achievement as an expression of the creative and sustaining image of God then we may see men's tendency to exclude women from certain activities as an expression of the original sin, or a marring of God's image. Women participate in God's creativity in ways men can't even imagine. It is the greatest gulf that separates women and men—conception, development, and birth. Men are directly involved in the creation of their children for only a fleeting moment. By the time conception has occurred, the father has been relegated to observer. Even the joy of their child's development holds the twinge of distance—as a kick felt only second-hand through the walls of the womb. It is the mother's blood that brings life to their child, not his. It is she who will give birth, not him. It will happen whether he is present or not. So he longs for a realm of creativity he can call his own, and in his self-centeredness (i.e. his sin) he carves out an area that is for men alone, where he can achieve something she supposedly cannot. It is not that "his maleness has to be underwritten by preventing women from entering some field or performing some feat."[28] It is that he desires a greater role in creation and gains it by claiming an achievement that is exclusively his. Thus it is not men's focus on achievement or performance that needs to be called into question, but the self-centered and exclusive expression of it.

---

25. In the study outlined above this is expressed in the "fulfillment" statement (#16).
26. Mead, *Male and Female*, 159.
27. Ibid., 160.
28. Ibid.

As a second example, let's look at men's hierarchical orientation.²⁹ The conventional wisdom, again, is that this is a flaw in the make-up of men. Elizabeth Dodson Gray interprets Psalm 8:3–5, "What are human beings that your are mindful of them . . . (NRSV)" in this fashion when she says, "And there you have the basic flaw in this mental picture, namely a cosmic hierarchical ranking of values. The illusion is that you can look at reality, find out what the value of each thing is, and then rank it according to that which is more valuable (and is always 'up') and has dominion over that which is of lower value (and is 'down')."³⁰

Gray and others are accurate in their description of how this hierarchical model has been used as a rationale for the domination of various classes of people as well as nature. Their solution is the replacement of hierarchical thought with systemic or "holistic" or "connectional" thinking which is exclusively lateral rather than vertical. Letty Russell writes, for example, that "the gift of New Creation by a loving Creator should be sufficient for us to see reality in a new way, so that we see all of creation, *not as a hierarchy*, but as an interdependent partnership of life in which we bring to the world signs of wholeness and shalom."³¹

Such reasoning, however, assumes that the hierarchical conception of reality is an entirely social construction. It holds that hierarchy is in no way woven into the fabric of creation, nor into our relationship with the Creator. It conceives of nature as a benevolent web of cooperative relationships in which individual creatures work together in an atmosphere of equality and affection. Yet the fact is that nature is rife with hierarchies, from the pecking order in every bird's nest to the system that produces an alpha female in every lion pride. And certainly our relationship with our Creator is hierarchical. Indeed, the first sin is set in the context of a refusal to accept this hierarchical relationship: "For God knows that when you eat of it your eyes will be opened, and you will be like God, knowing good and evil" (Genesis 3:5, NIV).

This reasoning also assumes that hierarchies are inherently evil, that the descent to domination is inevitable, as is evident in the thinking of emergent church leader and "theoblogian" Tony Jones. He writes, "A trinitarian hierarchy provides theological defense for other hierarchies, like men over women, clergy over laity, master over slave, and king over subjects."³² Such a view holds that there is no interdependence in a hierarchy and that no good

---

29. In the study outlined above this is expressed in the "place in the plan" statement (#7).
30. Gray, *Patriarchy*, 80.
31. Russell, *Growth in Partnership*, 27. Emphasis added.
32. Jones, "Some (Honestly) Bad Reformed Theology," 2013.

can come from a hierarchical relationship. Finally it holds that there is no sense in which there are hierarchical relationships within the Trinity. This is Nancy Hardesty's view: "The three persons are equal; they are not to be identified with each other or separated from each other; *they are not to be subordinated one to another. They do not represent a hierarchy.*"[33]

The question is, are these two assumptions warranted? Is it not possible that hierarchies exist, not merely as socially constructed realities, but as objective realities which were created by God as expressions either of God's plan or God's nature? Does hierarchy necessarily mean domination and oppression, or are these perhaps expressions of the fallenness of creation? I agree with my fellow egalitarian Kevin Giles that trinitarian hierarchy *has* been used to justify domination and oppression.[34] But I disagree with the assumption that it *must* be. Scripture suggests that there can be a redeemed expression of hierarchy that is neither paternalistic nor patriarchal. In 1 Corinthians 12, Paul ranks the gifts of the Spirit in clear hierarchical fashion:

"And in the church God has appointed first of all apostles, second prophets, third teachers, then workers of miracles, also those having gifts of healing, those able to help others, those with gifts of administration, and those speaking in different kinds of tongues" (1 Corinthians 12:28, NIV).

But he precedes this statement with a discussion of the church as an interdependent system in which all parts of the body are of equal importance and where "God gives greater honor to the parts that lacked it." He then follows his hierarchical description by identifying the love that characterizes God as its operating principle.

In using this pattern Paul was following Jesus's lead. Though the doctrine of the Trinity is not explicitly developed, John 12:44 through 17:26 provides the fullest treatment in Scripture of the relationship among the persons of the Trinity, most of it in words attributed to Jesus. In it we find an extraordinary mixture of hierarchical language coupled with expressions of unity and love. Jesus is sent by the Father (12:44, 15:21), and says and does only what the Father commands (12:49–50, 14:31, 15:10), but is *one* with the Father (12:45, 16:15, 17:10–11, 21). Jesus will *ask* the Father to *send* the Holy Spirit and *both* he and the Father *send* the Spirit (15:26, 16:7). The Spirit also speaks only as the Father *directs* (16:13) and brings glory to the Son (16:14). And the defining principle by which this mix of command, obedience and unity operates is love (17:22–26). All of this suggests that the Trinity may be, humanly speaking, a paradox of hierarchy and equality, directiveness and mutuality. This would make sense of the presence of intertwined hierarchies

---

33. Hardesty, *Inclusive Language*, 55. Emphasis added.
34. See Giles, *The Trinity & Subordinationism*, 2002.

and "communalities" throughout creation. It would also make sense of men's tendency to see things in hierarchical terms coupled with women's tendency to see things in communal terms in otherwise highly different cultures around the world. If both men and women carry the image of God, is it not logical to consider both men's and women's primary ways of perceiving reality as reflective of that image? And would not this understanding be supported by the fact that there is actually a spectrum, a mixture of these two ways of perceiving among both men and women? In this view, it would be not hierarchical thinking itself, but the tendency for it to be expressed in terms of dominance, exclusion, and oppression that would be reflective of the fallen nature of humankind.

Of course, an alternative view would be that expressions of hierarchical thinking in Scripture, whether by Jesus or anyone else, are indicative of the cultural context in which they are found, rather than any ontological or objective reality. Such would be the opinion of revolutionary feminist Mary Daly or reformist feminist Rosemary Radford-Reuther.[35] Yet even if we grant such a view, then Jesus's use of hierarchical language becomes an expression of God's accommodation to human limitations. The question then arises, in the context of evangelism is there not still a need for such accommodation?[36] This points to:

INCLUSIVE LANGUAGE AS AN EVANGELISTIC ISSUE

When it comes to the arena of evangelism there are unique considerations that bear on the inclusive language debate. In evangelism we are dealing with pre-Christian people who do not yet share significant portions of a Christian worldview, and who may consciously reject a Christian worldview as a whole. They frequently have misperceptions about the Christian faith and life, and make judgments about Christianity on the basis of limited, stereotyped information. This means that our first task in evangelism is to gain a *hearing* among pre-Christian people and, in many cases, overcome or correct their current image of Christianity, Christians, and the Church. It also means that in evangelism we must maintain our focus on the primary or ultimate issue—persons' relationship with God in Christ.

---

35. e.g. Radford-Reuther's comment that, "the feminist critique of sexism finds patriarchy not only in contemporary and historical Christian culture but in the Bible as well. The Bible was shaped by males in a patriarchal culture, so many of its revelative experiences were interpreted by men from a patriarchal perspective." Radford-Reuther, "Feminist Interpretation," 116.

36. Similar reasoning to that presented in the discussion of achievement and hierarchical thinking could be followed for each of the masculine themes.

Gaining a hearing and helping people have an accurate picture of the Christian faith requires adapting to their thought-world, using language, images, illustrations, and themes with which they can identify. In other words, it means being incarnational. God, who is wholly other than us, adapted or accommodated to us and came to us in human form. Throughout his ministry as he strove to reach people with the good news, Jesus continued to accommodate to his hearers. He used both masculine and feminine language, images, illustrations, and themes. He spoke of a woman baking bread or searching for a coin, of building a tower or preparing for battle, of a hen caring for her chicks, and of a builder building on a strong foundation. He did not refrain from using statements such as "I have come not to bring peace, but a sword" (Matthew 10:34, NRSV) because they might portray or imply endorsement of military conquest, for example. Neither did he allow himself to be distracted from the main issue by trying to correct "wrong thinking" on side issues. Take for example the Roman centurion who asked Jesus to heal his servant from long distance (Luke 7:2–10). Jesus didn't say to him, "You're thinking in hierarchical terms when you say you're a man under orders and you give orders to others. The universe doesn't actually work that way." No, instead Jesus said, "In all of Israel I have not seen such faith!" Or, as a more serious example, Jesus refused to be deflected by the woman at the well into a side debate over the hot topic of Jewish–Samaritan relations and the proper place to worship (John 4).

The apostles and the early church continued to be incarnational, as Jesus was. It took a vision from God to accomplish it, but Peter finally realized that he did not have to force Gentiles to come to God on Jewish terms (Acts 10). Paul continued that practice in more explicit terms, becoming all things to all people that he might by all means save some (1 Corinthians 9:22). The Jerusalem Council observed what God was doing among the Gentiles and concluded that they ought not require Gentiles to become cultural Jews in order to be Christians.

The message men have been hearing today is that they must come to God on women's terms; that to be Christian, they must *become* feminine. They must renounce concern for accomplishment or achievement, influence, power, position,[37] etc. and focus *instead* on mutual support, nurture, sharing of feelings, etc. Is that the message we really want to send? Though we may want men to open up to those so-called "feminine" characteristics

---

37. Position is used here not in the restrictive sense of organizational rank, but in terms of how men relate to one another socially. Deborah Tannen has pointed out that, while women use talk to make connection and build cooperation, men use talk to accomplish tasks and establish position. (Tannen, *You Just Don't Understand*, 1990). Notice how men's use of talk relates to achievement and hierarchical thinking? Hmm.

so that they might more fully experience life as God intends it to be, is that the place to begin? James Dittes says no:

> Some men (and some women) find it easy to suppose (and they may be right) that men would be better human beings if we were more like women. Because *social* wholeness requires the balance, blending, and equality between men and women that it does, it has been easy to surmise that wholeness requires a similar internal balance between male and female traits. (Sometimes anyone who resists such androgyny as a therapeutic formula is accused of resisting social justice.) This usually translates to making men more "vulnerable," more "sensitive," more "expressive," more "relational," or to "getting in touch with the feminine within." That may be a good goal, but is not a good starting point.[38]

It is not a good starting point sociologically because in most cultures men are less free to cross gender lines than women.[39] It places a greater burden on men than women and inevitably leads to a disparity of participation. It is also not a good starting point theologically. To begin at this point is to confuse the realm of prevenient grace with that of sanctifying grace. If we assume, as did John Wesley, that the Holy Spirit is active in the lives of pre-Christian men and women, "gently wooing" them back to God, then it is logical to assume that the Spirit is also accommodating to them. Surely the Spirit, as did the Son, would speak to them in terms with which they could identify. Surely the Spirit would whisper echoes of Eden in their ears, recalling deep memories of the unmarred image of God created in them, memories which would be consistent with their culture's gender definitions and their own identification with those definitions. If this is true, would not God's stated purpose to draw all people to Godself be better served by our cooperating with what the Spirit is doing, by presenting the gospel in language, images, illustrations, and themes with which they can identify?

Ironically, the results of the latest study described above indicate that if the church will place a strong emphasis on the so-called "masculine" themes expressed in its statements, both men and women will feel included. This is another confirmation that women are, indeed, more free to cross gender lines. If we will include these themes in our worship, our discipleship, our evangelistic and missional ministries, and our personal conversations, we will find both men and women responding in greater numbers.

---

38. Dittes, *Driven by Hope*, vii.
39. Feinman "Why is cross-sex-role behavior more approved for girls than boys?" 300.

To illustrate, after attending one of my seminars dealing with the problem of the missing men, Dorothy Cassel of Wesley United Methodist Church in El Reno, Oklahoma decided she would try to include as many of the masculine themes as possible in the next term of the *Experiencing God* class she taught at her church. She reported that in the two previous terms when she had taught the class, twelve to fifteen people, five to seven of whom were men, would come to the first session and that by the third session they had settled down to twelve to fifteen in attendance with only two men involved. After preparing the first session for the third term, Ms. Cassel went through her lesson and inserted as many of the ten masculine theme words[40] as she could appropriately use. She followed this practice for each session afterwards. Attendance at the first session was as before, nine women and six men. Unlike the other terms, however, by the third session attendance had increased to thirty-one, of which eighteen were men. Consequently, she began using the same practice whenever she preached as a lay speaker in area churches. "I could not believe the difference," she said. "Before, hardly a single man would comment on my message. Now the men seek me out to tell me how much my message spoke to them. It really does make a difference."[41]

The inclusive language debate to this point has focused on those women *within the Church* who feel excluded by the use of male referent language. The evidence of the missing men and the research into *why* they are missing takes the issue of inclusive language far beyond male referent nouns and pronouns. By choosing to focus its message on primarily feminine themes the church has, as a matter of practical effect, excluded men from its ranks. The church is not, however, faced with a choice between excluding women or excluding men. While the church is addressing the legitimate concerns of feminist Christians, it can also emphasize themes with which both men and women identify, illustrating them with metaphors, analogies and illustrations drawn from both women's and men's experience, and calling them to response in both male-and female-appropriate ways. The inclusive language debate need not be a "heads I win, tails you lose" proposition, but one in which everybody wins, especially those who do not yet know Christ.

---

40. See the words in parentheses in the "Masculine" Themed Christian Worldview Statements above.

41. Spontaneous comments offered by Ms. Cassel at a T.E.A.M. Leader Training event conducted by the author in Hinton, Oklahoma.

6

So What Do We Do about the Topics We Choose?

A NUMBER OF YEARS ago I was the spiritual director for a United Methodist conference's annual Youth Choir Tour. The theme of the tour that year was "Spreading Your Wings." The college campus where the pre-tour sessions were held was decorated with posters of butterflies and cocoons, and by the end of the second evening I was inspired to write a song using the same name and images. The words were uplifting, the music was bright and lyrical, and it was a hit. The evening after I introduced it, the organist for the camp invited me into his bed. When I made it clear that that was not my orientation, he said he had misread me and apologized. Fast-forward three months to the annual clergy conference. A pastor who had been present at the pre-tour sessions also invited me into his bed. I never put those invitations together with the song until years later when I used the song in a worship service. The music minister asked an effeminate male soloist to sing it and had him wear a pastel blue chiffon sash as he did so, strolling back and forth across the chancel. When I asked her why she had made those choices she said, "It just seemed to fit the character of the song." I said, "Really? A pastel chiffon sash? What were you thinking?" She said, "He was playing the part of Jesus. It was like Jesus's sash in the paintings." Both she and I had been oblivious to the messages we were sending. The men in the pews were not. They ribbed us about it for months.

Now, some of you are having a strong emotional response to the fact that two church leaders made homosexual advances to another church leader. Others of you are having a strong emotional response about homophobic stereotypical descriptions like "an effeminate male soloist" and "a pastel blue chiffon sash. . . ." If you are having either of those responses, you are being distracted from the point of the story—and in so doing are experiencing exactly what most non-church Action Men experience when it comes to church. They are distracted from our core message—the gospel of Christ Jesus—by subtle messages which are obvious to them but to which we are oblivious. That is the point of the story. I have a holy hunch that that music minister and I are not the only oblivious ones in the church. To determine where your church stands in that regard you will once again need to look back at what you have been communicating in the recent past. But before you do that, once again, you need to:

STOP READING AND PRAY

In my seminars, I have often encountered strong resistance to the notion of adding masculine themes to our message. It has come especially from pastors, regardless of theological perspective. In those settings our discussions have made it clear that, at its root, the resistance stems from an emotional response to a proposed change in the church's culture. It is couched in theological arguments, to be sure, but the emotional heat comes from a perceived threat to deeply held values. Jesus encountered the same response from the scribes and Pharisees. Such a response is natural. To a degree, it is also necessary in order to prevent the chaos of rapid or constant cultural change. But it also can stop us from having eyes to see and ears to hear what the Holy Spirit is saying to the church. The Sadducees and Pharisees so clung to their respective theologically justified cultures that most of them could neither see nor hear. As their philosophical descendants, we liberal progressives and conservative evangelicals run the same risk. We listen to someone who has a different view only long enough to catch the key words and phrases that allow us to choose which ammunition to fire back. That is what separates debate from dialogue. In dialogue we listen for and acknowledge common ground. With that foundation established, we can then examine and discuss our differences with less emotional interference. We can recognize where there is validity in the other's view and consider dispassionately the possibility of error or extremity in our own.

The polarization of society that characterizes the current stage of the generational cycle—when the Idealist (as in Boomer) generation is in power—has become extreme thanks to the shallow, buffered nature of social media. Its electronic fortifications allow us to fire potshots or barrages at the opposition while shielded by distance, electrons, and pixels. We have an endless stockpile of ammo in the form of posts and tweets and memes—none of which we have fully examined for the credibility of their source, nor for the veracity of their information, nor for the quality of their reasoning. And every time we fire one off, we get a neurochemical jolt of satisfaction for having "defended the faith," never realizing that we are actually only defending our own philosophical sub-culture within Judeo-Christian culture.

In such an environment, hearing the Holy Spirit say something different from the values, beliefs, and attitudes we already hold is next to impossible. We are like Saul on the road to Damascus (Acts 9:1–9). We are so focused on the world-view we have adopted that we are blind to what God has been doing right in front of us. We are so worked up about the mission in which we have invested ourselves that we can't feel the spiritual jolt of God's cattle-prod goading us in a different direction. In such an environment, we will only hear what the Spirit is saying to the church through submitting, surrendering, blood-sweating Gethsemane-prayer.

Now, if you read the previous paragraph thinking, "I sure hope those homophobic evangelicals are going to take this seriously and do it," you have missed the point, again! If you read the previous paragraph thinking, "I sure hope those Bible-hating progressives are going to take this seriously and do it," you too have missed the point, again! For each of us our prayer needs to be, "Oh great God of the universe, I have to admit that I think you think like me, even though you've said you don't. I have to admit that I think you would do things the way I would, even though you've said your way of doing things are as far beyond mine as the far reaches of the universe. Right now I choose to release my grip on my tightly held thoughts and step out of the rut of my unexamined ways. Show me the errors of my thoughts and the limitations of my ways. Give me eyes to see more like you see, and ears to hear as you do. Show me how you are working through those with whom I disagree, some of whom I can't stand. Show me how you are speaking through what they say and do. Show me how you want to change my thoughts and my ways. Show me how my thoughts and my ways are keeping people you love out of your church."

When you sense that you have become open to the Spirit enough to see and hear what you normally miss, you will be ready to assess the messages your church is sending to most men, and the many women who are action-oriented as well.

THE NEXT BABY STEP:
THE MESSAGES YOUR CHURCH SENT LAST WEEK

As before, you and your team should divvy up the past week's publications for review. This should include the sermon manuscript, bulletin and/or projection slides, worship songs/hymns, welcome/information packet, newsletter, blogs, social media posts, group studies, children's & youth materials—even the minutes from meetings. This time, however, you are looking for the "feminine" and "masculine" Christian themes discussed in the previous chapter. Each team member will sit down with whatever piece of communication they are reviewing, two different colored highlighters or pens, and the following cards:[1]

Table 6.1: Feminine Christian Theme Card

FEMININE CHRISTIAN THEMES	Hits
{BEING-OPEN/SHARING-FEELINGS}	
{SUBMISSION}	
{COMMUNITY}	
{NONVIOLENCE/NONAGGRESSION}	
{SUPPORT/NURTURE}	
{FORGIVENESS}	
{LOVE}	
{HUMILITY}	
{SERVICE/SACRIFICE}	
{BEING/BECOMING}	
Total Feminine Hits:	

---

1. Note the formatting in the cards. Throughout this chapter feminine themes are in {ALL CAPS}, masculine themes are in {All Italics}.

Table 6.2: Masculine Christian Theme Card

Masculine Christian Themes	Hits
{Influence}	
{Belonging/Teamwork}	
{Purpose/Place}	
{Character}	
{Courage}	
{Challenge}	
{Fulfillment}	
{Responsibility/Duty}	
{Discipline/Perseverance}	
{Strength/Power}	
Total Masculine Hits:	

Have everyone use the same colors for feminine themes and for masculine themes so that you can compare everyone's results. If you want to keep with American popular culture, you can use pink for feminine (like Major League Baseball on Mother's Day), and baby blue for masculine (like the Major League Baseball on Father's Day). If you hate all this gender stereotyping, pick whatever colors you like. Just make sure that they are used consistently by all members of your team. As you read your materials, highlight words or phrases that reflect one of the themes on the cards and write the theme beside it or in the margin. Sometimes the themes will be expressed using the exact words on these cards. Most times, however, you will have to interpret what you read in light of the themes on the card and choose the appropriate theme to identify. You will see examples of this in the analysis of one of my early sermons provided as an illustration below. Read this analysis before attempting your own.

Sermon Analysis: "The Message Is, 'I Love You'"

Scriptures: Genesis 2:18-24; Hebrews 2:9-11; Mark 10:2-16 (Lectionary, Year B).

(A word of caution: I wrote this sermon and the one that follows later in the chapter shortly after graduating seminary. As a result, it bears the marks of an inexperienced preacher. It is more a theological treatise than a sermon. Try to ignore its failings and focus on the issue at hand.)

I want you to visualize a rocky stretch of coastline. You are viewing that coastline through the gloom from the deck of a ship, tossed and battered by storm waves. Suddenly you catch sight of a lighthouse as it flashes from the top of a cliff on the shore—a warning that a treacherous coast is near. As you watch the flashing light, you realize there is a pattern to it. It is flashing a message in Morse code. So you watch, and decipher, letter by letter, until you get the whole message. And the message is, "I love you!" {LOVE}

That lighthouse does exist. It is called Minot's Light, and it lies off Cohasset, Massachusetts. Several years ago the Coast Guard decided to replace the old equipment at the lighthouse. But when they announced that for technical reasons the new equipment would not be able to flash messages, there was such a storm of protest that they backed off. The old equipment is still intact—still flashing it's message to weary seamen, "I love you!" {LOVE}

How like God that is! He, too, sent his light into a dark, gloomy world—the light of his son—as John 1:9 says, "A light that shines in the darkness." And that light, too, carried a message. At its very heart that message was, and still is, "I love you! I love you so much that I was not only willing to give, I gave my life for you." {LOVE}

How like that the lighthouse are God's people, as well. Jesus said, "You are the light of the world. Let your light so shine before men that they may see your

{FEMININE CHRISTIAN THEMES}
1. BEING-OPEN/SHARING-FEELINGS
2. SUBMISSION
3. COMMUNITY
4. NONVIOLENCE/NONAGGRESSION
5. SUPPORT/NURTURE
6. FORGIVENESS
7. LOVE
8. HUMILITY
9. SERVICE/SACRIFICE
10. BEING/BECOMING (as opposed to doing)

{*Masculine Christian Themes*}
1. *Influence*
2. *Belonging/Teamwork*
3. *Purpose/Place*
4. *Character*
5. *Courage*
6. *Challenge*
7. *Fulfillment*
8. *Responsibility/Duty*
9. *Discipline/Perseverance*
10. *Strength/Power*

good works and to give glory to your father who is in heaven." {SERVICE} {*Influence*} I hope people in our community see us as a lighthouse flashing out that message to each of them, "I love you!" {LOVE} Indeed, I hope each of us in our own way is a lighthouse. "This little light of mine, I'm going to let it shine." I hope we are flashing that message to each other. Jesus said, "By this they will know I am in you and you are in me—if you love one another." {COMMUNITY}

> Note the language of intimacy here, connecting intimacy with God with intimacy between husband and wife. If I were writing this sermon today I would replace this with "They were close to their Creator. They were close with each other."

You see, that is what the kingdom of God is all about. We were created for love—for relationship—for family. {LOVE}{*Belonging/Teamwork*}The Bible begins with a man and a woman in a garden. They were created out of love, for love. Their world was a paradise. They were on intimate terms with their Creator. They were on intimate terms with each other. They were in harmony with all of creation. That is what the kingdom is all about—love, relationship, family.

Jesus confirms the same principle in Mark's gospel. He is speaking about the sanctity of marriage. "From the beginning of creation," he says, "God made them male and female. For this reason a man leaves his father and mother and is joined to his wife and the two become one flesh." That is what the Kingdom is all about. It's about love, relationship, family. {LOVE} {*Belonging/Teamwork*}

A few moments after giving this teaching on marriage, some parents brought their children to Jesus, wanting him to touch them and bless them. Now this is an important moment in scripture. Watch what happens. The disciples rebuked the parents. I guess they were a lot like many adults in worship services today who view children as a distraction—a bother—as not belonging there until they reach the age of accountability. Or at least until they can sit still and be quiet for the entire time. I remember a conversation my parents had when I was little. A two-or three-year-old got fussy one of those few times when we did go to church, and Dad fidgeted and "humphed" the whole time. All the way home he fumed about "that woman and her kid!" "She shouldn't bring him in the service in the first place," he said. "That's what they've got a nursery for." Don't you think that's just what the disciples were saying? "Don't interrupt. Don't bother the Master. Take them to the nursery."

But what does the Scripture say? It says Jesus became indignant. He was angry! "Let the children come, don't hinder them, for to such belongs the kingdom of God." I believe children belong in church, including worship, from day one. Let me encourage you to bring your children with you to worship, every Sunday. We have a nursery for those rare occasions of unmanageability. But that's out of concern for the occasionally struggling parent, not for the convenience of the congregation. They belong in church—why? Because that's what the Kingdom is all about: man-woman-children.

The Kingdom is family. But more than the so-called nuclear family of mother, father, and 1.7 children, as statisticians are fond of saying. The Kingdom includes the whole family of God. In Hebrews 2:9–11 it says that Jesus, "who for a little while was made lower than the angels," and who "was crowned with glory and honor because of the suffering of his death, so that by the grace of God he might taste death for everyone"—this same Jesus "for whom and by whom all things exist"—the pioneer of our salvation and the perfecter of our faith—this same Jesus is not ashamed to call us sisters and brothers!

This is the most important family in the Scriptures—the family of God. Those who are in Christ are that family. That is who we are. That is why we were created. That is the cause for which Christ died—that we should no longer be strangers, but that we should be part of this family, the family of God. {COMMUNITY}{*Belonging/Teamwork*}

We were created for a family relationship. But because of sin, that relationship has been broken. If the kingdom is about family, then sin is the breaking of the family relationship. That's why Jesus spoke so strongly about divorce in Mark 10. Divorce strikes at the very heart of what the Kingdom is about.

That's not to say that people don't make mistakes in marriage. And sometimes what was once a strong, joyous relationship deteriorates to the point where reconciliation is no longer possible. Nevertheless, the scriptural attitude toward the ending of a marriage is that it is always a tragedy and never God's best will for the persons involved. Especially today when so many marriages are coming apart at the seams, we need to affirm the importance of the family relationship.

Unfortunately, we live in a broken world. We know that. After Adam and Eve left Eden, they had two sons—and one killed the other. Just imagine if they had been your boys. Yet this is the kind of world we live in. Ever since Eden, men and women have lived in awful disharmony with their neighbors, with their environment, with the very earth from which they were formed, and even with themselves.

Novelist F. Scott Fitzgerald knew that. After his death they found the plot for a novel he never got to write. The plot concerned a wealthy man who died and left a strange will. All his millions were to be divided equally among all his

> If writing it today I would add, "Most of us know what that's like. We have wounds that have festered between ourselves and our fathers or our mothers—wounds that affect everything else in our lives." While not a part of the "masculine" themes, mention of these wounds will connect with many men, and not a few women.

relatives, share and share alike. There was just one condition. They were to come and live together in his spacious mansion. Below the outlined plot was a note by Fitzgerald. It read, "This could be a little spot of hell."

We understand how it could be. We live in a broken world, don't we? Even with the best of intentions, many families are torn simply by the race for survival. As one person put it, "Nowadays, Dad works the night shift, Mom works the day shift, and the kids just have to shift for themselves."

But the greatest cause of our brokenness is a broken relationship with God. Nothing else can be right until our relationship with the Father is right. The good news is this: that relationship can be made right. It can be made right because of that light God sent into the world.

A woman wrote a letter to Billy Graham.

> "Until last January I was a stranger to Jesus," she wrote. "I was a rebel, a thief, a drunk, a drug abuser, and an adulteress. I was a self-centered, confused young woman. Well, somebody invited me to a Bible study about a year ago and I went, half out of curiosity, half just to stump everybody with my cynical questions. But that night I became seriously interested in the Bible. Finally, after reading and studying for months, John 3:16 spoke to my heart and I gave my life to Christ. I never knew this kind of happiness could exist. God shows you how to love and what it feels like to be loved. {LOVE} He was what I had been looking for since my early teens. It had seemed to me that drugs, liquor, free love and bumming around the country would make me free. But they were all traps that led me to confusion, unhappiness, guilt, and near suicide. Christ has made me free."

How do we turn a spot of hell, as Fitzgerald called it, into a showplace for heaven? We can't. But God can. We are not able, but God is able. Noted psychologist William Glasser in his book *Reality Therapy* writes, "At all times in our lives we must have one person who cares for us and whom we care for, ourselves. If we do not have this person, we will not be able to fulfill our basic needs." You may say, "I don't have anybody who cares for me like that." But think about it. You do have someone who cares for you. Indeed, he calls you sister. He calls you brother. Jesus is the one who says, "I love you." {LOVE}

Anyone who has a hint of a romantic nature thrills to the story

---

Note the use of romantic love to illustrate the point. It mirrors the connection made earlier with the language of intimacy. It would be better to use an illustration of sacrificial love, such as that of soldiers on the battlefield or fathers and mothers or brothers/sisters who gave their lives for their sibling(s). Such illustrations would give the opportunity to mention {Courage} {Character} {Responsibility} and/or {Perseverance}.

of poet Robert Browning and his equally talented wife, Elizabeth Barrett Browning. You recall the beginning of her Sonnets of the Portuguese: "How do I love thee? Let me count the ways. I love thee to the depths and breadths and heights my soul can reach . . . " But do you recall that Elizabeth Barrett was literally a shut-in, held captive by a domineering, tyrannical father? This beautiful poetry grew out of the love of this bold, brash young poet who carried her away. One day she went to his side as he had fallen asleep at his desk while working on his poetry and wrote a note on his paper: "My dearest Robert, my whole world, my whole life, my whole future has been different since that day I first felt thy footsteps walk across my soul." {LOVE}

Many of us never experience the grandeur of such love from a living, breathing person. But such love is available. There is a lighthouse with its beacon shining at us individually in our personal darkness. As we gaze at that lighthouse, we can make out a message blinking through the fog of our neglect and despair. It is one that has warmed and transformed the lives of countless persons just like you. And the message is, "I love you." {LOVE}

Table 6.3: Feminine Christian Themes in Sample Sermon One

FEMININE CHRISTIAN THEMES	Hits
{BEING-OPEN/SHARING-FEELINGS}	
{SUBMISSION}	
{COMMUNITY}	2
{NONVIOLENCE/NONAGGRESSION}	
{SUPPORT/NURTURE}	
{FORGIVENESS}	
{LOVE}	12
{HUMILITY}	
{SERVICE/SACRIFICE}	1
{BEING/BECOMING}	
Total Feminine Hits:	15

Table 6.4: Masculine Christian Themes in Sample Sermon One

Masculine Christian Themes	Hits
{Influence}	1
{Belonging/Teamwork}	3
{Purpose/Place}	
{Character}	
{Courage}	
{Challenge}	
{Fulfillment}	
{Responsibility/Duty}	
{Discipline/Perseverance}	
{Strength/Power}	
Total Masculine Hits:	4

The analysis above should give you a feel for the process. Once you have that feel, do the same kind of analysis on the pieces of church communication you have chosen. When you are finished, use the Masculine/Feminine Themes Summary Form below (see Table 6.5) to tally for each of the items you have reviewed and report the results. And, again, if you hate all this gender stereotyping replace Masculine with "Actional" and Feminine with "Relational". Just remember that "Actional" isn't just about taking action. It is most importantly about having an impact or affecting objects, people, processes, events, etc.

Table 6.5: Masculine/Feminine Christian Theme Summary Form

Masculine/Feminine Themes Summary Form	
Item(s) Reviewed:	Date:
FEMININE CHRISTIAN THEMES	Hits
{SUBMISSION}	
{COMMUNITY}	
{NONVIOLENCE/NONAGGRESSION}	
{SUPPORT/NURTURE}	
{FORGIVENESS}	
{LOVE}	
{HUMILITY}	
{SERVICE/SACRIFICE}	
{BEING/BECOMING}	
Total FEMININE Hits:	

Masculine/Feminine Themes Summary Form	
Item(s) Reviewed:	Date:

Masculine Christian Themes	Hits
{Influence}	
{Belonging/Teamwork}	
{Purpose/Place}	
{Character}	
{Courage}	
{Challenge}	
{Fulfillment}	
{Responsibility/Duty}	
{Discipline/Perseverance}	
{Strength/Power}	
Total *Masculine* Hits:	

As before, give your team several days to complete their reviews and then get together at a coffee shop or restaurant to discuss their findings. What tendencies are you uncovering? What themes are recurring? . . . missing? To what extent are these things an expression of external influences such as seasons of the year, recent significant events in your community or church, etc. To what extent are they in expression of internal factors in your church? In what way are those things positive or negative? What is the Holy Spirit saying? Once your team has done this exercise for a few weeks you will be ready to go on to:

TRACK THE TALK IN YOUR CHURCH

This is the same process you used in chapter 4 to track linguistic markers in your church's live talk. The only difference is you are listening for the masculine and feminine themes. In formal settings like worship or meetings you

SO WHAT DO WE DO ABOUT THE TOPICS WE CHOOSE?

can use the Theme Cards from Tables 6.1 and 6.2. In informal settings like conversations, simply keep a running mental tally of the feminine versus masculine themes. It may help to think of them in terms of their root meanings, relational versus actional. As soon as possible after the conversation make a note of your tally on your smart phone, tablet, or paper notepad. Keep a file of those tallies to report to the team. As much as possible, note which of the themes keep recurring and which are missing. Take note of who (including yourself) is speaking about which topics. This can be helpful for church leaders and staff. We all have our hobbyhorses and are often unaware that we are riding them. Continue to make the same observations for what you are hearing at the sports bar, at work, in the locker room, etc. Record all of this in the journal you have been keeping since chapter 2. Also record the insights the Holy Spirit gives you as you think and pray about what you are hearing. Talk about these with the other team members. Once you have a handle on both your own and your church's tendencies, you can begin recovering your thematic gender balance. If yours is like most churches, you will need to:

ADD MASCULINE THEMES

Notice, that says "Add" not "Replace." We are not talking about replacing feminine themes with masculine ones. We are not talking about removing the relational aspect of the gospel. We are talking about balancing it with the actional component. To illustrate, we will focus on worship which in my view begins with the Scriptures. Let's look at the lectionary readings for fall of 2017.[2] We will review in detail the readings for September 3, 2017, the 22nd Sunday after Pentecost and, in the USA, Labor Day weekend:

Lectionary Readings: September 3—December 26, 2017; end of Year A, beginning of Year B (Theme key: *{Masculine Themes}* {FEMININE THEMES})

September 3, 2017:

Exodus 3:1–15 and Psalm 105:16, 23–26, 45b • Jeremiah 15:15–21 and Psalm 26:1–8 • Romans 12:9–21 • Matthew 16:21–28

> In Exodus 3:1–15, Moses receives his call from God. In the process he begins to discover his *{Purpose}* and learn his *{Place}* before God.

---

2. Your church may not use the lectionary. of However, its use here illustrates the presence these themes throughout Scripture and their availability for every worship service.

This requires {SUBMISSION}, {HUMILITY}, and *{Courage}*—things Moses has had in short supply to this point in his life. God *{Challenges}* Moses to confront Pharaoh and lead the people, but also promises to provide the {SUPPORT/NURTURE} necessary for that mission. This is the beginning of Moses' {BEING/BECOMING} the man God intended and needed. Passages in the coming weeks will show how Moses *{Fulfills}* his *{Responsibility/Duty}* becomes a channel of God's *{Influence}* in the world.

Psalm 105:1-6, 23-26, 45b celebrates the *{Strength/Power}* of God made evident through God's actions and their *{Influence}* in the world. It reminds God's people that they are both chosen and servants; that they, like Moses, have a special *{Purpose/Place}* that requires {SUBMISSION} and {HUMILITY}.

Jeremiah 15:15-21 is part of a conversation in which Jeremiah bemoans his *{Purpose/Place}* and the treatment he has received as the Lord's spokesperson. God *{Challenges}* him to {SUBMIT} to God's will rather than fight it, and to exercise *{Discipline/Perseverance}* in the face of opposition so that he may *{Influence}* God's people rather than being influenced by them to turn from God *{Character}*. God promises his *{Strength/Power}* to enable Jeremiah to overcome the opposition.

Psalm 26:1-8 calls on God to fulfill that promise of vindication because the Psalmist has {SUBMITTED} to God's will and been a person of integrity *{Character}*.

Romans 12:9-21 spells out in detail what the nature of that *{Character}* is. Paul *{Challenges}* Roman Christians to live as a {COMMUNITY}, showing authentic {LOVE} and {HUMILITY} expressed by outdoing one another in honoring one another. Like Jeremiah they are to have the *{Courage}* to *{Persevere}* in the face of suffering and the *{Discipline}* to resist evil. Like Moses and Jeremiah, they are to allow God to handle the opposition, rather than to usurp God's *{Place}* and overcome evil by returning it with good {NONVIOLENCE/NONAGGRESSION}.

In Matthew 26:21-20, Jesus demonstrates that *{Character}* described by Paul. Jesus knows his *{Purpose/Place}*. He {SUBMITS} to the will of the Father, even when Peter gives him opportunity to opt out. He has the *{Discipline/Perseverance}* and *{Courage}* to face the suffering to come with {NONVIOLENCE/NONAGGRESSION}. Jesus then *{Challenges}* the disciples with the knowledge that his followers must make the same {SACRIFICE}. Then, in the assurance of knowing his *{Purpose/Place}* as the Son of Man, he promises the same vindication that God promised to Moses, Jeremiah, and Israel in the previous readings.

The thematic analysis demonstrated above is one more interpretive tool that can be used in preparation for preaching and worship. It enables you to see connections across the Scriptures. It informs your choice of vocabulary, imagery, and illustrations. It enables you to choose a theme or constellation of themes as the focus of the service toward which the prayers, music, décor, graphics, etc. can point.

Listed below for your own review are the remaining readings for fall of 2017, with the masculine and feminine themes present in each passage identified. Notice that most of the themes expressed in the September 3rd readings are present throughout the season, providing both consistency and balance. In the coming weeks, read through those passages and identify for yourself where each of the themes is expressed.

September 10, 2017:

Exodus 12:1-14 *{Discipline/Perseverance}* {COMMUNITY} *{Courage} {Strength/Power}* and Psalm 149 *{Strength/Power}* {HUMILITY};

Ezekiel 33:7-11 *{Discipline/Perseverance} {Character}* {FORGIVENESS} and Psalm 119:33-40 *{Character} {BEING/BECOMING} {Discipline/Perseverance}* {SUBMISSION};

Romans 13:8-14 {LOVE} *{Character} {Influence} {Courage} {Challenge}*;

Matthew 18:15-20 *{Influence} {Strength/Power} {Belonging/Teamwork}* {COMMUNITY}

September 17, 2017:

Exodus 14:19-31*{Strength/Power} {Courage}{Belonging/Teamwork}* and Psalm 114 *{Purpose/Place}*;

Genesis 50:15-21 *{Purpose/Place} {Belonging/Teamwork}* {COMMUNITY} {SUPPORT/NURTURE} {FORGIVENESS} *{Character}* and Psalm 103:(1-7), 8-13 {FORGIVENESS} {LOVE} *{Purpose/Place}*;

Romans 14:1-12 {COMMUNITY} {SUPPORT/NURTURE} *{Purpose/Place} {Belonging/Teamwork} {Character}*;

Matthew 18:21-35 *{Purpose/Place} {Belonging/Teamwork}* {COMMUNITY} {SUPPORT/NURTURE} {FORGIVENESS} *{Character}*

September 24, 2017:

Exodus 16:2–15 *{Character} {Discipline/Perseverance} {Courage} {Strength/Power}*; and Psalm 105:1–6, 37–45 *{Strength/Power} {Courage} {Purpose/Place}* {COMMUNITY} *{Belonging/Teamwork}*;
　　Jonah 3:10—4:11 {FORGIVENESS} *{Character}* and Psalm 145:1–8 *{Strength/Power}* {FORGIVENESS} {LOVE};
　　Philippians 1:21–30 *{Courage} {Influence} {Purpose/Place} {Character} {Discipline/Perseverance}*;
　　Matthew 20:1–16 *{Purpose/Place} {Character} {Responsibility/Duty}* {HUMILITY} {SUBMISSION}

October 1, 2017:

Exodus 17:1–7 *{Character} {Discipline/Perseverance} {Courage} {Strength/Power}* {FORGIVENESS} and Psalm 78:1–4, 12–16 *{Strength/Power} {Courage} {Purpose/Place}*;
　　Ezekiel 18:1–4, 25–32 *{Purpose/Place} {Character}* {FORGIVENESS} *{Discipline/Perseverance} {Responsibility/Duty}* and Psalm 25:1–9 *{Discipline/Perseverance}* {FORGIVENESS} {LOVE} {HUMILITY};
　　Philippians 2:1–13 *{Belonging/Teamwork}* {COMMUNITY} {LOVE} {HUMILITY} *{Purpose/Place} {Courage} {Challenge}* {SERVICE/SACRIFICE} *{Discipline/Perseverance}*;
　　Matthew 21:23–32 *{Purpose/Place} {Character}*

October 8, 2017:

Exodus 20:1–4, 7–9, 12–20 *{Purpose/Place} {Character} {Challenge} {Fulfillment} {Responsibility/Duty} {Discipline/Perseverance}* and Psalm 19 *{Purpose/Place} {Character} {Challenge} {Fulfillment} {Responsibility/Duty} {Discipline/Perseverance}*;
　　Isaiah 5:1–7 {LOVE} *{Responsibility/Duty} {Discipline/Perseverance}* and Psalm 80:7–15 {FORGIVENESS};
　　Philippians 3:4b–14 *{Purpose/Place} {Fulfillment} {Character}* {HUMILITY} *{Challenge} {Discipline/Perseverance}*;
　　Matthew 21:33–46 *{Purpose/Place} {Character} {Responsibility/Duty}*

SO WHAT DO WE DO ABOUT THE TOPICS WE CHOOSE?

October 15, 2017:

Exodus 32:1–14 *{Purpose/Place} {Character} {Responsibility/Duty} {Discipline/Perseverance}* {FORGIVENESS} and Psalm 106:1–6, 19–23 *{Purpose/Place} {Character} {Responsibility/Duty} {Discipline/Perseverance}* {FORGIVENESS};

Isaiah 25:1–9 *{Strength/Power}* {FORGIVENESS} and Psalm 23 {LOVE} *{Strength/Power}*;

Philippians 4:1–9 {COMMUNITY} *{Belonging/Teamwork} {Purpose/Place} {Character} {Courage} {Discipline/Perseverance}*;

Matthew 22:1–14 *{Purpose/Place} {Character} {Responsibility/Duty}*

October 22, 2017:

Exodus 33:12–23 *{Influence} {Purpose/Place} {Character} {Courage}* and Psalm 99 *{Purpose/Place}*;

Isaiah 45:1–7 *{Strength/Power} {Purpose/Place}* and Psalm 96:1–9, (10–13) *{Strength/Power} {Purpose/Place}*;

1 Thessalonians 1:1–10 *{Influence} {Purpose/Place} {Belonging/Teamwork} {Character} {Courage} {Strength/Power}*;

Matthew 22:15–22 *{Character} {Courage}*

October 29, 2017:

Deuteronomy 34:1–12 *{Influence} {Purpose/Place}* {SUBMISSION} {SERVICE/SACRIFICE} *{Character}* {HUMILITY} *{Courage} {Fulfillment} {Strength/Power}* and Psalm 19:1–6, 13–17 *{Purpose/Place} {Discipline/Perseverance}* {LOVE} {FORGIVENESS};

Leviticus 19:1–2, 15–18 *{Character}* {COMMUNITY} *{Belonging/Teamwork}* and Psalm 1 *{Character}*;

1 Thessalonians 2:1–8 *{Influence} {Purpose/Place} {Belonging/Teamwork} {Character}* {HUMILITY} *{Courage} {Strength/Power}* {SUPPORT/NURTURE} {LOVE};

Matthew 22:34–46 *Character} {Courage}* {LOVE}

November 5, 2017:

Joshua 3:7–17 *{Influence} {Purpose/Place} {Character} {Courage} {Fulfillment} {Strength/Power}* and Psalm 107:1–7, 33–37 {LOVE} *{Purpose/Place} {Courage} {Strength/Power}*;

    Micah 3:5–12 *{Character} {Strength/Power}* {NONVIOLENCE/NON-AGGRESSION} and Psalm 43 *{Character} {Discipline/Perseverance}*;

    1 Thessalonians 2:9–13 *{Influence} {Belonging/Teamwork} {Character}* {SUPPORT/NURTURE} {LOVE};

    Matthew 23:1–12 *{Purpose/Place} {Character}* {HUMILITY} {SUPPORT/NURTURE}

November 12, 2017:

Joshua 24:1–3a, 14–25 *{Influence} {Purpose/Place} {Character} {Responsibility/Duty} {Discipline/Perseverance} {Challenge}* and Psalm 78:1–7 *{Belonging/Teamwork} {Purpose/Place}* {SUPPORT/NURTURE};

    Amos 5:18–24 *{Character} {Responsibility/Duty} {Discipline/Perseverance}* and Psalm 70 *{Purpose/Place}* {LOVE};

    1 Thessalonians 4:13–18 *{Belonging/Teamwork} {Purpose/Place}* {LOVE};

    Matthew 25:1–13 *{Purpose/Place} {Responsibility/Duty} {Discipline/Perseverance}*

November 19, 2017:

Judges 4:1–7 *{Influence} {Purpose/Place} {Character}* {FORGIVENESS} and Psalm 123 *{Purpose/Place}* {FORGIVENESS};

    Zephaniah 1:7, 12–18 *{Character} {Discipline/Perseverance}* and Psalm 90:1–8, (9–11), 12 *{Purpose/Place}* {SUBMISSION} *{Strength/Power} {Character} {Discipline/Perseverance}*;

    1 Thessalonians 5:1–11 *{Character} {Discipline/Perseverance} {Belonging/Teamwork}* {FORGIVENESS};

    Matthew 25:14–30 *{Character} {Purpose/Place}* {SUBMISSION} *{Responsibility/Duty} {Discipline/Perseverance} {Challenge}*

November 26, 2017:

Ezekiel 34:11–16, 20–24 *{Purpose/Place}* {LOVE} *{Character}* {HUMILITY} {SUPPORT/NURTURE} and Psalm 100 *{Purpose/Place}* {LOVE};

Psalm 95:1–7a *{Purpose/Place} {Strength/Power}*;
Ephesians 1:15–23 *{Character} {Belonging/Teamwork} {Purpose/Place} {Strength/Power}*;
Matthew 25:31–46 *{Character} {Purpose/Place} {Responsibility/Duty}* {SERVICE/SACRIFICE} *{Challenge}*

December 3, 2017:

Isaiah 64:1–9 *{Strength/Power} {Purpose/Place}* {SUBMISSION} *{Character}* {FORGIVENESS};
Psalm 80:1–7, 17–19 *{Strength/Power} {Purpose/Place}* {FORGIVENESS};
1 Corinthians 1:3–9 {FORGIVENESS} *{Character} {Purpose/Place} {Strength/Power} {Discipline/Perseverance}*;
Mark 13:24–37 *{Purpose/Place} {Strength/Power} {Discipline/Perseverance} {Challenge}*

December 10, 2017:

Isaiah 40:1–11 {SUPPORT/NURTURE} {FORGIVENESS} *{Influence} {Discipline/Perseverance} {Strength/Power}* {SUBMISSION} *{Purpose/Place}*;
Psalm 85:1–2, 8–13{FORGIVENESS} *{Discipline/Perseverance}* {LOVE} *{Character} {Purpose/Place}* {HUMILITY};
2 Peter 3:8–15a *{Discipline/Perseverance} {Strength/Power} {Character} {Purpose/Place} {Responsibility/Duty} {Challenge}*;
Mark 11:1–8 {FORGIVENESS} *{Influence} {Character} {Purpose/Place}* {HUMILITY}

December 17, 2017:

Isaiah 61:1–4, 8–11 {SUPPORT/NURTURE} *{Influence} {Strength/Power} {Purpose/Place}* {SUPPORT/NURTURE};
Psalm 126 *{Purpose/Place} {Strength/Power} {Discipline/Perseverance}*;
or Luke 1:46b–55 {HUMILITY} {SUBMISSION} *{Purpose/Place} {Strength/Power} {Discipline/Perseverance}*;
1 Thessalonians 5:16–24 *{Discipline/Perseverance} {Challenge} {Character} {Purpose/Place}*;
John 1:6–8, 19–28 *{Influence} {Character} {Purpose/Place}* {HUMILITY} {SUBMISSION}

December 24, 2017:

2 Samuel 7:1–11, 16 *{Purpose/Place}* {HUMILITY};
    Luke 1:46b–55 {HUMILITY} {SUBMISSION} *{Purpose/Place}* *{Strength/Power}* *{Discipline/Perseverance}*; or Psalm 89:1–4, 19–26 {LOVE} *{Purpose/Place}* *{Strength/Power}*;
    Romans 16:25–27 *{Purpose/Place}* *{Strength/Power}*;
    Luke 1:26–38 *{Purpose/Place}* *{Strength/Power}* {HUMILITY} {SUBMISSION}

December 31, 2017:

Isaiah 61:10—62:3 *{Character}* {BEING/BECOMING} *{Purpose/Place}* *{Influence}*;
    Psalm 148 *{Strength/Power}* *{Purpose/Place}* {HUMILITY} {SUBMISSION};
    Galatians 4:4–7 *{Purpose/Place}*;
    Luke 2:22–40 *{Purpose/Place}* *{Character}* {BEING/BECOMING} *{Discipline/Perseverance}* {SUPPORT/NURTURE}

Think about what real-life stories, metaphors, and images would express each theme in each passage, while at the same time connecting well with the passage you are reading. What kind of vocabulary would connect well the passage and with the actional and relational people in your congregation? That is your challenge. As much as possible, try to have balance. Below is one of my sermons from the same time as the one above. Though I was unaware of the need for thematic balance at the time, it is a good example of achieving it.

> {FEMININE CHRISTIAN THEMES}
> 1. BEING-OPEN/SHARING-FEELINGS
> 2. SUBMISSION
> 3. COMMUNITY
> 4. NONVIOLENCE/NONAGGRESSION
> 5. SUPPORT/NURTURE
> 6. FORGIVENESS
> 7. LOVE
> 8. HUMILITY
> 9. SERVICE/SACRIFICE
> 10. BEING/BECOMING (as opposed to doing)
>
> {*Masculine Christian Themes*}
> 1. *Influence*
> 2. *Belonging/Teamwork*
> 3. *Purpose/Place*
> 4. *Character*
> 5. *Courage*
> 6. *Challenge*
> 7. *Fulfillment*
> 8. *Responsibility/Duty*
> 9. *Discipline/Perseverance*
> 10. *Strength/Power*

Sermon Analysis: "You Can Do It!"

Deuteronomy 30:9–14, Luke 10:25–37, Colossians 1:9–16
(Lectionary, Year C)

> *The Butterfly Who Never Was* {BEING/BECOMING}
> There once was a caterpillar green and fat,
> "Whose friends said, "How can you live like that?
> You just eat and sleep, and eat and squirm.
> You'll never be nothin' but an ugly old worm!"
> He heard it so much that he said, "They are right.
> I'm lumpy and spotted, just a horrible sight!"
> And a sad thing happened beginning that day;
> The fat, green caterpillar wasted away.
> It's a pity it happened, for on the inside
> The ugly caterpillar was a pretty butterfly.
> All he needed was time and encouragement, you see,

To become the wondrous creature that he was meant to be.
So when someone says that you won't amount to much,
That you're dumb and you're dull and you're dopey and such,
Remember, on the inside waiting to be free
Is the beautiful person God meant you to be.
(by Woody L. Davis, ©1983)

There is an historic teaching in the church that we are not now and never will be anything more then lowly worms. It comes out of a desire to emphasize God's grace—the fact that we deserve to be given hell, but receive Heaven instead. {FORGIVENESS} We sing, "Amazing grace, how sweet the sound that saved a wretch like me!" In the traditional communion liturgy we prayed, "Though we be unworthy to so much as gather up the crumbs from under Thy table. . . . "

It is true. Our salvation is totally undeserved. It can never be earned, only accepted as a free gift. It is true that we are fallen creatures—self-centered and sinful—far less than God intended us to be.

> After the service one of the men came up and sang the US Army's recruitment jingle of the day: "Be—all that you can be. You can do it, in the Army!"—exactly my intent, so the commercial would be a reminder of the sermon.

Yet, another truth rings throughout the Scriptures—YOU CAN DO IT! You can be the person God intended you to be. {BEING/BECOMING} *{Fulfillment}* Moses' farewell speech to the people was, "It is not too hard for you or beyond your reach . . . it is near you: in your mouth and in your heart, so that you can do it (Deuteronomy 30:11-14)." When a teacher of the law asked Jesus what he must do to inherit eternal life, Jesus didn't say, "You can't do it. It's impossible." He said, "Your answer is right—Love God with all your heart with all your soul with all your strength and with all your mind. And love your neighbor as yourself. Do this and you will live (Luke 10:25-28)." John Wesley, the founder of the Methodist movement, said the sole reason God raised up the people called Methodist was for the rediscovery of this truth. He called it the doctrine of Christian perfection—that we can, indeed must, be perfected in love in this life—that we can be all we are meant to be. *{Fulfillment}*

But a lethal lethargy has crept once again into the church today. Too long we have listened to the voices saying, "You'll never be nothin' but an ugly old worm," and we have begun to waste away. We need to hear once again that scriptural message: You can do it!

That is what the apostle Paul wrote to the Colossians in chapter 1, verses 9 through 14. He said that every time he prayed for them, he prayed

SO WHAT DO WE DO ABOUT THE TOPICS WE CHOOSE? 129

they would lead a life worthy of the Lord. And when Paul prayed for things, it was not with a forlorn hope. He expected them to happen.

Now that is a tall order. *{Challenge}* To live a life worthy of the Lord means that Jesus is our model. As we receive the body and blood of our Lord in communion today, we are united with him and receive a little more of his nature. Nothing less than the life of holiness he displayed is our goal. *{Character}* His active, self-sacrificing love is to characterize our lives. {LOVE} {SERVICE/SACRIFICE} Our motive is not the blessings we will gain, though they will surely come. Our motive is to be completely God-centered—aimed at pleasing God. *{Purpose/Place}*

That is even a taller order—to live a life fully pleasing to God. *{Challenge}* We are not talking about just fulfilling our duty to God, *{Responsibility/Duty}* living up to whatever minimum requirements there may be. We are talking about completely, or wholeheartedly, pleasing God—to love God with all our heart. {LOVE}

This week I left my Bible on the breakfast table after family devotions. Later that morning Leah came into my office carrying it and said, "Here Daddy, you forgot your Bible." It warmed my heart that my three-year-old took the initiative of doing that for me. The same is true in our relationship with God. Life for the Christian is not just a matter of putting away our toys and eating our peas. It's wanting to help fold the clothes {SERVICE/SACRIFICE} and saying, "Mommy, lets go for a walk." {COMMUNITY} It's not standing on a priest's religious ceremonies, or a Levite's legal loopholes, as we read this morning. It's stopping to help a beat up traveler, when you could just as easily walk on by (Luke 10:28–37).

It is a tall order, living a life worthy of the Lord, a life fully pleasing to God. *{Challenge}* Yet it's an order that can be filled. And Paul's prayer contains the means by which it can happen.

But before we look at that, let me speak briefly to the question of why we should want it to. After all, you might ask, "Why should I care about a life worthy of Jesus, or pleasing him? Really, what's he got to do with me?" Well, really, he has everything to do with us. Paul says, "Everything, seen and unseen, to the ends of the universe, was created and is sustained by, for, and through Jesus Christ." (Colossians 1:16)—"Everything, seen and unseen, to the ends of the universe, was created and is sustained by, for, and through Jesus Christ." In other words Jesus Christ is the clue to the universe, its center and explanation. He is the crux of reality.

> Today, after "It is a tall order . . . " I would add, "But I challenge you to do it." Replace "Yet" in the next sentence with "Because." Drop "And" in the next sentence.

Now if that is true, to live without Jesus as the center of life is to live in a false reality. You cannot live in harmony with the rest of creation; you cannot live up to your full potential {Fulfillment}; you cannot be all you were meant to be {BEING/BECOMING} if you leave Jesus out of your life—or give him some place other than center-stage. {Purpose/Place} Paul is saying, "Unless you want a big hole in your reality, live a life worthy of the Lord, fully pleasing to God."

So how do we do that? First, by being "filled with the knowledge of God's will." It's hard to hit a target you can't see. If you don't know what a life worthy of the Lord and pleasing to God is, it is hard to live it. That knowledge comes through "spiritual wisdom and understanding (Colossians 1:9)."

What is your picture of a person who is wise and understanding? Someone, maybe like a grandfather, with a long life and lots of experiences? That's one kind of wisdom. But spiritual wisdom—the kind that brings knowledge of God's will—comes not just through learning from past mistakes. It comes from the illumination of the Holy Spirit. Spiritual wisdom speaks of thinking that is not merely dependent on the unaided process of your own intellect, but is guided by the Spirit of truth. And understanding speaks of the application of that basic wisdom to the situations that arise in all of life, not just our spiritual life. And all of this speaks of a life of spiritual devotion, a life that soaks in God's word—both that which God has written in scripture and that which God writes in our hearts by the Holy Spirit. Remember what Moses said? "This is not too hard for you or beyond your reach. The word of God is near you—in your mouth and in your heart, that you can do it" (Deuteronomy 30:11–14).

If you would have spiritual wisdom and understanding so that you may be filled with the knowledge of God's will, live a life of spiritual devotion. Wouldn't you like to know what God wants you to do? You can, if you search God's Word diligently, and listen with the ears of your soul to God's still small voice. You can be a person with spiritual wisdom and understanding.

You can also be fruitful, for that is the second characteristic of a life worthy and pleasing to God. Paul said, "So that you may live a life worthy of the Lord and please him in every way: bearing fruit in every good work" (Colossians 1:9).

Someone has said things are unprofitable or misplaced when they do not seek or serve their end. {Purpose/Place} We are like the wood of the grapevine, good for nothing, not so much as to make a peg to hang anything on; good for nothing but to be cast into the fire, unless it is fruitful Jesus said, "By this is my Father

> Today I would add, "It could also be characterized by strength, vision, courage, perseverance, determination, integrity, wisdom, honor, discipline—for these are also fruits of the Spirit that Paul prays for his readers throughout his letters."

glorified, that you bear much fruit. (John 15:5-7)." What kind of fruit are you bearing? How is your life characterized? It could be characterized by love, joy, peace, patience, kindness, goodness, faithfulness, gentleness, and self-control—for these are the fruit of the Spirit. *{Character}*

Perhaps you have known someone like Lib Johnson. Lib was the head of the student nursing program at Lenoir Memorial Hospital. You couldn't be in her presence without having your spirits lifted. You felt better about life and you felt better about yourself. That was true even when she contracted terminal cancer. Through all the radiation treatments and the chemotherapy, though she felt sick and put on weight and lost all her hair, still she gave joyously to everyone she saw. *{Discipline/Perseverance}* {SUPPORT/NURTURE} And when we came to say goodbye to her in the sanctuary of the church, we didn't hold a funeral—we celebrated a resurrection. For we knew where Lib had gone. "A tree is known by its fruit," Jesus said, and Lib's fruit was the fruit of the Spirit.

> This point is grossly under-developed in the sermon. This lack of balance is a mark of an inexperienced preacher. I had spent so much time on the earlier points that I didn't have enough to give to the last one.

Lib had "the knowledge of God's will." She was a fruitful and fruit-filled person. She also had the third characteristic of a life worthy of the Lord and pleasing to God—an increasing knowledge of God. If you have ever known a person like Lib, you know that kind of person has strong faith. They are very close to God. Their faith is not static, or slowly slipping backward. It forges ahead. *{Discipline/Perseverance}* They are continually learning more of God—more of God's love, more of God's justice, more of God's grace, more of God's discipline. And as they learn more of God, they trust God with more of themselves.

We can be that kind of person, you and I. {BEING/BECOMING} We can be filled with the knowledge of God's will. We can bear fruit of the Spirit in our lives. We can continually grow in knowing God. In short, we can live lives worthy of the Lord and pleasing to God. We can do it.

Someone asked John Wesley, "If Christian perfection is possible, why are there so few perfected Christians?" Wesley answered, "Because so few expect it." I heard a high-jumper one time tell how he couldn't clear six feet because he was six feet tall and he'd always been told, "You can't jump your own height. It's impossible." Then he told the official to set the bar at six-one. He told himself, "If I can't jump my own height, why can't I jump one inch above my own height." And he did! For centuries we Christians have been telling ourselves, "You can't do it. It is too high. It is beyond you. It is impossible." But in fact, Jesus came to make it possible. He said, "I have come that you might have life and have it abundantly (John 10:10)." As one Christian businessman I know put it, "When I am at my best in Christ, I am better then I can be!" Christ sets the bar above our own height. And it is possible to clear it because we are not dependent on our own strength. {Strength/Power} Paul's prayer was, "That you may be strengthened with all power according to God's glorious might, so that you may have great endurance and patience, and giving joyful thanks to the Father, who has qualified you to share in the inheritance of his holy people in the kingdom of light. For he has rescued us from the dominion of darkness and brought us into the kingdom of the Son he loves, in whom we have redemption, the forgiveness of sins (Colossians 1:11–14)." {FORGIVENESS}

God's forgiveness *of* our sins through Jesus Christ sets us free from our slavery *to* our sins and connects us with the One who makes all things possible. As Paul said, "In Christ I can do all things." {Strength/Power}

Don't say, "They are right. I'm just a lowly old worm. I'll never amount to much." If you do, you will just waste away and miss the best part of life. The message of the gospel is a triumphant one. Its tone is caught very well by, of all things, a current bankcard advertisement—with a few editorial changes:

> You can open up your world and make it shine; you can do it.
> You can squeeze that something extra out of life; yes you can.
> You can set a goal and do it, bring your own style to it,
> In your world, in your life, it's God's plan.
> Every minute, you can do it.
> Every day, yes you can.
> You can grow in your own way; you can do it.
> And God wants to help—that's God's plan.

> It would have been better to say, "You can do it. I challenge you—let him help, today." It is more confident and assertive, rather than pleading.

Why don't you let him, today? Amen? Amen.

Table 6.6: Feminine Christian Theme in Sample Sermon Two

FEMININE CHRISTIAN THEMES	HITS
{BEING-OPEN/SHARING-FEELINGS}	
{SUBMISSION}	
{COMMUNITY}	1
{NONVIOLENCE/NONAGGRESSION}	
{SUPPORT/NURTURE}	
{FORGIVENESS}	2
{LOVE}	2
{HUMILITY}	
{SERVICE/SACRIFICE}	2
{BEING/BECOMING}	4
Total Feminine Hits:	12

Table 6.7: Masculine Christian Themes in Sample Sermon Two

Masculine Christian Themes	HITS
{Influence}	
{Belonging/Teamwork}	
{Purpose/Place}	3
{Character}	2
{Courage}	
{Challenge}	3
{Fulfillment}	3
{Responsibility/Duty}	1

Masculine Christian Themes	HITS
{Discipline/Perseverance}	1
{Strength/Power}	2
Total Masculine Hits:	15

An overall change I would make if I were writing this sermon today would be to take a cue from the experience of Dorothy Cassel from the last chapter—use the specific words from the lists of themes wherever appropriate. You could do the same. Whenever you are preparing a worship service, sermon, Bible study, vacation Bible school lesson, newsletter/ blog—whatever—keep those two lists where you can see them. Refer to them and use the words wherever you can.

As you do so, strive for balance. This is easier than it might seem because of the natural connections between the masculine and feminine themes. For example, {COMMUNITY} and {SUPPORT/NURTURE} have an obvious kinship with *{Belonging/Teamwork}*, but less obviously require that we fulfill our *{Responsibility/Duty}* to one another. Similarly, discovering or fulfilling our *{Purpose/Place}* requires {SUBMISSION} to God and others, which in turn requires {HUMILITY}, which in turn is a component of *{Character}*. Likewise, *{Influence}* may be achieved through {FORGIVENESS} and {NONVIOLENCE/NONAGGRESSION}, which requires *{Courage}* and *{Discipline}* to resist the temptation to retaliate and *{Perseverance}* in the face of suffering. Make these connections more explicit in all your church communications and in your conversations in and outside the church. Do it consistently and you will begin to see more men and more action-oriented women in your pews, your studies, and your ministries—provided that you, your team, and your congregation are spending time and sharing faith with such men and women outside your church walls.

7

How We Talk

AT AN URBAN MINISTRY convocation in Columbus, Ohio, the keynote speaker, a United Methodist District Superintendent, said, "I hate church meetings." After a pregnant pause she said, "It takes so long to get anything done. By the time we get around to making a decision I'm so damn tired I don't care any more!"

Her comment echoed words from a man I'd interviewed in my first research project on the missing men twenty years before. He was a new Christian and had been a church member for less than two years. I had asked,

> "Why do you think many men don't come to church?"
> "You don't have your best leaders in church," he said. "The best leaders do their leading in the business world or government-other places. They don't want to waste their time in church leadership."
> "What do you mean by 'waste their time'?" I asked.
> He hesitated a moment, deciding whether I could take the truth. Then he said with some heat, "I've been trying to help out. But I can't stand the committee work. They take forever! Everybody's always apologizing for their opinion. It's like they're so afraid of hurting somebody's feelings that it takes them three times longer to say what they think!"

I have heard words to that effect multiple times in the years since. It is one of the reasons men have become even scarcer on planning teams and committees in the church than they are in worship. As with worship, gender representation on church boards and committees was once 50/50. That ratio was largely split along the lines of programming vs. administration. That is, it mirrored the myth that religion (and its programs) were women's work and business (including church finance, trusteeship, etc.) was men's work. In the 1980s mainline churches began mandating that all church boards must include women. As a young pastor I welcomed the mandated change. I wanted to see balance across the whole of the church's leadership and especially hoped that we would begin to see more men on the program committees and more women on the administrative ones. No such luck. In fact as men rotated off the administrative boards and committees it became increasingly difficult to get new men to serve. I couldn't understand why men were suddenly abdicating from all the traditionally male boards.

It wasn't until I began researching the causes of the church's missing men that I began to understand. In that process I observed the same phenomenon among Jaycees chapters. Often the Jaycees would meet in a local bar & grill. After the decision to incorporate the Jaycettes into the Jaycees, I observed the men hanging out in the bar and poking their heads in the meeting room where the women were running the meaning, "just checking to see how y'all are doing." Why? One man summed up what many of them told me: "Well, everything's different with the wives being there. We spend a lot of time on stuff that doesn't matter. I get lost before we get anything done. So we just hangout here—talk sports and stuff—and then do whatever they tell us once they've decided."

The same turned out to be true among male church abdicators. It was the character of the talk that drove these men out of leadership. They had neither the perspective nor the patience to wade through the sea of estrogenized language. What is the character of that language? In a word, it is "powerless."

THE GENDER-LINKED LANGUAGE EFFECT

The originator of the label, "powerless language" is our old friend, Dr. Robin Tolmach Lakoff from chapter 2. The thesis of her ground-breaking book, *Language and Women's Place*, was that women find themselves stuck in a subordinate, powerless position in society because they use language that is consistent with that state. You will recall that she originally called this language "the Feminine Register." However, subsequent research showed that some men also used this style of language, and that the common thread that ran through it for both men and women was powerlessness. That finding touched off a decade or so of trying to show that there were *no* differences between women's and men's talk.[1] No such luck with that one either. Gender differences in language use remained stubbornly resistant. Over

---

1. e.g. Mills, *Gender and Politeness* 2003.

thirty research studies have uncovered such differences and have led to the understanding of what is now called the Gender-Linked Language Effect.[2] In summary, the Gender-Linked Language Effect is this: 1) There *are* differences between women's and men's talk; 2) Regardless of the receiver's sex or age, men's and women's talk causes them to be evaluated differently on personal characteristics; 3) It is the language differences, not other factors like stereotypes, that produce the evaluations; and 4) This effect is consistent with, while still independent of, gender stereotypes.[3]

The Gender-Linked Language Effect, particularly in its evaluative consequences, has critical implications for church talk. Women's talk receives high ratings for "Socio-Intellectual Status" (i.e. sociability and literacy) and "Aesthetic Quality" (i.e. niceness and beauty), while men's talk is highly rated for "Dynamism" (i.e. strength and aggressiveness). In the church sociability, literacy, niceness, and beauty are all highly valued. Strength, on the other hand is highly suspect (remember our discussion of weakness in chapter 3) and aggressiveness is downright taboo. So at the general level at which men's and women's talk is unconsciously evaluated there is already a bias toward women's talk and away from men's talk. But the Devil is in the details, as the saying goes, and it is at the detail level that the evaluative impressions of powerlessness are formed.

Components of the Gender-linked Language Effect

Linguists and communication scholars from the 1970s on have identified a number of differences between men's and women's talk. For example, among other things women generally focus on relationships, use more intensive adverbs (e.g., "really," "so") and references to emotion (e.g., "excited," "sad"), whereas men focus on actions and events, and tend to use more elliptical sentences (e.g., "Great picture.") and references to quantity (e.g., "40 feet tall"). But the key differences for our discussion at this point lay in the details that make up the category labeled "Tentativeness." I add the label "Communalness" to that category. By labeling the elements of talk below as "Tentativeness/Communalness" I am highlighting the disconnect between most men's and most women's interpretation of them. Due to their tendency toward an action-orientation, for most men these elements express weakness and uncertainty. Because of their tendency toward a relational orientation, for most women they express openness and community. In other words, men perceive

---

2. Mulac, et al., "Gender-linked Language Effect" 2013.
3. Mulac, "A General Process Model" 2003.

these communicative behaviors as negative while women perceive the same things as positive.[4] Bear in mind that disconnect as we take each in turn.

Hedges or "Pre-Apologies"

Hedges can provide the speaker with psychological space ("Let me take a moment..." "I wanna... or think... or believe" or "We would like to..."). Using this kind of hedge can be taken by the hearer to mean the speaker is weak him/herself, they s/he doesn't have the confidence to say it firmly. Hedges can also be an indication that the speaker is about to say something the hearer won't like. These hedges' purpose is to soften the blow by indicating the speaker knows there are other views ("You may disagree, but..." "I affirm your..., but..."—*and no, I do not mean "I affirm your butt"!*), or by apologizing in advance for breaking social convention ("To be honest?..." "I'm only saying this because..."). Take these phrases away and you have strong, direct statements. Include them and you'll get mixed results. You may think you are being polite (another high value in the church—see below, "Super-polite Language") but you may be perceived as being false. Commenting on the use of hedges for a Wall Street Journal article, James W. Pennebaker, chair of the psychology department of the University of Texas at Austin, said, "Politeness is another word for deception. The point is to formalize social relations so you don't have to reveal your true self. If you're going to lie, it's a good way to do it—because you're not really lying. So it softens the blow. Of course, it's generally best not to lie. But because these sayings so frequently signal untruth, they can be confusing even when used in a neutral context."[5]

Another reason people use hedges is a desire to avoid conflict. NPR journalist, Ashley Milne-Tyte, reported on the mixed results these verbal gymnastics produce: "Those tactics keep women in their comfort zone, but tend to rob us of authority. The key words here are "avoiding conflict." Women, on the whole, can't stand it. So we perform linguistic somersaults to get around a hairy situation without upsetting anyone. But to men, being self-deprecating and speaking indirectly can come across as weak."[6]

Avoiding conflict, or at least the appearance of it, has become one of today's church's highest values. We have come to believe that unity means uniformity, that disagreement shows lack of love, that argument expresses disloyalty. This stands in stark contrast to the working world, particularly among men. Helena Morrisey, CEO of the £47 million financial firm,

---

4. Murphy, "Corpus and Sociolinguistics." 56–57.
5. Bernstein, Elizabeth. "Verbal Tee-Ups" (2014).
6. Milne-Tyte, "Women's Words," (2011).

Newton Investment Management in London, UK, describes life in the corporate world this way:

> It is hard to generalise [sic] because there is a spectrum, but actually the women I have worked with over the years certainly don't seek confrontation and would tend to try to avoid it, which would be consistent with this pre-empting of criticism and anxiety, I suppose; hedging, using humour [sic] to soften things.
>
> There are some men who enjoy a good fight, enjoy confrontation, but I don't think I have met any women who want to spark an argument, while I have seen men in the context of mainly male-orientated [sic] boardrooms or senior discussion almost seem to push somebody to have that discussion in a quite confrontational way. It is not only that women speak differently, but they are also trying to avoid what will happen next, and this is their style to get there.
>
> It may be seen as a bit of weakness on the part of women, because you are not playing the game in the same way. Maybe subconsciously there is a feeling that this person isn't as decisive, can't hold her own, is unsure of her arguments.[7]

Men enjoy and value argumentation. If you don't believe it, go to the local place where men gather to solve the world's problems—the sports bar, the fast-food joint, the coffee shop. Listen to their conversation. Notice the give and take, the challenge and response in it. One newly-converted Christian man I interviewed said, "My pastor and I disagree at first on most things. Sometimes we go toe to toe with each other over them. But afterwards we put our arm around each other's shoulder and walk off friends. That's what got me coming here. I might not agree with him, but at least he's willing to take a stand. A lot of pastors won't. A man ought to stand for something!" Also notice the directness of his statements, the lack of hedges, the unapologetic nature of them. They are strong and direct. The interview was one of many at a church that was effective in reaching men, and a running theme in all of them was the strength of the pastor's talk in sermons, meetings, and conversations.

Finally, research suggests that the desire to communicate openness is counter-productive in situations involving persuasion. When a speaker uses informal language to hedge on a data claim, it leads to negative perceptions of the policy, source, and argument. Only if the speaker uses professional language to hedge (i.e. cites data indicating exceptions to the case) do these negative perceptions not occur.[8]

---

7. Guardian, "Women Told To Speak Their Minds," 2011.
8. Durik, "Effects of Hedges," 217.

Qualifiers

Qualifiers are people's answer to generalizations. Words like "most," "some," "might," and "may," show that the speaker knows what she/he is saying is not true in every instance. Others, like "hopefully," "I think," "as far as I know," and "I guess," indicate the speaker's awareness that he/she is not the final expert on the subject. Others ("kind of, a little, slightly, somewhat, pretty, a bit, rather, reasonably, fairly, relatively, just, like, sortof, kindof) say, "Hey, there's some wiggle room here." In that regard you could think of them as "detensifiers," reducing the intensity of the statement.

The thing about qualifiers is that women use them frequently whereas men seldom do.[9] Now, if that statement bothers you—if you are saying "Hey, wait a minute, you can't make a generalization like that,"—then you are illustrating the difference between men's and women's approach to talk, in general. (Those last two words are a qualifier, by the way. Feel better?) The thing is, research has repeatedly born this out.[10] For example, a study of business leaders by British linguist, Judith Baxter, found women were four times more likely to use tentative language elements such as qualifiers than were men.[11]

So why is it that women use qualifiers more than men do? One reason is men think and talk in generalities, whereas women focus on particulars. Hugo Liu of M.I.T. and Rada Mihalcea of the University of North Texas analyzed 150,000 weblog entries, half by men and half by women, in order to

> ... gain insights into how men and women perceive day-by-day events, and what they most value in their daily experiences, by looking at a very large number of diary entries extracted from the blogosphere. Our analysis of gender distinctions revealed that women's and men's sensibilities exhibited a particularity-generality dichotomy that swept all dimensions of gender space. Women focused on immediate time, nuanced colors, close-knit relationships, objects describable by size, the flavors of food, and were disposed to happiness and sadness. Men focused on months and years, primary colors, social hierarchies, abstract ideas, food as a tool for sating hunger, and were disposed to anger and arousal. These findings generally agreed with previous research in gender psychology ... "[12]

---

9. Pennebaker, "Psychological Aspects," 547.
10. e.g. Fahy, "Use of Linguistic Qualifiers," (2002).
11. Baxter, "Is it all tough talking," 197.
12. Liu and Mihalcea. "Men, Women, and Computers," (2007).

Let's make that contrast more visible:

Table 7.1: Gender and the Particularity-Generality Dichotomy

WOMEN (particularity)	MEN (generality)
Immediate time	Months and years
Close-knit relationships	Social hierarchies
Nuanced colors (e.g. fuchsia, aqua, azure)	Primary colors (e.g. red, green, blue)
Objects by size (e.g. little chair)	Abstract ideas (e.g. theology)
Foods' flavor	Food's function

Think of it this way: Men see forests; women see trees. One perspective is not better than the other. Both are valuable and important. Men think and talk in terms of the large central portion of the bell curve of life (see Figure 7.1), whereas women want to make sure the tail portions of the curve get included (see Figure 7.2), especially when it comes to people.

Figure 7.1: The Focus of Men's Attention

Normal Distribution (The Bell Curve)

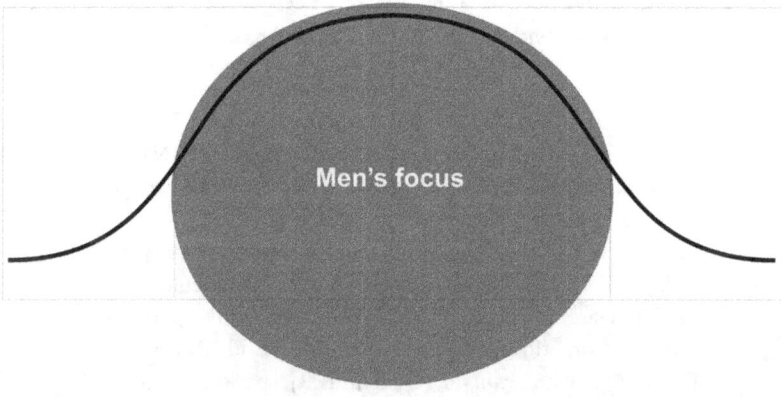

Figure 7.2: The Focus of Women's Concern

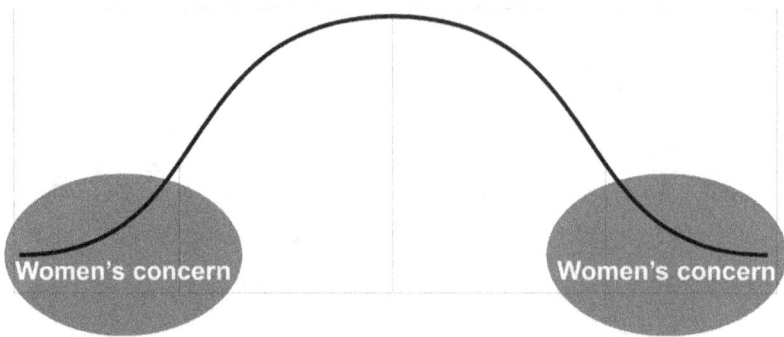

Men assume everyone knows the exceptions exist, but they want to place the emphasis on what is most often or most generally true. For them adding qualifiers reduces the impact of the statement and reflects uncertainty, weakness, or incompetence. For men the regular use of qualifiers erodes credibility. The men who hear it think, "Don't be so damn mealy-mouthed. Just say it already." Research has found that using language with qualifiers and the like can help women influence men on some issues, but it was only true for women speakers and only on a few issues.[13] Let's look at Helena Morrisey's statement above again with the qualifiers italicized as an illustration:

> *It is hard to generalise because there is a spectrum*, [HEDGE-INCLUSION CONCERN] but *actually* [INTENSIFIER] the women I have worked with over the years *certainly* [INTENSIFIER] don't seek confrontation and *would tend* [QUALIFIER] *to try* [QUALIFIER] to avoid it, which *would be* [QUALIFIER] consistent with this pre-empting of criticism and anxiety, *I suppose*; [QUALIFIER] hedging, using humour to soften things.
>
> There are *some men* [QUALIFIER] who enjoy a good fight, enjoy confrontation, *but I don't think* [QUALIFIER] I have met any women who *want to* [QUALIFIER] spark an argument, while I have seen men *in the context of mainly male-orientated* [QUALIFIER] boardrooms or senior discussion *almost seem* [QUALIFIER] to push somebody to have that discussion in a *quite* [INTENSIFIER (see below)] confrontational way. It is not only that women speak differently, but they are also *trying* [QUALIFIER] *to avoid what will happen next*, [CONFLICT AVOIDANCE] and this is their style to get there.

---

13. e.g. Carli, "Gender, Language, and Influence," (1990).

It *may be seen* [QUALIFIER] as *a bit of* [QUALIFIER] weakness on the part of women, because you are not playing the game in the same way. *Maybe* [QUALIFIER] *subconsciously* [QUALIFIER] *there is a feeling that* [QUALIFIER] this person isn't *as* [QUALIFIER] decisive, can't hold her own, is unsure of her arguments.

Now read that statement with all the powerless language removed:

[T]he women I have worked with over the years don't seek confrontation. They avoid it, which is consistent with this preempting of criticism and anxiety; hedging, using humour to soften things.

There are men who enjoy a good fight, enjoy confrontation, but I have [not] met any women who [purposefully] spark argument[s], while I have seen men in boardrooms or senior discussion push somebody to have that discussion in a confrontational way. It is not only that women speak differently, but they also [intentionally prevent] conflict and this is [how they] get there.

It is seen as weakness on the part of women, because you are not playing the game in the same way—this person isn't decisive, can't hold her own, is unsure of her arguments.

Notice the increase in the strength, the power of the statement. Note also it's crispness—there are 29% fewer words in the latter. This is one source of the misperception that women talk more than men. Research has shown that they don't. Women and men use about the same number of words per day, but women use more words per sentence. The reason? All the hedges, qualifiers, and the other powerless language we're about to discuss.

Uncertainty Signals

If qualifiers undermine persuasion, uncertainty signals destroy it. These are words, vocalizations, or a tone of voice that say, "I don't know . . . what to say, . . . what I'm doing, . . . if I belong here, . . . if I can do this." Consider this example from Sherry Surratt and Jenni Catron's *Just Lead!: A No-whining, No-complaining, No-nonsense Guide for Women Leaders in the Church*:

My first leadership lesson came to me when I was nineteen years old from a beautiful, take charge person of confidence named Jeanette, my youth pastor's wife. She asked me to lead the children's choir and assist in directing the upcoming musical they would perform in the adult service. The kids ranged in age from kindergartners to sixth-graders and were noisy, boisterous, and quite vocal in their skepticism that I could lead them in anything, much less a musical production. Jeanette came to my aid after one particularly unproductive choir practice when I think I said something like, "Um, would anybody, like to, um sing?" It was, of course, a question that I never should have asked, and it was met with a resounding NO! She quietly observed the chaos, then gently chided me with some simple words: "You are the leader. So lead."[14]

We'll overlook all the qualifiers in that paragraph and focus on that one quotation: "Um, would anybody, like to, um sing?" That sentence illustrates the two types of uncertainty signals we employ, verbal commas and turn-signals. Verbal commas can be the ubiquitous "Um" or "Uh," as above. Or they can be words and phrases such as "just," "like," "okay," "you know," or "I mean." These words can mean other things or perform other functions, but frequently they are nothing more than fillers. For example, when I was 13 or 14 years old my speech therapist mother drove me nuts for a while. Daily we would have conversations like this:

Woody: We were going to lunch (you know) and

Mom: No, I don't know.

Woody: and a bunch of girls came out of class and (you know) started talk—

Mom: No, I don't know.

Woody:—ing . . . Mom, cut it out!

Mom: Well I don't know. So stop saying I do. Just tell me what happened.

It took a while, but she finally drummed "you know" out of my system—to be promptly replaced by "okay," which was then replaced by "Um/Uh," and so on. I'm still working on it, Mom. It takes continual effort. When I told one church staff that such an effort was necessary for them, one of them said, "But, everybody knows you're just thinking of the next thing you want to say. It just means you're not prepared." "Yes," I said, "and that's the point. Whether you are making announcements in worship, or preaching, or leading a Bible study or meeting, the last thing you want people thinking is, 'S/He's unprepared.'" The same is true when leading prayer. Contemporary evangelical prayers have become so full of "Fathergod," "Lord," "Lordgod" "Father," "Lordjesus,"

---

14. Surratt and Catron, *Just Lead*, 4.

"wejust," "wewanna," etc. in every sentence that it is hard to follow the meaning of the prayer. Verbal commas like these are another thing that make you seem, as Nicholas Palomares found, "less competent, intelligent, confident, and powerful."

So too are turn-signals. These are cues at the beginning or end of a sentence that say "I am about to say something," or "I'm not done yet, so don't interrupt." "Um/Uh" can serve this purpose as it does in the quote above, "Ummm, would anybody, like to, um, sing?" Worship leaders or people giving announcements in contemporary services are fond of "Hey . . . " as the lead-in when they first step on stage. If they were in North Carolina I would think they're saying "Hi," but in Ohio it comes across as, "I'm a little nervous so I need a folksy way to get everyone's attention. Another favorite, "Well hey . . . " leaves that impression even more. In conversations, the popular "so" can serve as either this kind of turn-taking announcement: "So—I was thinking . . . " It also often shows up as the nebulous end of a sentence: " . . . and then he went in his office and closed the door—so . . . " It is like a filibuster in the legislature; it holds the floor in case you think of something worthwhile to say.

"Uptalk" is another type of floor-holding mechanism. It refers to finishing a sentence with an upward inflection as if you were asking a question, even though you are not: "So, I was going down the street. ↗ And there was this girl. ↗ And she looked, kinda, like, homeless ↗ . . . " It is as if a silent "you know?" was tacked on to the end of each sentence, as if the speaker was silently asking "Are you with me? Am I communicating this well?" All the while the listeners who value strong, direct talk are thinking, "less competent, less intelligent, less confident, less powerful."

Lakoff identified this rising intonation as one of the components of women's language that keep women in a subordinate social position because it often reveals the speaker's tentativeness and uncertainty. Fellow linguist, Sally McConnell-Ginnet, illustrates it by pointing out the power dynamics in the following exchange:

> Husband: When will dinner be ready? ↘
>
> Wife: Around 6 o'clock. ↗
>
> Answers to questions normally end with a falling intonation, providing a sense of strength and certainty. But here, the husband uses a falling intonation to ask a question, asserting his strength. The wife answers with a statement using rising intonation, the opposite of normal, as if seeking approval. It shows uncertainty about her husband's wishes or response.[15]

15. McConnell-Ginet, et al. "Women and Language," 1980.

This oft-cited example has been re-interpreted by others to emphasize the wife's motives in this exchange. In this interpretation, the uptalk shows that the wife is open to her husband's wishes. In other words, she is being polite and considerate. These differing interpretations illustrate well the Tentativeness/Communalness dynamic. We may choose our phrasing or intonation out of a desire to communicate openness or flexibility or politeness, (i.e. Communalness), but it may turn out to be counter-productive to our ultimate goal: "Some people believe the phenomenon is used by uncertain speakers hoping to win their audience over. It acts as a constant check that listeners follow—phrasing every sentence, no matter how declarative, *is a subconscious begging by the speaker to be reassured* [emphasis added]."[16]

About ten years ago I was one of the speakers at a conference on ministry in a post-modern world. One of the other speakers was an emerging leader in the Emerging Church movement. He was passionate about reaching the post-modern people with whom the church has failed miserably to connect. He talked about how these are people who value openness, and then he said, "So, you notice how I've got this, sort of, cool Po-Mo style of talk going? Where I end all my sentences like they're questions even when they're not? Well that's to say, 'Hey, I'm open to new things, to different, like, ideas and stuff.'" In other words, he was tailoring his speaking style to his target audience, and I applaud that. But while those of the PoMo subculture may have found it cool, I'd wager that most men and many women outside that subset would have thought him "less competent, intelligent, confident, and powerful." Indeed, the fact that studies among post-modern college students have had the same findings suggests that what he gained in coolness he probably lost in credibility. It may have been entertaining, but it would not have been convincing. For example, the other day I overheard a comment by a man in his thirties as he and a friend walked by our table at Starbucks—"Some people's voices go up at end of sentences. Like my dermatologist, he does that. I don't trust them."

Quest-ments and State-tions

These hybrid utterances make explicit what is implied in Uptalk. They state a claim, or propose an action, or present an argument indirectly by putting it in the form of a question. Sometimes it is simply the statement with what Lakoff called a "tag question" attached, such as, "People just don't think church is important like they used to, *do they?*" She observed, "This sort of tag question is much more apt to be used by women than by men in conversation. Why

---

16. BBC News Magazine, "The Unstoppable March," http://www.bbc.com/news/magazine-28708526, accessed 8/11/14.

is this the case? The tag question allows a speaker to avoid commitment, and thereby avoid conflict with the addressee. The problem is that, by so doing, speakers may also give the impression of not really being sure of themselves, or looking to the addressee for confirmation of their views."[17]

Other instances are more complex, involving phrases like "Don't you think that . . . " or "Why don't we . . . " or " . . . don't you agree?" These are indirect ways of stating a claim or making a proposal. In women's language culture it's being open and inclusive. But men hear it as manipulation or misdirection. Far from being inclusive, for men "Don't you think that . . . " feels like being maneuvered, being told what they *should* think rather than being asked what they *do* think. Men prefer direct statements and questions like, "I think your inclusive language excludes me." In men's language culture, a direct statement carries with it an unspoken "What do you think?" Unlike the tag question, " . . . don't you agree?" it leaves the hearer free to respond as they wish rather than matching the speaker's expectation. Structures like, "Why don't we . . . " can have the same manipulative feel, but may also misdirect or confuse the hearer. In men's talk, the speaker is asking for an explanation. In other words, men will answer the direct question, "Why . . . ?"

Super-polite Language, "Communitifiers" and Approval-seeking

In recent years I have noticed a new trend among pastors and worship leaders. When it is time to lead the congregation in prayer, they will say, "May we pray . . . " How nice! How polite! How—wimpy. You're leading worship and you're asking permission to pray?! It is another expression of Communalness, with the added dimension of what Lakoff called "super-polite forms." These, she said, were another characteristic of women's talk. "May we pray" is a step further along the politeness continuum from "Let us pray," a phrase that direct individuals find weak enough as it its. Other examples include "If you would, turn with me to the fifth chapter of Matthew . . . " or "Let me encourage you to think about . . . " Such sentence structures may seem polite to the speaker, but to those who value direct communication they sound mealy-mouthed. This is especially true for men, who from an early age grow accustomed to directives. Marjorie Harness Goodwin documents this difference in a study among school children. She notes the contrast between the frequent use of commands and directives among the boys, as opposed to the girls' use of words such as "we" and "let's" and structures that include all the participants. This "softens the directive meaning into a

---

17. Lakoff, *"Language and Women's Place,"* 49.

kind of suggestion and shortens the mutual distance" between them.[18] At one time this would have been simply noted as a difference between boys' and girls' communication. But current academic culture has become more evaluative than descriptive, casting the former in a negative and the latter in a positive light. It is part of the belief that all things hierarchical are evil.

That belief is related to, perhaps even founded upon, the belief that all men want to be top dog—that they all want to be the leader. That was my assumption when I began doing research among men, whether because I was projecting my own desires or simply operating within the culture of academia. Either way, imagine my surprise when in study after study I found that the overwhelming majority of men did *not* want to be leaders. Overall, only about 15% of those surveyed had any desire for such a role. The other 85% did not. They did, however, want to *have* a leader. And they wanted that leader to be strong, clear, competent, and trustworthy. Direct communication like, "Pray with me," or "Turn in your Bibles to Matthew, chapter 5," or "Consider this," inspire confidence and trust. It says, "This is a leader I can follow." There are situations that call for directives, even imperatives.

The thing is, even young girls know this. Amy Kyratzis and Şeyda Deniz Tarım studied middle class Turkish girls during play in their preschool classroom. They found that

> Group members explicitly sanctioned one another not to differentiate themselves, and used egalitarian forms ... when engaged in task activities or pretend play with one another. The same girls, however, used imperatives when they enacted the role of mothers, or played with boys. Results suggest that in peer group conversations among young Turkish preschool-aged girls, group members socialize one another that girls should speak in ways that enact egalitarian forms of social organization when with other girls, *but they make local, strategic uses of these norms, competently enacting alternative, hierarchical forms of social organization in other contexts* [emphasis added].[19]

The authors did not indicate the reason the girls used imperatives when playing with boys—whether because they were still enacting the role of mothers, or adapting to the boys' pattern of talk. The point is there are times when direct, even directive, and yes, even imperative talk is appropriate. Why then is it so absent from church talk? The answer I have received from both the pulpit and the pew is, "People will be upset by being told instead of asked." In other words, we fear damaging our Communalness.

18. Goodwin, "Directive-Response Speech Sequences" 169–70.
19. Kyratzis and Tarım, "Using Directives," 490.

That brings me to an issue that has surfaced repeatedly in interviews with men who had given up on church: approval-seeking. Sometimes it is in reference to announcements in worship services: "It doesn't matter who it is or what it's about. It's always, 'Please, please . . . '—like they're afraid they're asking too much and you'll disapprove. They need to just put it out there and let it stand on it's own merit." Sometimes it is in sermons: "A lot of times the pastor got into this pleading tone at the end of his sermons. There's no confidence there. I got the feeling he's mostly afraid people won't like him." Sometimes it is in ministry planning meetings: "The committee meetings were like everybody was walking on eggshells. It was 'if you don't mind,' or 'I'd appreciate it if' or 'Would you mind,' or 'Okay?' or 'Right?' After a while I got tired of the time it took for people to get stroked." This is not how people talk in business team meetings, or during lunch break at the factory, or in the deer shack on the hunting trip. And for direct individuals such superpolite language, like the uptalk discussed above, speaks of insecurity and an over-developed desire to please.

Intensifiers or Vocal Italics

When you take all the strength and power out of your language, you have to have something to give it some "umph." Irish linguist, Bróna Murphy, notes that women's tendency to use intensifiers has a long history:

> From the mid-18th century, amplifiers become particularly associated with women. . . . Lord Chesterfield (c.1694–1773 cited in Ito and Tagliamonte 2003:260), one of the most influential politicians at that time, writes in 1754 that his "fair countrywomen" have extended the word "vastly" to a generalised [sic] intensifier function. He reports having heard a woman describe a very small gold snuff-box as "vastly pretty because it is so vastly little" (cited in Jespersen 1922:249–250). Stoffel (1901:101) highlights the use of "so" as an amplifier by women, for example, "He is so charming!" and refers to it as a "purely feminine expression".[20]

In her discussion of the Feminine Register (later redefined as Powerless Language), Lakoff dedicated a whole section to the word *so*, noting that while men do use it, it "occurs more frequently in women's than men's language" and is used with "vocal italics" to intensify their (women's) feelings.[21] Look at the difference between women's and men's language usage from an analysis of

20. Murphy, "Corpus and Sociolinguistics," 113.
21. Lakoff, *Language and Women's Place*, 81.

"700 million words, phrases, and topic instances collected from the Facebook messages of 75,000 volunteers ages thirteen to sixty-five (See Figure 7.3).[22]

Figure 7.3: Frequency Of Word Usage On Facebook By Gender

There are sixteen instances of "so" ranging in intensity from "so" to "soooooo" among the females' posts, but not a single one among those of the males.[23]

The intensified use of "so" shows up frequently in today's church, both in talk and in print. Sometimes the intensification is increased by repetition

---

22. Schwartz, et al. "Personality, Gender, and Age," 8.

23. There are, however, thirteen instances of profanity, which Lackoff observed is the male's preferred choice of intensification.

within the sentence, like this: "Here is another seed story from Matthew 13 of how God can take something *so* tiny and produce *so* much with it."[24] Neither "so" adds anything of substance to the sentence. In fact, it is stronger without them. The contrast between "tiny" and "much" (or "large" or "great") is sufficient. The addition of "so" is redundant.

At other times the intensification is increased by lengthening the "so." The Jesus Daily Facebook page is again instructive. Again, take note of the words and phrases I have italicized for you:

> Jesus Daily
> LIKE if GOD IS *SOOO GOOOD!*
> LIKE if GOD IS *SOOO GOOOD!*
> LIKE if GOD IS *SOOO GOOOD!*
> LIKE if GOD IS *SOOO GOOOD!*
> LIKE if GOD IS *SOOO GOOOD!*
> LIKE if GOD IS *SOOO GOOOD!*
> LIKE if GOD IS *SOOO GOOOD!* January 25, 2014 at 10:00am ·
>
> LIKE if GOD is *sooooooo* GREAT to you*!!!* January 5, 2014 at 11:19pm ·
>
> LIKE if GOD is *sooooooo gooooood* to you*!!!* December 29, 2011 at 8:19pm ·
>
> JESUS, I don't tell you enough . . . I LOVE YOU *SOOOOOO MUCH!!!* ♥ December 22, 2011 at 9:15am

The ALL CAPS and "Sooo" and "goooood" and "!!!" and "♥" are pictures of the vocal italics we would hear in a conversation. And they are the source of sarcastic humor in television programs, such as The Simpsons's Ned Flanders and Saturday Night Live's Church Lady.

Lakoff, Murphy, and others have identified a number of other intensifiers that are more prevalent in women's talk, including *too(ooo), very (very-very), really (really-really), such (suuuch), quite, definitely, totally (toooa-tlly), completely, extremely, simply, tremendously, altogether, absolutely, super-(as in "super-pleased"),* etc. The purpose of all these is to raise the emotional ante of the statement. Consider these italicized examples from church websites and Christians' Facebook posts:

---

24. https://www.facebook.com/asburyseedbed (accessed January 4, 2012).

We had the *most wonderful* [empty adjective] worship experience this morning. I was *so* blessed by the congregation and pray that everyone there came away feeling touched by God in a profound way. God is good.[25]

We are *so excited* [empty adjective] about our preschool program, Lil' K. I think you'll be *very* pleased with what your child will be learning and the ways in which he/she will be growing spiritually![26]

I am enormously excited [empty adjective] about this book . . .[27]

So *wonderful* [empty adjective]*!* We so very much enjoyed our time at your *special* [empty adjective] place!*[28]

Thank you so much for inviting me to come back and speak at your church. I had *such a wonderful time* catching up with people and meeting your youth. Hands down, that was the best youth talk I've ever had! The guys had *such wonderful* [empty adjective] questions. I was *so encouraged* by them. I felt *so* honored and welcomed. Thank you *so much* for your support, prayers, and advocacy over the years. You all are *truly* a blessing to my family and me.[29]

I am so *incredibly proud* of Generation Student Ministries! They Served and Worshiped with all of their hearts this week.[30]

Men's Ministry is *so much more* than a Bible study or a class. It is *a community [re. "commuuuuunity"]* of Christian men that *seek to* [QUALIFIER] encourage one another in Christ and grow together.[31]

"We are *super excited* [empty adjective]] to bring an *amazing* [empty adjective] marriage conference to LifeWay on Feb 14th

---

25. Facebook post, accessed August 11, 2014.
26. Church webpage, accessed July 29, 2014.
27. Facebook post, accessed July 28, 2014.
28. Facebook post (accessed July 27, 2014).
29. Church webpage (accessed July 16, 2014).
30. Facebook post (accessed July 12, 2014).
31. Church webpage (accessed May 16, 2014).

and 15th. . . . We have over 100 people already signed up, so don't wait to [sic] long to get your ticket.³²

God is *SO amazing* [empty adjective]*!!!!* I can't even put it in words*!!* Today at [the high school] God totally touched a young man who is an athlete on campus*!*³³

Take our Time & Talent offering ONLINE NOW! We are *so excited* [empty adjective] to reach our goal of 200 submissions of the Time & Talent*!*³⁴

"*We had such* a great family summit*!*"³⁵

"I *am so excited* [empty adjective] to attend this conference tomorrow with my two best friends*!*"³⁶

Again, the purpose of all those italicized words and exclamation points is to raise the emotional ante. It may come from a desire to be positive, encouraging, and to promote involvement. But when it comes to Action Men it is not only ineffective, it can be counter-productive. Research has consistently shown that men are reluctant to show emotion and to respond to others emotions, particularly if the others are also men.³⁷ For almost four decades leading communication scholar, the late Brant Burleson, studied how people provide support to others in difficult circumstances. Among other things, his research showed a significant difference between women's and men's use of what he called "Highly Person-Centered (HPC) comforting messages"³⁸ to provide emotional support to others. In explaining that difference, he pointed out that:

32. Church Facebook page (accessed February 6, 2014).
33. Facebook post (accessed January 23, 2014).
34. Church webpage (accessed December 10, 2013).
35. Church webpage (accessed November 24, 2011).
36. Church Facebook page (accessed November 30, 2011).
37. e.g. Jansz, "Masculine Identity" 2000. Also, Jakupcak, et al. "Masculinity and Emotionality," 2003.
38. "Highly person-centered (HPC) comforting messages explicitly recognize and legitimize the other's feelings by helping the other to articulate those feelings, elaborate reasons why those feelings might be felt, and explore how those feelings fit in a broader context." In contrast, ". . . messages that exhibit low person centeredness (LPC) deny the other's feelings and perspective by criticizing or challenging their legitimacy, or by telling the other how he or she *should* act and feel. Moderately person-centered (MPC) comforting messages afford an implicit recognition of the other's feelings by attempting to distract the other's attention from the troubling situation, offering expressions of

Most men seek to think and behave in ways consistent with prevailing cultural notions of masculinity while avoiding patterns of thought and behavior inconsistent with the cultural masculine image.[39] Some argue that the demand on men to maintain a masculine image "becomes culturally elaborated as a way of rejecting cultural definitions of women and femininity. In this line of reasoning the most important, ongoing challenge for maleness involves proving that one is not feminine or homosexual."[40] In particular, *"men may be less expressive with their male friends out of concerns that they will appear weak or homosexual"*[41] . . . *Men [who are] schematic on gender [i.e. Action Men] are especially invested in the masculine image, and are particularly disturbed* by departures from it by other men.[42] Thus, highly gender-schematic men should view the use of HPC comforting messages by men as less normative [i.e., less typical and desirable], as well as be less likely to use such messages when they seek *to provide emotional suppor*t to others, especially other men [emphasis added].[43]

Remember from chapter 3 that, outside the church, Combination Men also self-edit to comply with social norms. Add that 20 percent of the non-church male population to the 69 percent of non-church men that are Action Men and you get 89 percent of non-church men who are reluctant to show emotions in ways associated with women. This has huge implications for ministry with men, where it has become an axiom that true men's ministry must get men to open up about their feelings. (More about this later. Stay tuned.)

In the cartoon, Zits, for July 18, 2013 Jim Borgman and Jerry Scott distinguish between a paraphrase and a "Saraphrase:"

> Paraphrase: A restatement of a text or passage giving the meaning in another form.
>
> Saraphrase: Same, but with drama.
>
> Sara says to Jeremy, "And so she *literally SCREAMED HER HEAD OFF* until this **super nice guy** came along and **swept** her off **her** feet*!!!* [Emphasis in original]

---

sympathy and condolence, or presenting explanations of the situation that are intended to reduce the other's distress." (Brodie, et al., "Explaining the Impact," 230.

39. See Athenstaedt, et al., "Gender Role Self-concept," (2004).
40. See Johnson, *Speaking Culturally*, (2000).
41. Leaper, et. al., "Self-disclosure," 388.
42. e.g. Lindsey and Zakahi, " Perceptions," 1998; Markus, et al., "Self-schemas," 1982.
43. Burleson, et al., "Guys Can't Say *That*," 452.

Jeremy responds, "Wait-is that really what happened or are you saraphrasing?"

An exchange of comments under the cartoon on the website, Arcamax.com is telling:

> Michael: Gay men and stay at home mom's do the same thing.
>
> Brian: I can believe it. Another well-known figure named "Sarah"[44] does that all the time. (Problem is, it's not as funny as it is here.)

One could just as easily call it "Churchaphrasing" and the same associations would be made. In fact, they are made by non-church men all the time, and they don't think it's funny either.

"OH C'MON, ARE YOU FOR REAL?"

Just Ask TED

You may be thinking that. Is this really such an issue? Is church talk that much different? Yes, it is. Carmine Gallo, author of *Talk Like TED: The 9 Public-Speaking Secrets of the World's Top Minds* (St. Martin's Press), notes,

> TED [Technology/Entertainment/Design] talks have been viewed online more than one billion times. TED videos are viewed at the rate of two million times per day. TEDx events are organized eight times a day and have been held in 145 countries. Like it or not, your next presentation is being compared to TED. Business leaders, entrepreneurs, pastors and spiritual leaders are being asked by their audiences, investors, and congregations to be more "TED-like."[45]

So how does church talk stack up against TED talk? My research team reviewed over 100 TED talks and church sermons, tracking the number of Powerless Language Indicators per minute used in each. TED speakers included such well known persons as Microsoft founder Bill Gates, singer/songwriter Sting, and long distance swimmer Diana Nyad, as well as numerous people known only within their fields and, now, in the TED community. Church speakers also included well known persons, such as Fred Craddock, Rick Warren, Barbara Brown Taylor, Chuck Swindoll, Brian McLaren, Andy

---

44. That well-known figure is former Alaska governor, Sarah Palin, of course, and her church connections have also been well-known. So another association between intensives, vocal italics and the church is made, albeit indirectly.

45. Forbes Network, "TED Talks."

Stanley, Beth Moore, Kirbyjon Caldwell, Ravi Zacharias, Vashti Murphy McKenzie, Tony Jones, Adam Hamilton, Joyce Myer, Steven Furtick, Craig Groeschel, Judah Smith, and T. D. Jakes, in addition to a number of pastors from smaller congregations. On average, church speakers used 9.94 Powerless Language Indicators per minute (PLIpm) in sermons and conference talks, whereas TED speakers used 1.74. (See Figure 7.4.) So sermons had almost six times the amount of powerless language as TED talks.

Figure 7.4: Ted Talks vs. Sermons, Powerless Language Indicators per Minute

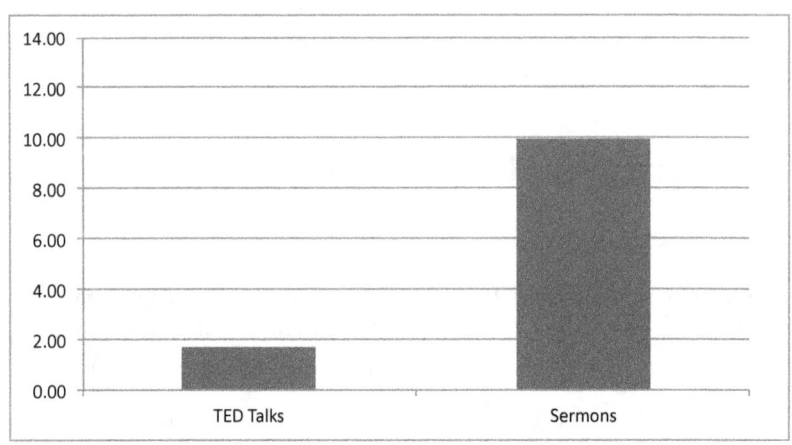

The range was also greater among church leaders, from a low of 1.1 to a high of 25.6 PLIpm, as opposed to a range of 0–4.5 PLIpm among TED speakers. Those church speakers who were in that comparable 0–5 PLIpm range were lead pastors, often of mega-churches, and mega-conference speakers.[46] Still, a number of notable mega-church/multi-site pastors and conference speakers had PLIpm rates ranging from 10.5 to 20.3.[47]

Since church guests begin forming their impressions from the moment of their first contact whether on-line or on-site, we also tracked powerless language use during portions of worship services leading up to the sermon. The overall average for words of welcome, announcements, music introductions and comments, communal prayers, and pre-sermon comments was 11.73 PLIpm. When we removed lead/senior pastors from this analysis and looked at worship leaders', lay leaders'/liturgists', and associate pastors' rates, the average jumped to 13.54 PLIpm, almost eight times that of TED talks. (See 7.5.)

46. e.g. Cynthia L Hale (1.1), Dwight Mason (1.1), Ravi Zacharias (1.3), Bill Chaney (3.5), Steven Furtick (3.6), Louie Giglio (4.5).

47. e.g. Joel Osteen (10.5), Adam Hamilton (11.3), Matt Chandler (13), Andy Stanley (13.3), Carl Lentz (18), Tony Jones (20.3).

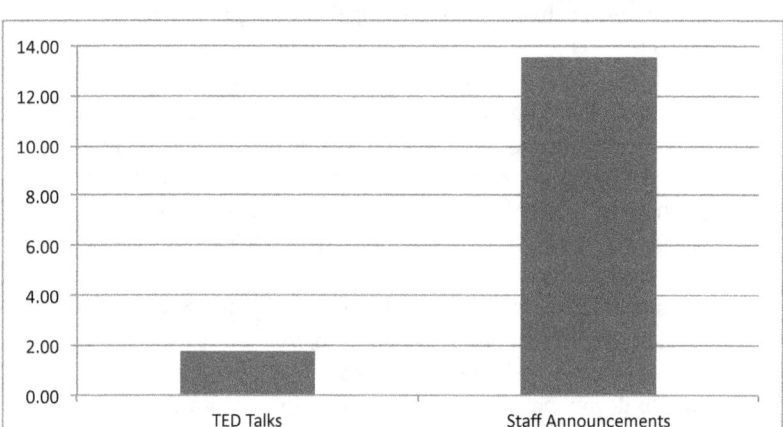

Figure 7.5: Ted Talks Vs. Staff Welcome/Announcements, Powerless Language Indicators Per Minute

So, even if the lead pastor is a strong and direct communicator, most men and many women will have already mentally left the building before he or she says a word. This helps explain why many of them don't come in until the sermon is about to start.[48] It explains why so many of those we have interviewed in mega-churches have expressed the sentiment, "I'm just here because of (the lead pastor). If it weren't for him/her, this place wouldn't have anything for me." And it explains why most men and many women have left and never come back.

The Power of the Powerless Pews

Even with a strong and direct lead pastor, the cumulative effect of all the other people using powerless language in the church's services, group studies, team meetings, social gatherings, etc. is to spread and solidify its use by those new participants who do stay. Take, for example, the following testimony by a young man in one of those multi-site churches with one of those strong and direct lead pastors (powerless language in italics):

> My life before Christ, I was all into drugs . . . I liked to shoot heroin up my arms at the time. I was into coke, I was into marijuana . . . I was angry all the time, I never had, I never had any joy in my life. I was always evil with people. I ended up choking my wife out 'cause I ended up going through withdrawal with

---

48. This analysis is important because in multi-staff churches and many single staff churches these other people handle the non-sermonic elements of the worship service.

> heroin. I'd watched my father do it all the time, so I thought it was ok to do drugs. So when I did 'em I didn't have a problem with it, *um*, I actually enjoyed doing them. I enjoyed the high so much that I enjoyed the high better than life.
>
> I was sittin' in jail one night, lookin' at all the walls around me, and I picked up the Bible one night and *just* started reading it. For some reason, Christ *kinda like* came through me. *I-I-I just* started reading the Bible *more and more and more*, and started jottin' down verses for my wife to read and that's when I knew Christ was in my life. Now it did take me a while to get involved with the church *or anything like that*, because when I first started I was an atheist. And now that I'm a Christian there's these miraculous things that *just* keep happenin', *like*, in my life. *I mean*, I'm happy now, I'm hardly angry ever. I read the Bible every day and do devotionals. I do, *uh*, I try to, help out with the church *whenever I can*, and *uh, I try to* lead a path with Jesus, to make my life that way as well. The reason I want to be baptized is, *uh*, I want to show everybody that, *uh*, I'm with Christ now. I'm for the good now and not for the bad. The bad used to be controlling, but *uh*, not any more. It's all about the good and Jesus—Jesus Christ.

Note that in the first paragraph when he is talking about his former life there is only one powerless language indicator. The impression he makes in this portion of the video is that of a strong, mountain of a man who knows he's done wrong and is unafraid to face it. But when he moves to his Christian life, the character of his talk changes. It becomes halting and uncertain, with twelve Powerless Language Indicators per minute. Read that second paragraph again, this time with the highlighted words removed:

> I was sittin' in jail one night, lookin' at all the walls around me, and I picked up the Bible one night and started reading it. Christ came through me. I started reading the Bible more and started jottin' down verses for my wife to read and that's when I knew Christ was in my life. Now it did take me a while to get involved with the church, because when I first started I was an atheist. And now that I'm a Christian there's these miraculous things that keep happenin' in my life. I'm happy now, I'm hardly angry ever. I read the Bible every day and do devotionals. I do help out with the church and I lead a path with Jesus, to make my life that way as well. The reason I want to be baptized is, I want to show everybody that I'm with Christ now. I'm for the good now and not for the bad. The bad used to be controlling, but not any more. It's all about the good and Jesus—Jesus Christ.

See how much more powerful it is? That is how he talked in the first paragraph, when his mind was on his life outside the church. Unfortunately he had absorbed the lesson that church talk is powerless. Powerless language is, in fact, connected with women's talk. Its prevalence in church communication confirms the myth in the minds of men that church *is* feminine or at least for women.

IMPLICATIONS FOR THE CHURCH

To summarize the above: *Hedges* are counter-productive because they communicate falsehood (hypocrisy, posing, mask), send conflict underground to fester, and undermine the speaker's credibility. Similarly, *qualifiers* and *uncertainty signals* erode our ability to lead because they make us seem "less competent, intelligent, confident, and powerful than direct individuals." *Quest-ments* and *state-tions* can either feel manipulative or confuse people who are direct communicators. *Super-polite language* gives the impression that the speaker is desperate for approval. *Intensifiers* and *vocal italics* express emotions with which most men and many women do not identify and do so in a way that most men consider inappropriate for men. And finally, church leaders as a whole are about six to eight times more likely to use these expressions of powerlessness. As a result they are rarely able to persuade others to adopt a new belief or set of values or to take an action. And at its root, all this stems from an extreme concern for Communalness.

What does this mean for the church today? It is time we recognize that that over-emphasis is counter-productive. With a large section of the population it undermines our attempts to help people come to faith and mature as disciples. And within the church it undermines our efforts to lead the church through today's tempest of internal and external change.

8

So Now What Do We Do?

> "When you lived in North Carolina and told me about what hunting doves was like, it completely changed how I taught about the Holy Spirit."

I HAD JUST ASKED if New York had a dove season as we passed a row of them sitting on a wire. My brother, Casey—a New Testament scholar[1] and biblical studies professor—and I were returning from a morning of fishing on Lake Ontario.

"How's that," I asked.

"Your description of their speed and the way they changed direction in a heartbeat didn't match the picture in my head of the Holy Spirit descending on Jesus at his baptism. I had this image of a gentle, cooing bird fluttering down onto his shoulder. But the Greek word that is used for the Spirit's descent is a violent word."

He's right. It is a word that conveys power, not gentleness. The same word is used when James and John ask Jesus if he wanted them "to call fire to come down (καταβῆναι—katabēnai) from heaven and consume" the Samaritan village that refused to welcome Jesus because he was going to Jerusalem (Luke 9:54). I have to admit, I had the same image as Casey. And I would bet you do, too. It is one more example of how we have "gentled" God—and Jesus—and even the "Sons of Thunder."[2] That is why, once again, you need to:

1 See Davis, Oral Biblical Criticism.

2. Yes, Jesus rebuked them, but that was for their intended misuse of the power they had recently been given (Luke 9:1). Luke then illustrates the attitude they are to

STOP READING AND PRAY

We in the church have a problem with power. We are afraid of it. It makes us nervous. And we certainly don't want to be accused of wanting it, having it, or using it. So we use powerless, tentative language that undermines our credibility. It was not so with Jesus. When he spoke, people marveled at his authority (Matthew 7:28–29). It was not so with Peter and John. When they spoke before the Sanhedrin, "they saw the courage of Peter and John and, realizing that these were unschooled, ordinary men, they were astonished and took note that these men had been with Jesus" (Acts 4:13). Peter and John were able to speak with courage and authority because they had "stayed in Jerusalem until they were clothed in power from on high" (Luke 24:49) when the Holy Spirit descended on them (Acts 2) just as on Jesus at his baptism. Pray that you and your church will be clothed afresh with power. Pray that we will speak again with authority; and that we will speak words, not of anger and self-righteousness, but of faith, hope, and love (1 Corinthians 13)—words of the one who is the way, the truth, in the life (John 14:16). Let that be your daily prayer, as you "pray in the Spirit on all occasions with all kinds of prayers and requests. With this in mind, be alert and always keep on praying for all the Lord's people. Pray also for me, that whenever I speak, words may be given me so that I will fearlessly make known the mystery of the gospel" (Ephesians 6:18–19).[3]

As you pray that prayer, understand that you will be taken to a place we do not want to go. The reason our powerless language undermines our credibility is, ironically, because our talk is rife with power moves. We have heard Jesus's words about being meek, about being the last rather than the first, and so we phrase our talk to give the appearance of meekness and humility. But we are still convinced of our own importance, and so the veil is a thin one to those who have not bought into modern western church culture. They see through the veil that our powerlessness, like our humility, is pseudo-powerlessness. It is one reason many non-church people believe church folk present a false face. And in many cases they are right. Unless and until we go to the place of true powerlessness, we will continue to be deceived by our own false face. We will manipulate and maneuver to preserve our places within the power structure of the church, whether formal or informal. This

---

have—focusing on the cost of following Jesus rather than the power—with the story of the three men who tell Jesus they want to follow him (Luke 9:57–62). Luke 10 then reports how the same power that had been given to the twelve is extended to the seventy-two. When they return rejoicing at their power over demons, Jesus warns them against reveling in the power, not against having or using it.

3. I mean that last sentence. I am not just quoting Scripture for the sake of quoting it.

is the truth Fr. Richard Rohr uncovered in his cross-cultural study of male initiation rituals: "This was the rather universal conclusion: *Unless the male is led into journeys of powerlessness, he will invariably misuse power.* He becomes a loose cannon in the social fabric, even dangerous to the family, always seeking his own dominative power and advancement to the neglect of others."[4] It is true for women as well as men. And none of us want to go there. It is a journey to a place of pain because we are confronted with our ultimate inadequacy. "In the larger-than-life people I have met," Rohr writes, "I always find one common denominator: in some sense, *they have all died before they died*—and thus they are larger than death too! . . . they were led to the edge of their private resources, and that breakdown, which surely felt like dying, led them into a larger life. They went through a death of their various false selves and came out on the other side knowing that death could no longer hurt them."[5] When we reach that point—when we fall to our knees and surrender our self-sufficiency and self-importance—we fall into the all-sufficient arms of the God who is love. We discover that we are meant to be an instrument in God's hand, not a recipient of God's plan. And we discover that our small place in God's great plan has more meaning and worth than any plan we have imagined for ourselves.

I am convinced that Peter and John, as well as the other disciples, were able to receive the power of the Holy Spirit because they stayed in Jerusalem as Jesus had commanded. Good Friday and Black Saturday had scoured the vision of position, power, and glory from their souls and left space for the Holy Spirit to work. As you pray for the power of the Holy Spirit, prepare to be taken to that place where your resources will be stripped bare. In that place, in that condition, ask the Holy Spirit to make you a fit tool in the hand of God.

THE NEXT BABY STEP: YET ANOTHER LOOK AT ANOTHER WEEK

By now you are familiar with this process. But before you start tracking powerless language live in worship, classes, meetings, or conversations, you need to get familiar with the Powerless Language Indicators (PLI). As before, that will be easier if you review written rather than spoken forms first. So, you and your team should again divvy up the past week's publications to review. Also as before you can use different colored highlighters to identify the different PLI. Just be sure your team is consistent in how the colors are used.

---

4. Rohr, "Jesus's Invitation." Emphasis in original.
5. Rohr, "Passing from Death." Emphasis in original.

Figure 8.1: Powerless Language Indicator Card

<u>Hedges</u> or <u>Apologizers</u>
"You may disagree, but" "I affirm your . . . , but" "To be honest?" "Let me take a moment" "I wanna (think) (believe)"
<u>Qualifiers</u> or <u>Detensifiers</u>
Most, some, hopefully, might, may, like, kind of, maybe, a little, I guess, I just
<u>Quest-ments</u> or <u>State-tions</u>
"Don't you think that" "What if we" "How would it be if" "wouldn't you?" "don't we?"
<u>Super-polite language</u>, "<u>Communitifiers</u>" & <u>Approval seekers</u>
"May we" "Let me encourage" "If you would" "if you don't mind." "Okay?" "Right" "Please, please" Uptalk or upward inflected phrases
<u>Intensifiers</u> or <u>vocal italics</u>
So(ooo), very, really, quite, such, totally, plus repeated words ("very very"), etc.
<u>Verbal commas</u> & <u>Uncertainty signals</u>
Just, like, you know, I mean, Lord, God, Uptalk, Um/Uh
<u>Turn signals</u> or <u>Verbal Stop Signs</u>
Hey, Well, Well hey, Now, Um/Uh, Uptalk, . . . so . . .

A word about your Powerless Language Indicator Card (see Figure 8.1): You will notice that some words or phrases are used as indicators in more that one category. Uptalk can be an Approval Seeker or an Uncertainty Signal or a Verbal Stop Sign, for example. Or "so" can be an intensifier or a turn signal. You must determine its function within the statement. Do not get overly concerned about this, especially to start. The most important issue is how much powerless language is showing up. Helping people deal with the PLI types they are most likely to use will come later. Use the following Powerless Language Data Sheet to record your observations (see Table 8.1):

Table 8.1: Powerless Language Data Sheet

Date: Service or Publication	Speaker:	Part of Service:	Time: Duration (minutes)	Totals	WPM
Hedges or Pre-apologies	I think/guess	I wanna	Don't know about you, but		
	I believe	I mean	To be honest		
	You may disagree...	I'm sorry, but...	Other		
Qualifier or Detensifier	just	some/sometimes	kinda/sorta		
	a little/a bit	may/maybe/might	most/many		
	probably/possibly	hope/hopefully	Other		
Verbal Commas or Uncertnty Signals	just	you know	you see		
	Um/Uh	Lord	God		
	well/hey	So,...	Other		
Super-polite Language or Approval Seekers	May we...	Let me encourage	If you would...		
	Right?/Ok?	If you don't mind	Please, please or Pleeease		
	Let me take a moment...	Let's/Let us	Other		
Quest-ments & State-tions	Don't you think...	What if we...	Why not...		
	How about...	Uptalk	Other		
Intensifier or Vocal Italics	so(ooo)/so much/such	very	really/especially		
	honestly	quite	totally		
	Breathiness	Extreme Inflection	Repeated word/Other		

Print a copy of this sheet for each speaker. Place marks under each word or phrase as they occur. Write the totals for each row in the Totals column. Enter the data in this Excel file and email the file to research@teaministries.com.

To help you get you started, here is a powerless language analysis of the first sermon we analyzed for feminine and masculine themes in chapter 6.[6]

Sermon Analysis: "The Message Is, 'I Love You'"

Scriptures: Genesis 2:18-24; Hebrews 2:9-11; Mark 10:2-16 (Lectionary, Year B)

I want [HEDGE] you to visualize a rocky stretch of coastline. You are viewing that coastline through the gloom from the deck of a ship, tossed and battered by storm waves. Suddenly you catch sight of a lighthouse as it flashes from the top of a cliff on the shore—a warning that a treacherous coast is near. As you watch the flashing light, you realize there is a pattern to it. It is flashing a message in Morse code. So you watch, and decipher, letter by letter, until you get the whole message. And the message is, "I love you!"

That lighthouse does exist. It is called Minot's Light, and it lies off Cohasset, Massachusetts. Several years ago the Coast Guard decided to replace the old equipment at the lighthouse. But when they announced that for technical reasons the new equipment would not be able to flash messages, there was such a storm of protest that they backed off. The old equipment is still intact—still flashing it's message to weary seamen, "I love you!"

How like God that is! He, too, sent his light into a dark, gloomy world—the light of his son—as John 1:9 says, "A light that shines in the darkness." And that light, too, carried a message. At its *very* [INTENSIFIER] heart that message was, and still is, "I love you! I love you so much that I was not only willing to give, I gave my life for you."

How like that the lighthouse are God's people, as well. Jesus said, "You are the light of the world. Let your light so shine before men that they may see your good works and to give glory to your father who is in heaven." *I hope* [QUALIFIER] people in our community see us as a lighthouse flashing out that message to each of them, "I love you!" Indeed, *I hope* [QUALIFIER] each of us in our own way is a lighthouse. "This little light of mine, I'm going to let it shine." *I hope* [QUALIFIER] we are flashing that message to each other. Jesus said, "By this they will know I am in you and you are in me—if you love one another."

You see, [VERBAL COMMA] that is what the kingdom of God is all about. We were created for love—for relationship—for family. The Bible begins with a man and a woman in a garden. They were created out of love, for love. Their world was a paradise. They were on intimate terms with their Creator. They were on intimate terms with each other. They were in

---

6. You don't have to read the whole sermon again. Just note the PLIs in all-caps.

harmony with all of creation. That is what the kingdom is all about—love, relationship, family.

Jesus confirms the same principle in Mark's gospel. He is speaking about the sanctity of marriage. "From the beginning of creation," he says, "God made them male and female. For this reason a man leaves his father and mother and is joined to his wife and the two become one flesh." That is what the Kingdom is all about. It's about love, relationship, family.

A few moments after giving this teaching on marriage, some parents brought their children to Jesus, wanting him to touch them and bless them. *Now,* [VERBAL COMMA] this is an important moment in scripture. Watch what happens. The disciples rebuked the parents. *I guess* [QUALIFIER] they were a lot like many adults in worship services today who view children as a distraction—a bother—as not belonging there until they reach the age of accountability. Or at least until they can sit still and be quiet for the entire time. I remember a conversation my parents had when I was little. A two-or three-year-old got fussy one of those few times when we did go to church, and Dad fidgeted and "humphed" the whole time. All the way home he fumed about "that woman and her kid!" "She shouldn't bring him in the service in the first place," he said. "That's what they've got a nursery for." *Don't you think* that's just what the disciples were saying? "Don't interrupt. Don't bother the Master. Take them to the nursery."

But what does the Scripture say? [QUEST-MENT] It says Jesus became indignant. He was angry! "Let the children come, don't hinder them, for to such belongs the kingdom of God." *I believe* [HEDGE] children belong in church, including worship, from day one. *Let me encourage you* [SUPER-POLITE LANGUAGE] to bring your children with you to worship, every Sunday. We have a nursery for those rare occasions of unmanageability. But that's out of concern for the occasionally struggling parent, not for the convenience of the congregation. They belong in church—why? Because that's what the Kingdom is all about: man-woman-children.

The Kingdom is family. But more than the *so-called* [QUALIFIER] nuclear family of mother, father, and 1.7 children, as statisticians are fond of saying. The Kingdom includes the whole family of God. In Hebrews 2:9–11 it says that Jesus, "who for a little while was made lower than the angels," and who "was crowned with glory and honor because of the suffering of his death, so that by the grace of God he might taste death for everyone"—this same Jesus "for whom and by whom all things exist"—the pioneer of our salvation and the perfecter of our faith—this same Jesus is not ashamed to call us sisters and brothers!

This is the most important family in the Scriptures—the family of God. Those who are in Christ are that family. That is who we are. That is why we were created. That is the cause for which Christ died—that we should no longer be strangers, but that we should be part of this family, the family of God.

We were created for a family relationship. But because of sin, that relationship has been broken. If the kingdom is about family, then sin is the breaking of the family relationship. That's why Jesus spoke so strongly about divorce in Mark 10. Divorce strikes at the *very* [INTENSIFIER] heart of what the Kingdom is about.

That's not to say that people don't make mistakes in marriage. And sometimes what was once a strong, joyous relationship deteriorates to the point where reconciliation is no longer possible. Nevertheless, the scriptural attitude toward the ending of a marriage is that it is always a tragedy and never God's best will for the persons involved. Especially today when so many marriages are coming apart at the seams, we need to affirm the importance of the family relationship.

Unfortunately, we live in a broken world. We know that. After Adam and Eve left Eden, they had two sons—and one killed the other. Just imagine if they had been your boys. Yet this is the kind of world we live in. Ever since Eden, men and women have lived in awful disharmony with their neighbors, with their environment, with the *very* [INTENSIFIER] earth from which they were formed, and even with themselves.

Novelist F. Scott Fitzgerald knew that. After his death they found the plot for a novel he never got to write. The plot concerned a wealthy man who died and left a strange will. All his millions were to be divided equally among all his relatives, share and share alike. There was just one condition. They were to come and live together in his spacious mansion. Below the outlined plot was a note by Fitzgerald. It read, "This could be a little spot of hell."

We understand how it could be, *don't we?* [STATE-TION] We live in a broken world. Even with the best of intentions, many families are torn *simply* [QUALIFIER] by the race for survival. As one person put it, "Nowadays, Dad works the night shift, Mom works the day shift, and the kids *just* [QUALIFIER] have to shift for themselves."

But the greatest cause of our brokenness is a broken relationship with God. Nothing else can be right until our relationship with the Father is right. The good news is this: that relationship can be made right. It can be made right because of that light God sent into the world.

A woman wrote a letter to Billy Graham.

> "Until last January I was a stranger to Jesus," she wrote. "I was a rebel, a thief, a drunk, a drug abuser, and an adulteress. I was a self-centered, confused young woman. Well, somebody invited me to a Bible study about a year ago and I went, half

out of curiosity, half just to stump everybody with my cynical questions. But that night I became seriously interested in the Bible. Finally, after reading and studying for months, John 3:16 spoke to my heart and I gave my life to Christ. I never knew this kind of happiness could exist. God shows you how to love and what it feels like to be loved. He was what I had been looking for since my early teens. It had seemed to me that drugs, liquor, free love and bumming around the country would make me free. But they were all traps that led me to confusion, unhappiness, guilt, and near suicide. Christ has made me free."

How do we turn a spot of hell, as Fitzgerald called it, into a showplace for heaven? We can't. But God can. We are not able, but God is able. Noted psychologist William Glasser in his book *Reality Therapy* writes, "At all times in our lives we must have one person who cares for us and whom we care for, ourselves. If we do not have this person, we will not be able to fulfill our basic needs." You may say, "I don't have anybody who cares for me like that." But think about it. You do have someone who cares for you. Indeed, he calls you sister. He calls you brother. Jesus is the one who says, "I love you."

Anyone who has a hint of a romantic nature *thrills* [INTENSIFIER] to the story of poet Robert Browning and his equally talented wife, Elizabeth Barrett Browning. You recall the beginning of her "Sonnets of the Portuguese:" "How do I love thee? Let me count the ways. I love thee to the depths and breadths and heights my soul can reach . . . " But do you recall that Elizabeth Barrett was literally a shut-in, held captive by a domineering, tyrannical father? This beautiful poetry grew out of the love of this bold, brash young poet who carried her away. One day she went to his side as he had fallen asleep at his desk while working on his poetry and wrote a note on his paper: "My dearest Robert, *my whole world, my whole life, my whole future* [INTENSIFIER] has been different since that day I first felt thy footsteps walk across my soul."

Many of us never experience the grandeur of such love from a living, breathing person. But such love is available. There is a lighthouse with its beacon shining at us individually in our personal darkness. As we gaze at that lighthouse, we can make out a message blinking through the fog of our neglect and despair. It is one that has warmed and transformed the lives of countless persons *just like* [INTENSIFIER] you. And the message is, "I love you."

SO NOW WHAT DO WE DO?

Table 8.2: Powerless Language Indicators in Sermon

POWERLESS LANGUAGE INDICATORS	HITS
HEDGES OR PRE-APOLOGIES	2
QUALIFIERS OR DETENSIFIERS	7
QUEST-MENTS OR STATE-TIONS	2
SUPER-POLITE LANGUAGE OR COMMUNITIFIERS	1
INTENSIFIERS OR VOCAL ITALICS	6
VERBAL COMMAS OR UNCERTAINTY SIGNIALS	2
TURN SIGNALS OR VERBAL STOP SIGNS	
TOTAL POWERLESS LANGUAGE HITS:	20

As you can see from Table 8.2, there are twenty instances of powerless language in the sermon. That is not bad in a fifteen to twenty minute sermon—on a par with the TED Talks' rate discussed in chapter 7. But notice the effect when you add that to the fifteen instances of the Feminine Christian Themes (see Table 8.3) discussed in chapter 5 and the twenty-seven instances of the Feminine Register vocabulary (see Table 8.4) discussed in chapter 3. The result is sixty-two experiences of potential disconnection for the majority of men and many women who are action-oriented. That works out to one every fifteen to twenty seconds.

Table 8.3: Feminine Christian Themes in Sermon

FEMININE CHRISTIAN THEMES	HITS
{BEING-OPEN/SHARING-FEELINGS}	
{SUBMISSION}	
{COMMUNITY}	2
{NONVIOLENCE/NONAGGRESSION}	
{SUPPORT/NURTURE}	

FEMININE CHRISTIAN THEMES	HITS
{FORGIVENESS}	
{LOVE}	12
{HUMILITY}	
{SERVICE/SACRIFICE}	1
{BEING/BECOMING}	
TOTAL FEMININE THEME HITS:	15

Table 8.4: Feminine Register Vocabulary in Sermon

FEMININE REGISTER VOCABULARY	HITS
Beautiful [EMPTY ADJECTIVES/ OVERSTATEMENTS]	1
Heart [ROMANTIC EMOTIONS]	1
Care [S'MOTHERING]	4
Intimate [ENMESHMENT]	2
Relationship [ENMESHMENT]	10
Dearest [ENMESHMENT]	1
Broken [WEAKNESS/BROKENNESS]	5
TOTAL FEMININE REGISTER HITS:	27

To make it worse, because this analysis is from the sermon text only, it does not include all the verbal commas and uncertainty signals that were rampant in my preaching at this stage. No wonder there were no men among those who responded.[7]

That awareness raises the issue of paralanguage. Paralanguage refers to those elements of communication that stand alongside (hence "para-") our language—tone of voice, tempo, volume, vocal emphasis, etc. We touched on this topic to an extent when we dealt with uptalk, but it is also a key part of

---

7. See the beginning of chapter 1.

Intensifiers and Vocal Italics. For example, it is vocal tone, timbre,[8] and tempo that distinguishes men's use of "so" as an adverb (e.g. "That was so great!") from the drawn out Feminine Register version, the "sooooo".[9] Paralanguage also shows up on your Powerless Language Indicator Card (see Figure 8.1) as *"breathiness, pleading, begging, etc."* I recently spent several days with a friend I had not seen in a number of years. He was a no-nonsense engineer who had previously spoken with directness and no frills. By the end of the second day I wondered if I was with the same person. The directness was still there, but there was a lot of vocal emphasis in the form of raised pitches, lengthened words, and breathiness, accompanied by more and larger gestures than he had ever used. The effect was remarkable. Where previously he had been steady and calm, now he came across as emotional. Where he had been a commanding presence, he now gave the impression of trying too hard. I cannot say for certain what caused the changes. But I have a holy hunch that his conversion and subsequent twenty-plus years in a large nondenominational church was a contributing factor. His primary social network became the church, and with that came the church's pattern of talk.

Paying attention to our paralanguage is important because much of how we are perceived is influenced by it. Men who speak in a lower pitch range are perceived as stronger, more authoritative, respected, influential, and often as a leader.[10] Significantly for female pastors, this is also true for women, despite higher-pitched voices being perceived as more socially attractive for women.[11] For both men and women, voices pitched higher than normal conversational tones—as they often are in announcements, sermons, and contentious leadership meetings—are associated with negative emotions such as panic, fear, and stress.[12] Men who use this higher pitch range regularly are perceived as weak, effeminate, incompetent, less truthful

---

8. Tone refers to the pitch (or frequency) you hear, whereas timbre (pronounced "tamber") refers to "the distinguishable characteristics of a tone. Timbre is mainly determined by the harmonic content of a sound and the dynamic characteristics of the sound such as vibrato and the attack-decay envelope of the sound." http://hyperphysics.phy-astr.gsu.edu/HBase/sound/timbre.html#c4. Accessed October 21, 2016.

9. Lakoff, *Language and Women's Place*, 81.

10. See Anderson and Klofstad, "Preference for Leaders," 2012; Feinberg, et al., "Manipulations," 2005; Klofstad, "Sounds like a Winner," 2012; Puts, et al., "Dominance," 2006; Puts, "Masculine Voices," 2012; Puts, "Men's Voices," 2007; and Tigue, et al., "Voice Pitch," 2012.

11. See Borkowska and Pawlowski, "Female Voice Frequency," 2011; and Jones, et al., "Domain-specific Bias," 2010.

12. See Banse and Scherer, "Acoustic Profiles," 1996; Weeks, et al., "The Sound of Fear," 2012; Wittels, et al., "Voice Monitoring," 2002.

and less emotionally stable.[13] At the same time, staying exclusively in a lower pitch range is counter-productive. Listeners perceive male voices with a greater variation of pitches and vocal intensity, as well as a faster speech rate, to be more extroverted, confident, bold, authoritative, and influential.[14] Speech rate influences listeners' perceptions differently depending on the characteristic being considered. Perceptions of competence vary directly with higher and lower speech rates, within limits. Perceptions of benevolence, on the other hand, have an inverted U relationship with speech rate. In other words, intermediate levels of rate being rated as most benevolent, while both high and low rates lead listeners to doubt that the speaker has their best interests at heart.[15] In summary, a speaker's pitch range, variation of pitches and vocal intensity, and speech rate all have a direct impact on his/her credibility. That means they are worthy of intentional review and improvement for anyone in a leadership position.[16] Once you have familiarized yourself with the Powerless Language Indicators by reviewing written materials, you will be ready to do the analysis live or with recordings. Then you will be able to include the paralanguage components as well. Here is an example done from an online source (see Table 8.5):

---

13. See Apple, "Effects of Pitch" 1979; Scherer, "Personality Markers," 1979.
14. See Aronovitch, "The Voice," 1976.
15. See Burgoon, "Attributes," 1978; and Burgoon, "Nonverbal Behaviors," 1990.
16. Mahew, et al. found that among male public-company Chief Executive Officers "an interquartile decrease in voice pitch (22.1Hz) is associated with a $440 million increase in the size of the firm managed, and in turn, $187 thousand more in annual compensation. Deep voiced CEOs also enjoy longer tenures." (Mahew, et al. "Voice Pitch," 243).

Table 8.5: Powerless Language Data Example

Date Accessed	Date Publishd	Church	Speaker	Http://Www.Austinnewchurch.Com/Media.Php?Pageid=5	
9/11/12	9/9/12	In Touch Podcast	Joel Osteen		
Powerless Language Type	Time Code:	Part of Service:	Duration	Totals	PLIpm
	3:00–4:45	Welcome	1.75 Min.	35	20
Hedges or Apologizer	I think, guess	I wanna, gonna	I don't know about you, but …		
		2		2	
	I believe	I mean	To be honest/ Honestly		
		1		1	
	You may disagree …	Not every-one …	I'm sorry, but …		
				0	1.7
Qualifier or Detensifier	Just	Some/ Some-times	Kinda/ Sorta		
	7			7	
	A little/ A bit	May/ Maybe/ Might	Pretty/ Pretty much		
				0	
	Probably/ Possibly	Hope/ Hope-fully	Most/ Many		
				0	0
Verbal Commas Or Uncertnty Signals	Just	You know	You see		
				0	
	Um/Uh/ And-uh	Like	God/ Lord FatherGod		
				0	0
	Well/ Hey	So … / Ok	Stuff like that/And everything		
				0	0

Super-Polite Language Or Approval Seekers	May we...	Let me encourage	If you would...		0	
	Right?/ Ok? Agree?	If you don't mind	Please, please/ Pleee-ase		0	
	Let me take a mo-ment...	Let's/ Let us	Cooing/ Droning/ Pleading	9	9	4.5
Quest-Ments & State-Tions	Don't you think...	How would it be...	What if we...		0	
	How about...	Why not...	Uptalk (rising pitch at end)	1	1	.5
Intensifier Or Vocal Italics	So(ooo)/So much Such	Very/ Quite a lot	Really/ Especially/ Truly			
				1	2	3
	Awesme Precious	Wow	Totally		0	
	Breathi-ness	Extreme Inflection	Repeated Word			
	6	14	1		21	13.7

SO NOW WHAT DO WE DO?

And here are some of the results of one of our client churches' powerless language tracking (See Figures 8.2–8.4):[17]

Figure 8.2: Galilee Church Staff Members' Powerless Language Indicators per Minute (PLIpm) in Worship, 10 Week Average

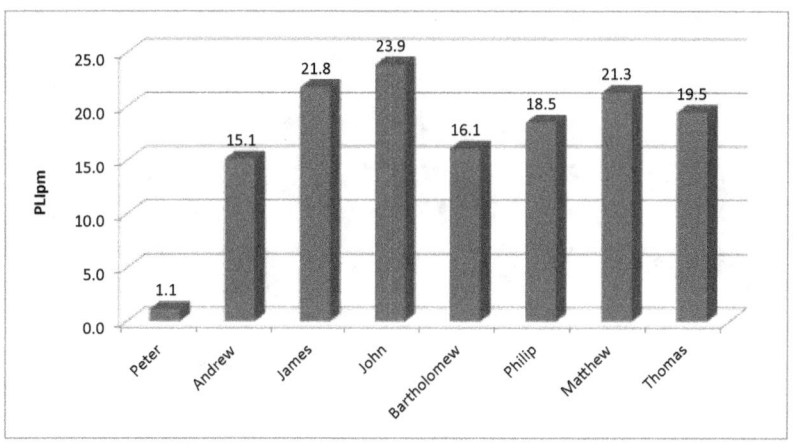

Peter is the lead pastor of this multi-site megachurch. James, John, and Matthew are each pastors of one of the campuses. Andrew, Bartholomew, Philip, and Thomas are the worship leaders for the four campuses. At each of the satellites, the campus pastor sets up the incoming video feed of the lead pastor's sermon. As you can see from Figures 8.2 and 8.3 there is a marked difference between their talk and that of the lead pastor. It is a pattern we see often and may point to one of the key qualifications for becoming and remaining a lead pastor.

---

17. The data you are about to see are true. Only the names (including the church's) have been changed to protect the innocent.

Figure 8.3: Galilee Church Campus Pastors' Powerless Language Indicators per Minute (PLIpm) in Pre-Sermon Set-Up

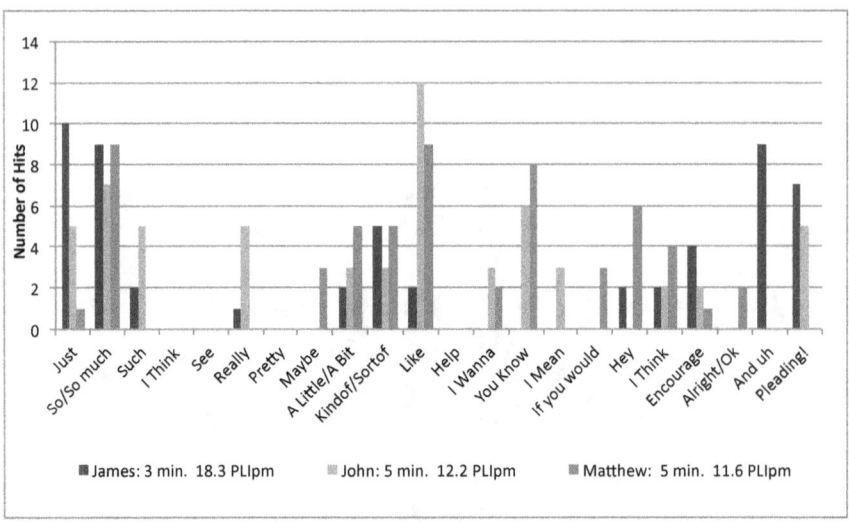

Lest you think that this difference can be attributed to the nature of giving announcements and leading worship compared to that of preaching, look at the data in Figure 8.4.

Figure 8.4: Galilee Church Lead Vs. Campus Pastor's Powerless Language Indicators per Minute (PLIpm) In Sermon

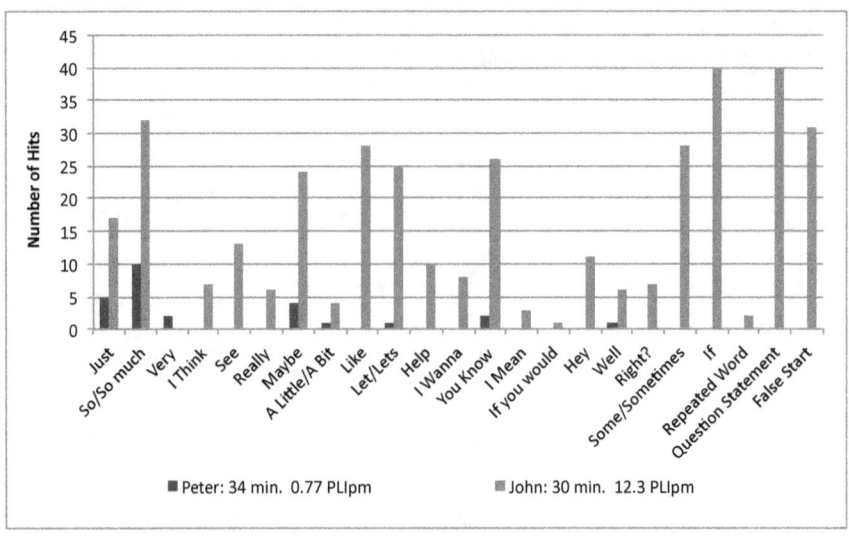

During the period Galilee Church was under study, one of the campus pastors provided the sermon in the lead pastor's absence. Figure 8.4 is a comparison of his sermon with one of the lead pastor's sermons. As you can see, while the sermons are approximately the same length, the difference in PLIpm mirrors that between Peter and the rest of the staff (see Figure 8.2). In addition, Peter used only eight different Powerless Language Indicators compared to John's twenty-one. That difference explains in part the fact that, despite working hard to reach men, this church's gender mix before the sermon was close to the 61/39 national average. On any given Sunday, roughly one third of the congregation—the majority of them men—remained in the gathering area outside the worship service drinking coffee and talking until just before the sermon. They felt no connection with the first half of the service and those who led it. We interviewed a number of men from the various campuses. One of the questions we asked was, "What keeps you involved here?" Most of them, regardless of which campus they attended, responded with some variation of, "I come here because of Pete. If he weren't here, I wouldn't bother."

PUTTING IT ALL TOGETHER

I have left this chapter on how we talk until the end because *how* we talk is the most difficult thing to change. It is the most unconscious part of our communication, and therefore requires greater effort and diligence to learn new patterns. We are also adding yet another level to the analysis and transformation. That makes the discipline and perseverance I mentioned chapter 4 even more important. You will be even more tempted to stop short. You will be even more tempted to slip back into old patterns. At the same time, you will have to exercise healthy self-criticism. You will have to be open to your teammates' critical analysis of the way you talk. You will have to learn to give healthy criticism to your teammates in a way they can hear it. And you and your teammates will have to be intentional about the process of change as well as supportive of one another throughout.

How To Use The Information

Each of you should summarize his/her tendencies from their data sheets (see Figure 8.2) on a single sheet. As you have previously, use your summary sheet as a filter in all your writing and preparations for church events and meetings. Unlike your previous efforts, however, your aim is not to replace these with alternative expressions. It is to eliminate them. You will never do so completely, but your efforts will reduce them to a more appropriate level. Keep a running mental tally of the Powerless Language Indicators used by the men you have come to know at the sports bar, gym, etc. and compare it to what you have used at church. Also as before, make a game of catching each other's slips into old patterns in your conversations with your teammates. The staff of Galilee Church began to address their high PLIpm rate by "calling" each other on each instance the Feminine Register and Powerless Language in staff meetings. This group of eight male and two female pastors said it was so prevalent that they had trouble getting any work done at first. They started carrying cricket clickers to help keep other aware throughout the day. As the daily awareness grew, the productivity in meetings grew as well. This is vital because if we do not change the way we talk throughout church life, we will not see increasing numbers of men throughout church life.

If you serve in any kind of leadership capacity, I recommend that you record yourself in the settings in which you serve. Then, analyze your paralanguage in terms of pitch range, variation of pitches, vocal intensity, and speech rate.[18] Because we have a natural tendency to speak in a higher range with a higher rate when addressing a group, it will take conscious effort to slow down and drop the range you use to a lower level. As you do so, keep that lower range within what is natural for your voice. A forced, unnatural, low voice can have as negative an effect on one's credibility as the higher voice. Keep your rate conversational. Work especially hard to keep it fluid. It is primarily the hesitations and extra pauses that cause the negative response to a slower rate. Ask your teammates, family, and friends to help you determine the range and rate that is best for you and work together in the coming weeks to help you make the transition. Just remember that you can do more with your voice than you think you can. You can widen the range at both ends by working to get your voice in shape. That will mean exercising the muscles that control the vocal chords like you exercise the rest of your body to build strength and flexibility. And that means investing time and effort to exercise, to practice, to prepare. It is that issue to which we will turn in the next and final chapter.

---

18. Several voice or pitch analyzer apps that can help you track your pitch range are available in both iOS and Android.

9

Where Do We Go from Here?

A RUDE AWAKENING

ORIGINALLY THIS CHAPTER BEGAN with the next section, "Calf Fries, Rough Edges, and Niceness." Then I sent the chapter to a friend and colleague whom I wanted to quote later in the chapter. I was surprised to receive an email saying not to use the quotation, as my friend was for various complex reasons uneasy with "the tone and language of the piece. This is about me, not you." When I asked what the issue was, this was the response:

> I'll be blunt with you, Woody. I am pretty sure any publisher whose editors are spiritually grounded people will be offended by the coarse story at the beginning of the chapter. It left me feeling kind of sick. I am absolutely certain that women readers and many men would also feel that the story is inappropriate... The words at this time are an assault.

Apparently this really was about me, not my friend. I had been weighed on the balance of spiritual groundedness and found wanting. I was no longer a friend; I had become the assaulting enemy.

I tell you this story for several reasons. First, it perfectly illustrates the point of the story that follows. Just reading about the incident below produced the very response in my friend that the man in that story was hoping to get from me. I was shocked that it did so. My friend had always related to people outside our walls with grace, not hostility and judgment. It was clear that, had my friend been in my shoes, in this instance the response would not have been grace. Yes, the man in the story was a bozo[1] (remember chap-

---

1. "A stupid, rude, or insignificant person, *especially a man*." Google Search, emphasis added.

ter 3?), but unless we are willing to condemn the bozos out of hand, we cannot allow their words to manipulate us into a graceless response. The world outside our walls is not a pretty, polite place. If we are to reach the people outside our walls, we will need thicker skin and more compassionate hearts.

That brings me to the second reason. The topic, language, and imagery used by the man below has become much more common and accepted than we inside our cloistered walls realize. Take, for example, an article written by columnist Kate Rice in the University of Santa Barbara's award winning independent student newspaper, the Daily Nexus. Titled "Say Hello to My Little Friend,"[2] it extols the virtues of masturbating in front of one's sexual partner and gives helpful tips for enhancing the experience. Or take psychologist and family physician, Dr. Leonard Sax's report that "fourth grade boys, referring to oral sex, casually ask girls whether they spit or swallow.[3] My daughter, a middle school teacher in the Bronx in New York City says that this kind of language is common among the students. In fact, she says it was common among the students when she was in high school. (*Now* she tells me!) And it doesn't get any better among the adults. A few years ago my wife attended a divorce party for one of her colleagues where the ice cubes were in the form of erect male genitalia. (She was not pleased!) Again, the world outside our walls is not a pretty, polite place. This is nothing new. It would not surprise me if Jesus had an experience similar to the one described below while eating goat or lamb fries (a Middle Eastern delicacy) at a party at, say, Levi the tax collector's house. The world was not a pretty, polite place Jesus's day either. The purpose of this book is to prepare you for that world. Part of that preparation is to decide where you stand—with the Pharisees who are picking up stones or with the supposed drunkard and glutton, Jesus. He hung out with bozos like Levi—who became Matthew the apostle—because he loves *all* sinners, including us.

The third reason I tell you the story above is to give you fair warning. If you have suffered sexual abuse you may want to skip the "Graphic Imagery" section in the story below, as it may access painful memories and emotions that have not yet been healed.

---

2. http://dailynexus.com/2004-01-21/say-hello-to-my-little-friend/. As of February 2017, The Daily Nexus had been ranked in the top 10 best college newspapers by Princeton Review two out of the previous three years.

3. Sax, *Why Gender Matters*, 240.

CALF FRIES, ROUGH EDGES, AND BEING NICE

When I was the Teacher of Evangelism for the Oklahoma United Methodist Conference in the late 90s, I was invited to give an evangelistic talk at a district Men's "Calf Fry" dinner. For those of you who don't know, calf fries are bull testicles that have been sliced and fried. The Calf Fry is a cultural event each year in ranch country when they castrate the young bulls to turn them into steers. As we were standing around the shelter eating plates full of calf fries, Jim, one of the non-church men came up to me and said,

> ### WARNING: GRAPHIC IMAGERY
>
> "I hear you're the preacher tonight. I bet you don't know what you're eating."
> "Sure I do," I said, "though growing up back in southern Ohio we called them mountain oysters."
> "Oh." he said, "Well, can't you just feel the . . . [grossly explicit reference to oral sex deleted]?"

If you are feeling disgust and revulsion and maybe a little sick to your stomach as the possibilities for what he said cycle through your mind, you know how I felt at that moment. It was clear that Jim was challenging me. He intended to shock me into a response that would legitimize him dismissing anything I might say later in my talk. It was a test. Fortunately, the Holy Spirit had prepared me for this moment. Two weeks prior I had eaten calf fries at a steakhouse on the other side of the state with several couples who were church leaders. They were solid, spiritually grounded, salt-of-the-earth ranch folk. During the meal, the wives said this was the only restaurant where they would order calf fries because they knew they would be cleaned properly. Then they discussed how awful calf fries tasted if they weren't. The Holy Spirit brought those comments back to me as Jim stood there, waiting to see what I would do.

"Naw," I said, "I've had some like that before, but they cleaned these up pretty good."

Jim gave me a quizzical look, a nod, and then turned and walked away.

To start my talk I told about my coming of age experience when I was twelve. My grand-dad taught me how to handle bringing a young bull in from the field—

> "Always carry a walkin' stick; always look him in the eye; if he ain't movin' give him a whack; never turn your back on him, and never. never. run.."

He put me up on a box so I could be face-to-face with the bull as it stood on the other side of the stall gate. Then he handed me his old, octagonal barreled Winchester pump-action rifle and showed me where to shoot.

> "You gotta hit him smack dab between the eyes or the .22 won't put him down."

Grandpa had me sit on the tractor fender as we dragged the carcass up from the basement stalls to the main floor of the barn. We hoisted it from the rafters and my older brothers and I helped butcher it. When we finished the butchering Grandpa asked me how I felt.

> "Like a man," I said.
> "Well son," he said, "you're not a man till you've had a meal of bull's balls."

Later as we ate, he talked about the bull's strength and power, and how it protects its herd.

> "If you're gonna be a man," he said, "You gotta have bull's balls."

In my talk I said eating bull's balls was not enough to make us the men we are meant to be—that the power that raised Jesus from the dead was available to us and would make each of us the men we really wanted to be, and more. Afterwards Jim, came up and said,

> "I never had much use for preachers, but you're for real. You can take it, and you can give it right back. You know, this is the first time I ever thought I might want to be a Christian."

A little while later Jim's friend, Tom, came up to me.

> "I saw you talking with Jim. I'm glad—I invited him. I liked what you had to say tonight," he said. "I think it helped him. But . . . you said we could be more. I been in the church my whole life and I don't see how. I'll never be a good Christian."
> "Why not?" I asked.
> "I got too many rough edges," he said. "I just don't fit, and I'll never measure up."

As we talked it became clear that Tom had the same picture of what it meant to be a good Christian as the one I uncovered in my "Perceptions of Christians" study discussed in chapter 1. He saw himself as having more in common with the "Not Like a Good Christian" column in Table 1.1 in that chapter than with the "Like a Good Christian" column.

> "Keep your rough edges," I told him. "The world is full of people with rough edges. Without people like you we will never reach them. If you didn't have rough edges, Jim would not be here tonight."

As I drove home I realized that Tom had been saying he was not polite enough; he was not "Nice" enough to be a good Christian. It put me in mind of C.S. Lewis's take on our fixation with niceness.

> "Niceness"—wholesome, integrated personality—is an excellent thing. We must try by every medical, educational, economic, and political means in our power to produce a world where as many people as possible grow up "nice"; just as we must try to produce a world where all have plenty to eat. But we must not suppose that even if we succeeded in making everyone nice we should have saved their souls. A world of nice people, content in their own niceness, looking no further, turned away from God, would be just as desperately in need of salvation as a miserable world—and might even be more difficult to save.[4]

Through the years when I have asked men why they have chosen to stay away, one of the things they have consistently said is, "Church people are nice—on the surface. Underneath?—They're nasty!" It always makes me think of "whitewashed tombs" (Matthew 23:27)—especially when they proceed to tell me a story or two to prove it. You and I know that is only true of a few. But those few, and the stories they generate, are enough to confirm the stereotype. What is important to our discussion here, however, is non-church men's choice of "Niceness" as the characteristic to describe church folk. They could have chosen a number of others, but they didn't. It made it a double-barreled slam. They had no interest in niceness. To them it was always a sham. In contrast, when we asked the men of Galilee Church what it was about Pastor Peter that made them want to stay (see chapter 8), we heard over and over, "He's *real*." "You can trust him to say what he thinks, even when he knows you're not going to like it." "He's not afraid to get dirty. He'll get right down in the muck with you if that's what you need." The buzzword is "Authenticity," but I like the first guy's statement, "He's *real*."

Pastor Peter's response at the close of our sessions at Galilee Church shows just how real he is. He said, "I am challenged. Have I just been playing at ministry, being satisfied with surface change instead of real

---

4. Lewis, *Mere Christianity*, 215–16.

transformation?" Then he invited any of the staff that wanted to, to join him in the worship center for an hour on their knees, listening for the Holy Spirit's guidance. Within six weeks he had led his staff in rewriting their vision, mission, and values statements. Those changes began moving Galilee Church from being satisfied with relational, communal inertia towards actionable, impactful transformation of self and the world.

UNEASY QUESTIONS

C. S. Lewis's observation and Pastor Peter's question raise a number of other questions that are not easy, and should make us uneasy.

The Critical Question: What is our mission?

You may be wondering why this is leading a section devoted to uneasy questions. After all, there is widespread agreement across most of the church that our mission is to "Go and make disciples of all nations, baptizing them in the name of the Father and of the Son and of the Holy Spirit, and teaching them to obey everything I have commanded you" (Matthew 28:19-20). In this day of declining membership and attendance even churches that had been the most resistant to just the mention of "the e-word"[5] have come to recognize that the Great Commission was so central to the early church that a version of it shows up in all four gospels.[6] The reason I have placed it first in the discussion of uneasy questions is that, at least in the North American church, most of us are doing a poor job of fulfilling it. Instead, we have stopped short. We have settled for less, and as a result we are operating under the Muddled Mainline Version:

> Stay, therefore, and make compliant members of our people,
> Socializing them in the ways of Grandpa and Grandma and old Preacher Jones
> And teaching them to do everything "the way we've always done them."
> And remember, I am with you most of the time—even to the edge of the church lot.

---

5. It is demoralizing how many times someone has said in my evangelism seminars and consultations, "We can't use the e-word at our church."

6. cf. Mark 16:14-20, Luke 24:36-4; Acts 1:4-9, John 20:19-23. The version of the Great Commission associated with Mark's gospel is not found in the earliest manuscripts of Mark. Scholars are generally agreed that Mark 16:14-20 dates from the second century. It is, in effect, a summary of the other versions written in light of the second century church's situation and recalling events that occurred in relation to the spread of the gospel.

But the true Great Commission requires us to go, to take the initiative, even as God has done throughout the history of God's relationship with humankind, rather than to sit passively saying, "If they are interested, they will come." It requires us to reach out to *all* peoples, not just those who look like us or act like us or talk like us; not just to those who are on our side of town or our side of the country or our side of the world. It requires us to initiate people who do not yet know Christ into a relationship with a God who is far greater than they have ever imagined, or ever could—a God who created the vast expanses of the universe and all that is in it, who redeems a creation marred by the willful self-centeredness of the very children God created and loves. It requires us to connect them with the God who not only holds that creation together in spite of the flaws we have introduced into it, but who works within it to accomplish God's original purpose for us and all creation (Romans 10:10). Finally, the Great Commission requires us to weave those who are initiated into a community where we are all being transformed by an ever-deepening bond of our whole person with God. The result of that deepening bond in the context of the community of Christ is that we not only have a different worldview, we have a different lifestyle. We have a lifestyle that so closely matches the Sermon on the Mount that it can only be described as "the good and acceptable will of God" (Romans 12:2), for it is the embodiment of the Great Commandment—to love God with our heart, soul, and mind; and to love our neighbor as ourselves (Matthew 22:38–39). Where we first get into trouble is when we focus on the second half of the commission while neglecting the first. We focus our attention and efforts on the people we already have and unthinkingly remain content with letting the rest of the world go to hell in a hand-basket.

Without the act of crossing our barriers, without the initiation and the connection, the lifestyle becomes about maintaining church culture rather than living the life of the Age to Come in this present age.[7] And when the lifestyle becomes about church culture, it is easy to import the assumptions of whatever subcultures we have chosen, whether from within the church or without. The result is that we end up modern day Pharisees who have the form of godliness without the power (2 Timothy 3:5)—nice, but nasty—unable to connect with or even gain a hearing among sinners and tax collectors, drunkards and gluttons (Matthew 11:19), or even your average everyday Joe or Josephine.

Some of my clergywoman friends have said that *this* is the cause of the missing men. It is not that the church is feminized but that it is losing

---

7. New Testament theologian, George Eldon Ladd, said this is the core of the gospel as presented in the book of Matthew. See *The Presence of the Future*, 1974.

its soul. Its disengagement from its God-given mission with its message, its lifestyle, and its actions affects the women as well as the men. And they are right; at its deepest level it is not about gender. But at the level where most men live it is, because men live in an actional world. To be a people set aside for the mission of God[8] is to be actional. And because we live in a world where most men are actional while most women are relational, when the church turns aside from the mission of God in this world—that is, "loses its soul"—it has a disproportionate effect on men, as well as those women who are also actional. In each revolution of the generational cycle since at least the 1850s (see chapter 1), the wake-up call that signaled the church's loss of its soul has been the missing men. The alarms went off and the church responded. To date, the critical component in that response has been a rediscovery of the first part of its mission—the realization that the men had gone missing led the church to once again *go* beyond its barriers to connect men with Christ. It engaged the culture by adapting its actions and its talk so that it once again related to men in terms with which they could identify.

At the same time, the critical limitation in the church's response has been its failure to fulfill the second half of its mission by living the life of the Age to Come. Too often the church has settled for clichés and stereotypes in its efforts to reach men, and never moved beyond them. We have simply substituted one subculture for another. From the Men and Religion Forward Movement's "religion from the businessman's point of view," and the Institutional Church Movement's turning churches into athletic facilities and health spas complete with Turkish baths in the 1910s, to the contemporary men's movements' military-or adventure-or mancave-themed retreats, our temptation and our tendency has been to stop short—to confuse the means with the mission. I have nothing against any of these things as means. In chapter 1 we saw how effective they could be. Indeed, my great-grandfather came to faith through "the first institutional church known in Ohio." According to that church's published history,

> Institutional features included reading rooms in the basement, two fully equipped bathing departments, each containing Turkish, Russian, shower, tub and plunge baths, lavatory, lockers and dressing rooms, and a splendidly equipped gymnasium. The Institutional Methodist Church was dedicated June 6, 1904 . . . Great revivals occurred during this golden era of the church, with membership at about 1,000.

---

8. Which is the biblical definition of holiness—to be set aside for God's purpose (1 Peter 2:9).

According to census records, the town population at this time was 3,985. A quarter of the population in that one church—I would call that effective. But like many similar edifices that sit mostly empty today, it easily became *about* the edifice:

> "GREENFIELD'S CALAMITY" was the headline in the Greenfield Republican of May 1, 1910. The newspaper described how "the First M.E. Church, the pride of the city and one of the finest church edifices in the state," was wiped out by fire, with the loss set at more than $100,000. [After the church was rebuilt,] the next several decades were relatively tranquil. One highlight was the establishment of the Memorial Room in 1937 for literary and social purposes.

The rest of the history recounts the various remodeling projects of subsequent years. There is no mention of revival, or redemption, or mission.

Stopping short with Institutional Features in the early 1900s or today with, let's say, Adventure, or say, Correcting Gender Stereotypes is no different from stopping short with Niceness. It is a danger we all face, no matter what its expression. And so we must go on to ask more uneasy questions, questions that will reveal how far we may be settling for less than the true Great Commission.

What are the real aims of our ministry?

Take a look at your checkbook and calendar. The way you spend your money, your time, and your attention will reveal your priorities in life. The same is true in your ministry, personally and as a church. Whether you are a layperson or clergyperson, you are in ministry and your priorities show up in your life, even on your face. If one of my priorities were being "holy" in the sense that it commonly is understood, it would have shown up on my face at Jim's opening line at the Calf Fry. If I had shown shock or offense—had I said I resented his language, had I so much as flinched or stood there with a blank, "I don't know what to say" look on my face—I would never have gained a hearing with that man. He would have shut me down. Pre-Christian people can read our attitudes in a flash without our ever uttering a word. That's why we have a reputation as self-righteous, holier-than-thou prigs. Being nice is nice, but it can also get in the way.

Similarly, correcting gender stereotypes is a good and worthwhile aim. I do not want my children or my children's children to be limited by culturally defined characteristics or opportunities. And it is possible to address gender stereotypes within the context of our mission.[9] At the same time, concern over gender stereotypes can so fill our view that it becomes the priority of our ministry or a required component of a faithful discipleship. When that happens we have become distracted from our mission by the values of a subculture with which we have identified.[10] That distraction can have a major impact when we are engaged in a cross-cultural ministry. And it is important to recognize that any ministry outside the church walls is cross-cultural. Nice is nice, but it can get in the way.

As you look at how you have invested yourself, as you look at issues or concerns in which you have invested, as you look at the outcomes you hope will result from your investment, what are the real aims of your ministry? Spend some time right now in prayer asking the Holy Spirit to help you answer that question. Make a note of the answer on your iPad or paper journal.

What are the sources of those ministry aims?

I mentioned in chapter 1 how pastoral training had become heavily influenced by psychology and pastoral care had become psycho-social support rather than the "cure of souls." That process has continued to the point that discipleship ministries have more in common with self-help support groups than anything particularly spiritual. Take, for example, the goal of getting people to talk about their hurts and fears in a group setting as a prerequisite to spiritual growth. While this can be helpful and healthy for some people, for others it can cause them to become mired in the past. Apart from this, it also has a built-in bias against men, who are notoriously more reticent about this than are women.

It turns out there is a neurological reason for this difference. Studies using PET scans have demonstrated that most men process emotional experiences through the right amygdala while most women process them through the left amygdala.[11] This difference "stimulates more activity downward in the male brain towards the brainstem (and thus more quickly into the physical body), and more often upward in the female brain toward

---

9. See Csinos, "Correcting Gender Stereotypes," 23–28.

10. It is important to note that this is true whether we are seeking to overcome traditional gender roles or preserve them.

11. There is an amygdala deep in each temporal lobe of the brain. It is involved in the processing of emotions such as fear, anger, and pleasure. The amygdala also determines what memories are stored and where they are stored in the brain.

talking centers."[12] In addition most women activate more brain regions that correlate with both ongoing evaluation of emotional experience and later recall.[13] This difference leads to most men's emotional memory being limited to central information about the event (what the authors called "the gist" of it) while most women have enhanced memory for peripheral details.[14] I say "most" because it turns out that gender schematicity plays a role (remember chapter 3?). It is actually Action Men and Women whose emotional memory focuses on the gist. Similarly, the Relation Women and Men showed greater recall of the peripheral details.[15] So, once again our ministry practices selectively attract relational people and exclude actional people, the great majority of whom are men.

The reality of that discrimination was brought home forcefully to me in a listening session with the youth group of a church with which I was consulting. As they recounted their experiences and discussed their likes and dislikes, what was helpful and not, one young man began to grow increasingly agitated. I finally said to him, "You look like you want to say something."

> "No," he said. "I don't belong here. I only been comin' a few weeks. I shouldn't say nothin'."
>
> "If you've just started coming, we really need to hear what you think," I said.

It took a little while for him to work himself up to it, but finally he fairly exploded with,

> "You got to do somethin' besides sittin' in a chair!"
>
> "What do you mean?" I asked.
>
> "Okay, I've been coming here for three weeks and all we done is sit and talk."
>
> At that the rest of the group chimed in with, "Yep, that's pretty much it."

As I listened to the adults in the various other listening sessions that weekend, that young man's statement kept echoing in my mind. The majority of our ministry in the local church could be described as "sitting in a chair, talking."

The process that started with the psycho-social captivity of ministry has expanded over the last forty years. Because of the educational requirements for ordination and the ongoing requirement of continuing education, contemporary Euro-American academic ideology as a whole has a major

---

12. Gurian and Annis, *Leadership*, 40.
13. Canli, et al. "Sex Differences," 10789.
14. Cahill and van Stegeren, "Sex-related Impairment," 81.
15. Cahill, et al. "Influence of Sex," 391.

influence on ministry priorities. As a social scientist trained in that environment I have no problem with that, so long as we examine and consciously choose those aims. As we do so in the context of the missing men some alarm bells should go off. As legitimate concern over the negative effects of patriarchy has taken hold and efforts to dismantle it have grown, a subtle anti-male environment has developed. And in some instances it is not quite so subtle. Take for example the book, *Single by Chance, Mothers by Choice: How Women Are Choosing Parenthood without Marriage and Creating the New American Family*. The author, sociologist Rosanna Hertz, a women's studies professor at Wellesley College basically states that mother-and-child[ren] are the core of the family and men are obsolete. Similarly, Cornell University professor of psychiatry Peggy Drexler in her book *Raising Boys without Men: How Maverick Moms Are Creating the next Generation of Exceptional Men* argues that men are not just unnecessary, they are in the way, and that boys are sometimes better off being raised by single mothers or in lesbian homes. The fact that Hertz's book is number fifty-nine in Amazon.com's Single Parents category ten years after its publication and Drexler has appeared on and written for a wide range of national and international media—including The *Today Show, Good Morning America*, NPR, The *New York Times, USA Today, Good Housekeeping and Parents magazines*—shows how widespread acceptance of such views has become.

As you look at the real aims of your ministry, to what extent are they grounded in secular Euro-American academic ideology? Spend some time right now in prayer asking the Holy Spirit to help you answer that question. Make a note of the answer on your iPad or paper pad.

What assumptions make up the foundation of those ministry aims?

One of the assumptions we need to address is actually a holdover from the Victorian era. Succinctly put, it is:

"Sugar & Spice vs. Rats & Snails"

The notion that women are good and men are bad is so prevalent that Kathleen Parker devoted a whole chapter to it in her book, *Save The Males: Why Men Matter And Why Women Should Care*. She cites the work of Dr. Jim Macnamara to illustrate.[16] The professor of public communication at the University of Western Sydney, Australia, analyzed over 2000 mass media

---

16. Parker, *Save the Males*, 20.

portrayals of men and male identity. Seventy-five per cent of all mass media representations of men portrayed them as either "villains, aggressors, perverts or philanderers." The only positive portrayals showed men as sensitive, emotional or caring—describing these as men's and boys' "feminine side."[17]

Education journalist, Peg Tyre, describes the impact such negative images have had in the American system of education. She cites a case study where several parents insisted that their children be assigned to another classroom when they discovered the kindergarten teacher was male.

> "I know kids. I have to. I worked in a day care. I subbed all through my undergraduate work," [the teacher] said. "I knew I'd be a great kindergarten teacher. But the first things most parents think is that you are a pedophile or a homosexual." ... By the end of the year, the parents who had complained nominated him for new teacher of the year.... [However], the following September, two mothers of incoming kindergartners were standing about six feet away from him and one said loudly to the other, "Can you believe they allow him in a room with a group of kids?"[18]

Tyre found the "men bad" assumption applied to boys as well. She tells of early education expert, Susan Horn's experience in helping preschools identify "kids who might have serious developmental or neurological problems" in the public schools of St. Louis. In the first eight months of the program Horn was called to observe fifty problem students. Not one of them was a girl. In each case she found no diagnosable problem. "What I'm finding is that many urban teachers I talk to, especially ones that don't have brothers and don't have sons, simply don't understand what little boys are like."[19] And unfortunately, when they don't understand boys they assume the worst. Men's frustration with having been treated like this all their lives is summed up well by the late Robert Jordan in his international best selling series, *The Wheel of Time*:

> "Women were always happy for a chance to educate a boy when he was young; Mat thought they assumed they could educate him out of becoming a man if they tried hard enough."[20]

It is little wonder they feel that way, given a second widespread assumption I call,

---

17. Phys.org, "Men Become," para 5–9.
18. Tyre, *Trouble with Boys*, 128–29.
19. Ibid., 79–80.
20. Jordan, *The Towers of Midnight*, 252.

"Testosterone is from the Twilight Zone."

When I was growing up the television show, *The Twilight Zone*, scared me to death. Since the mid-1980s a lot of people have felt the same way about this essential male hormone. A host of articles and books linking testosterone with words like "anti-social," "misbehavior," "criminal," "violence," "delinquency" and the like[21] forged the link and has kept it strong in the common mind. I see it frequently on the faces of people in my seminars about reaching men when we talk about how church folk's aversion to risk excludes men.[22] I have heard it in pastors' and seminary faculty members' criticisms of various contemporary men's ministries as "little more than a glorification of testosterone." It is as though they think testosterone is at best a necessary evil that leads *inevitably* to the worst in men.

Rather than wishing it would go away or looking for ways to reduce its influence in men, we should be looking for ways to channel testosterone's influence in positive directions. It is, after all, an integral part of God's original plan in creation. In other words, it is a gift of God, and ought not to be denigrated.

One way to channel its influence positively is particularly appropriate to church talk. We have already seen that men and women who speak in a lower pitch range are perceived as stronger, more authoritative, respected, influential, and as leaders (see chapter 8). We have known for some time that higher testosterone levels correlate with lower pitched voices in men.[23] Other research has shown that testosterone levels vary throughout the day and that the fundamental frequency of voice pitch lowers as testosterone levels increase in men.[24] In addition, Harvard social psychologist Amy Cuddy set the world on fire in June 2012 with a TED talk[25] citing research showing that testosterone levels in the brain can be intentionally raised by "power posing" for as brief a period as two minutes.[26] "These expansive pos-

---

21. See Dabbs, "Saliva Testosterone," 1987; "Testosterone, Social Class," 1990; Brooks and Reddon. "Serum Testosterone," 1996; Aromäki, Anu S., et al. "Testosterone," 2002; Coccaro, et al. "CSF Testosterone," 2007.

22. It has been demonstrated that men in general are far higher sensation-seekers than are women (see Kurtz and Zuckerman. "Race And Sex Differences," 1978) and that testosterone is a key factor in that difference since it is highly correlated with sensation-seeking (see Gerra, G., et al. "Neurotransmitters," 207–13).

23. Though not in women (see Dabbs and Mallinger, "High Testosterone Levels," 801–04).

24. Evans, et al. "Testosterone and Vocal Frequencies," 783–88.

25. To date, since its posting Cuddy's TED talk has been viewed over 37 million times.

26. Carney, et al. "Power Posing," 536–47. There has been a lively debate among social scientists about this research and the conclusions reached by Cuddy and her

tures[27] both reflect and produce power.... [They] boost feelings of power, confidence, self esteem, risk tolerance, mood, action orientation, memory for positive words and concepts, and pain tolerance, while reducing feelings of fear.... [These effects] cause a bevy of psychological and behavioral changes that could improve a person's performance and outcomes in stressful social situations."[28] In Cuddy's latest research, participants enacted expansive power poses for a period of six minutes while thinking about a self presentation speech which they then gave in a simulated job interview. Though the power posers were unseen by the interviewers, they positively affected *the interviewers' perceptions* of the interviewee.[29]

So here we have a simple, easily done action that raises testosterone levels, thus unconsciously lowering male speakers' voice pitch, which in itself raises hearers' perceptions of the speaker.[30] And at the same time it raises their feelings of power, confidence, self esteem, memory for positive words and concepts, etc., while reducing feelings of fear. And all of that also has a demonstrable positive effect on the hearers' perceptions, whether the speaker is a male or female.[31] For anyone who is preaching, teaching, or leading meetings that is a helpful tool.

Another activity raises testosterone in both men and women and results in positive effects—competition. For some of you that statement has raised your hackles, because it is based on another assumption:

"Competition is demolition."

This belief has made its way not only into the church but also into society as a whole, especially youth sports programs. Children routinely receive "participation trophies" out of concerns that competition—or rather, being on the short end of it—will damage their self-esteem. "Not so," says Ashley Merryman, co-author with Po Bronson of *NurtureShock: New Thinking About Children*, as well as *Top Dog: The Science of Winning and Losing*.

---

colleagues. They have responded with additional studies as well as a re-examination of their previous research. Refinement of the research is contributing to a clearer picture of the factors involved and has provided further support for their original conclusions.

27. e.g. standing with feet shoulder width apart, hands on hips.
28. Cuddy, et al. "Preparatory Power Posing," 1288–89.
29. Ibid., 1303-4.
30. Cheng, et al. "Listen, Follow Me," 536-37.
31. "Neither gender nor race of participant interacted with the power pose condition or affected any of the dependent variables" (all p's > .70). Ibid., 1301.

By age 4 or 5, children aren't fooled by all the trophies. They are surprisingly accurate in identifying who excels and who struggles. Those who are outperformed know it and give up, while those who do well feel cheated when they aren't recognized for their accomplishments. They, too, may give up. It turns out that, once kids have some proficiency in a task, the excitement and uncertainty of real competition may become the activity's very appeal.[32]

Unquestioning adoption of these assumptions led us to ministry choices with unintended consequences. I was a young youth minister in the late 70s when The Ungame and "endless volleyball" became hot choices for weekly programming. Endless volleyball was a game with no points. The idea was to eliminate competition and experience the joy of cooperation by keeping the ball in the air as long as possible. The Ungame is a board game designed to get participants to "share." We played them both faithfully, and then wondered why the boys began to disappear and the group got younger. I don't know if endless volleyball is still around, but the Ungame is. The following review by one of its online purchasers is instructive:

Great game to get people to open up. My daughter and I tried to get my psyzoid husband to talk about his feelings—it worked somewhat. My daughter and I found it useful to understand each other. Good tool for a family that doesn't talk much about feelings.

Competition suffers from the same problem as testosterone—the belief that it leads *inevitably* to the worst in people. Competition suffers in addition from the belief in some people's minds that it is an entirely human creation—that there is nothing inherent in God's creation that involves competition and that it just might be an expression of the Fall. Shirl James Hoffman, Professor Emeritus Of Exercise And Sports Science at the University of North Carolina at Greensboro, seems to advocate such a view:

Competition might more fittingly be seen as a distortion of the created essence of "human relationship" or "community." Unlike competition, a library of theological opinion can be mustered to support the contention that God created humans as relational beings, designed to relate not only to each other but also to him [sic]. However the form that relationship takes is left up to his [sic] children. Could it be that competition is a perversion of this created essence of relationship?[33]

---

32. Merryman, "Losing Is Good," para 8.
33. Hoffman, *Good Game*, 159.

He never really answers that question—so I will. I disagree that the universal urge for competition is not self-evident. On the contrary competition is everywhere. It exists in every expression and at every strata of human society. Indeed, it is not limited to human life. It is present among all of the life forms on the planet, even plant life and microscopic life. It is so woven into the warp and woof of life on earth that I have to ask, how can it not be part of God's creation? Perhaps this explains Dr. Hoffman's ambivalence. After picking apart arguments in defense of competition Hoffman goes on to say:

> These serious reservations about competition notwithstanding I don't hoist my flag with those who believe competition is irredeemable. Converting sports into entirely cooperative ventures or opting for the . . . school of "winning–isn't–everything–its–nothing" are not paths to redemption as much as they are paths to extinction.[34]

He later goes on to give good suggestions for redeeming sports in his chapter, "Notes on a Well-Played Game."[35] So perhaps competition isn't so bad a thing after all.

Michael Gurian and Barbara Annis point to competition as the means by which men naturally nurture.

> Male biochemistry and brain structure, as well as socialization, create a leadership style in men that shows primal devotion to the overall protection of a competitive system itself—that is, the "big picture."[36] Male leaders tend to protect the corporation's success not through caring immediately for an individual's feelings and emotions but through the breaking down and building up of competitive relationships that support a large system of accomplishment. . . . Women tend to nurture through direct empathy with individuals in immediate situations. Men tend to nurture in deference to the aggression/competition hierarchy to which they have become loyal. . . . American psychologist Shelley Taylor[37] has proven it through oxytocin and brain chemistry research. The empathy/aggression difference is wired into us via brain structures, blood flow in the brain, biochemistry, and, of course, socialization.[38]

---

34. Ibid., 164.
35. Ibid., 263–97.
36. Remember Figures 7.2: The Focus of Men's Attention and 7.3: The Focus of Women's Concern?
37. See Taylor, *Tending Instinct*, 2002.
38. Gurian and Annis, *Leadership*, 156–57.

A simple way to think of it is that men think in terms of self-confidence building rather than self-esteem raising. Self-esteem raising says, "Competition is bad because if you lose, you hurt." Self-confidence building says, "Competition is good because when you lose, you learn." You learn from your mistakes, you learn from those who are better than you, and you learn to persevere.

I was six years old when my father took the job of head baseball coach at a small rural high school. He immediately began increasing the number of games and the level of competition the team played. He caught a fair amount of flak from people in the community. His answer was, "You don't learn to win by practicing. You learn to win by playing games. And you don't get better by playing teams at your own level. You get better by playing people who are better than you. We are going to get beat a lot—for a while. But eventually we are going to be winners." It became a mantra and guys in those early losing years bought in. They sacrificed immediate personal success for the larger long-term success of the program. By the time I was a freshman we were playing against nationally ranked all-star teams and winning championships—with just guys from our little high school. Dad was named one of the top five high school baseball coaches in the country that year and eventually was named to the state baseball coaches' Hall of Fame. Coaches from other schools kept asking him where he found all those good ballplayers. Dad would tell them, "I don't have any better players than anybody else. I just expect more of them." Years later when they named the new baseball field after him, a number of former players came to the dedication. They had gone on into all walks of life and been successful. The most consistent thing they said was, "Coach Davis didn't just teach me baseball. He taught me life." The most telling thing about that is that a number of them were on the team, but never made it onto the field. They lost out in the competition for playing positions and still felt that being on the team had been the biggest single positive influence in their lives outside of their parents. Not only that, it was clear that the baseball team and all the team members' families had become one family. In the midst of high-pressure competition they had created community.

I see no reason for that to not be possible in the church. Hebrews 10:24 says, "Let us consider how we may *spur one another* on toward love and good deeds (NIV)." Does this not point us toward the way to do so? Romans 12:10 says, "Love one another with brotherly affection. *Outdo* one another in showing honor (ESV)." That became my aim when I pulled into the parking lot as the newly appointed lead pastor of a medium-sized church. The first thing I saw was a row of signs on the parking spaces closest to the main entrance of the educational wing. The one nearest the door said "Reserved for Senior Pastor." The next one said, "Reserved for Associate Pastor." The next one said, "Reserved for Director of Christian Education." The next one said, "Reserved for Director of Music Ministries." The next one said, "Reserved for Director of Youth Ministries." When I stood up to preach the next Sunday morning I pulled the senior pastor sign out of the pulpit and said, "I found this when I pulled into the lot parking lot this week. I took it down because we are not going to have royalty parking anymore. I am going to park in the space farthest away from the doors, so that our guests can have the best parking spaces. I invite you to join me. There is going to be one reserved space other than those for our handicapped folks and our guests, however." Then I pulled out a sign that I had had made during the week. "This is going to go in the place that had been my parking space," I said, turning it around so it could be seen. The sign said, "Reserved for Lay Minister of the Month." The rest of the sermon laid the groundwork for the series that came in the following weeks: "The Character of a Christian." The series emphasized that every layperson is a lay minister, whether they are ministering in the context of the church or of the world. During the series the lay leadership, and any others who cared to join in, studied with me the qualities of a servant-leader, as these should epitomize the character of a Christian. We put together a team to draft a statement of the qualifications for the Lay Minister of the Month based on that study. That team was then charged with the task of reviewing nominations from the congregation.

There was a bit of nervousness the first few weeks. This was a church that was explicitly anti-hierarchy[39] and anti-competition. According to the Director of Christian Education, "Lay Minister of the Month" came awfully close to hierarchical competition. Still, by the end of the summer things had settled in and we had our first Lay Minister of the Month. Everyone in the church was energized and enthused about where we were headed—I thought. Then the winter doldrums set in. I began to hear rumblings and grumblings. Nothing direct, mind you, just, "People are saying . . . " "How come *she* was chosen?" "How did he get on the selection committee?" "What are we doing picking one person over another, anyway?" "Well it seems to me this is just setting us all against each other." It took a while to trace it down, but it turned out to be a small knot of people who wielded considerable informal power. They had not participated in the Bible study on servant-leadership and, with the exception of the Christian Education Director, did not serve in any official capacity other than in the Women's Society. It was the power center that had kept the church inner-focused and stagnant for decades.

As it turned out, what had been before continued to be. When it became clear that the funds to be sent to the denomination would be choked

---

39. A bit ironic, given the clear order of the staff parking spaces.

off, the denominational leadership caved, and I was gone. Had this church been accustomed to open competition, things might have been different. Open competition provides an opportunity for learning to deal with conflict effectively. It also provides an opportunity to learn that one competition or conflict or confrontation does not define a whole relationship, a lesson today's church sorely needs.

Though addressing the American educational system rather than the church, Peg Tyre illustrates it well. She tells the story of a school superintendent who investigated why there were so few male teachers in his district. He found that the mostly female hiring committee found typically male answers to standard interview questions unacceptable. He asked the male teachers who were most loved by students, parents, and staff to respond anonymously to the questions and then had the committee evaluate them.

> For example, the hiring committee frequently asked how a prospective teacher would respond to a difference of opinion in a staff meeting. Acceptable answers, according to the committee, included words like *understanding* and *collaboration*. The best male classroom teachers, though, answered the question by suggesting they were not particularly interested in coalition building. One male teacher said that he "respected other people's right to disagree"—a response that the committee judged to be too confrontational. Prospective guy teachers, it seemed, didn't use the buzzwords that made their potential female colleagues comfortable.[40]

The church today is enamored of the same buzzwords as the educational system, and competition is not one of them. But there is no human system that is devoid of competition. And it is not the exclusive domain of men.

> Brain chemistry and hormone-based studies do not show women to be noncompetitive. They show, instead, different ways of competing, with men spending more time focusing their energies on hierarchical competition—in part because their blood stream is constantly flooded with aggression, competition, and territoriality chemicals—and women spending more of their time competing through verbal interactions in smaller groups.[41]

If competition is not allowed open expression it goes to dark places and gets ugly. Because Relation Women's competition will be more verbal and Action Men's more actional, it parallels the amygdala findings we discussed

---

40. Tyre, *Trouble with Boys*, 130.
41. Gurian and Annis, *Leadership*, 48.

earlier regarding emotions.[42] Whereas for the men experiences of competition are mostly acted on and only the gist is stored in the memory, for the women competition is experienced and then mostly stored—in language and in detail. That means it has a better chance of being repeated. And if it has gone to a dark place and turned ugly, it is going to be bad for that church.

The last assumption we will look at is this:

"Men are mere brutes."

It is rarely stated as baldly as this, but the feeling is out there nonetheless. Dr. Adair Lummis's statement, cited in chapter 3, from the oral presentation, "Men's Commitment to Religion," hints at it: "If real men support the church financially and approve of their family members attending, why be concerned that men are not present? Solution: let the jocks be and let the more spiritually advanced women and men both people and manage the congregations!"[43] Another statement expressing the same sentiment shows up in the final published version of this study: "On the question of how congregations can get "real men" (and particularly those who are younger *as well as not arrogant, lazy or grouchy*) to become more involved the answer seems to be that some measures can be taken which may improve men's participation, but dramatic improvements are unlikely."[44] The article states that those measures likely to attract these men would be more "agenic" (i.e. actional) in character, but that those men will not be interested in the more spiritual offerings of the church. In other words, things that are actional are by definition not spiritual.

---

42. Andersen and Williams found that "feminine females had significantly more competitive trait anxiety [and therefore more emotion-producing] than all other groups and androgynous females were more anxious than masculine males ($p < .05$)." See "Gender Role and Sport," 55.

43. Lummis, "Men's Commitment," §4, emphasis in original. Apparently it was too bald for publication, as it was struck from the version that made it to print. It became instead, "Congregations will likely continue to thrive as long as the "real men" support the church financially and approve of their family members attending." (See Lummis, "A Research Note," 412.)

44. Lummis, "A Research Note," 411, emphasis added—that is how the question in the survey was phrased (see chapter 3, note 16). I cite Dr. Lummis because she is highly respected in the religious research community, and rightly so. She has served as an officer and regular presenter/convener at annual meetings of the Society for The Scientific Study of Religion, the Association for the Sociology of Religion, Religious Research Association. Through her presentations and publications Dr. Lummis not only reflects, but also has helped establish and reinforce beliefs and attitudes among academics in that field, which then filter into others' publications and presentations.

Such a view has a long history the church. In the mid-seventeenth century Thirty Years War veteran, Nicholas Herman, joined the Discalced Carmelite Prior in Paris as a lay brother and took the name of "Lawrence of the Resurrection." Brother Lawrence, as we know him today, was looked down upon by others in the priory and so he was given the most menial of tasks. I am sure there are several reasons for this. He was of the peasant class and insufficiently educated to be a cleric. But I have a holy hunch that he was thought to be not spiritual enough because he found little use or positive effect in the usual spiritual/devotional practices, and apparently was not shy about saying so:

> Men invent means and methods of coming at God's love, they learn rules and set up devices to remind them of that love, and it seems like a world of trouble to bring oneself into the consciousness of God's presence. Yet it might be so simple. Is it not quicker and easier just to do our common business wholly for the love of him?[45]

He told Father Joseph de Beaufort, later vicar general to the Archbishop of Paris, "That he was more united to God in his outward employments than when he left them for devotion and retirement."[46]

In other words, Brother Lawrence was a man of action and found his greatest connection with God in contemplating God's love while in the midst of his daily activities. An intellectual, language-oriented approach to God did nothing for him. He spent the hours appointed for private prayer focusing his attention on God's *existence* and immediate *presence*, "rather than by studied reasonings and elaborate meditations."[47] Words were not his strong suit.

Brother Lawrence's conversion was like that of many of the new Christian men I have interviewed—outdoors, alone, in silence.

> In the deep of winter, Herman looked at a barren tree, stripped of leaves and fruit, waiting silently and patiently for the sure hope of summer abundance. Gazing at the tree, Herman grasped for the first time the extravagance of God's grace and the unfailing sovereignty of divine providence. Like the tree, he himself was seemingly dead, but God had life waiting for him, and the turn of seasons would bring fullness. At that moment, he said, that

---

45. Quoted in Cheney, *Men Who Have Walked*, 303.

46. Lawrence, *The Practice*, 17. Father de Beaufort is the reason that we even know about Brother Lawrence since it was he who compiled published the materials in *The Practice of the Presence of God*.

47. Ibid., 23.

leafless tree "first flashed in upon my soul the fact of God," and a love for God that never after ceased to burn.[48]

He reminds me of Ronald. Ronald was a tenant farmer who never had gone to church. Words were not his strong suit either. His wife, Betty, had come to the spring revival at the invitation of their landlord. A few weeks later she came to faith during that period I mentioned in chapter 1. When we began to meet for discipling she asked me if I did marriage counseling. She and Ronald were on the brink.

The three of us had been meeting for five weeks when my office phone rang. It was Ronald.

> "Preacher, can I come see you?"
> "Sure Ronald, come on over. What's it about?"
> "I don't know—I can't say—I just don't know."

When he arrived I asked him what was on his mind.

> "Well, I . . . I was out plowin' the 'baccer,[49] and I got to the end of a row, and . . . it was like . . . I don't know . . . somethin' was there . . . it was . . . it said . . . I gotta change! Was that God . . . talkin'? . . . to *me*?!"

In the following months Ronald came to the Bible study I led for the new Christians—him, me and a bunch of women. One day I stopped by the farm during the tobacco harvest. After we had chatted a bit Ronald said,

> "I'm glad you showed up. I been wantin' to talk to you about them Bible studies. They don't do much for me. I feel kinda bad about it, 'cause I know I'm s'posed to get something out of it, but . . . I don't. God don't feel close to me there. It's out here on the tractor or sittin' in my tree stand that I feel him."

Over the years I have known men like Ronald who came to faith, came to the group Bible studies for a while, gave them up, and yet had the gall to continue to grow stronger in their faith and connection to God. That reality has bothered me. It flies in the face of all my training, from InterVarsity Christian Fellowship to seminary and beyond. Then it hit me; all my training was designed for and led by people like me—intellectual, relationally oriented, word-merchants. These men were all obviously Action Men. You might even say they were brutes. Yet despite their not having language to describe it, God

---

48. Zwart, "Brother Lawrence," para 6.
49. That's "tobacco" to us Yankees—and this time I'm not talking baseball.

was connecting with them on an intuitive level and changing them from the inside out. And that flies in the face of the common belief about men.

The stereotype in most people's heads is that *women* are intuitive—men are clueless. Perhaps one source of that belief is that men are less able to read the emotional cues on women's faces.[50] Another source may be that most men don't have the language capabilities of women. Psychologist Susan Pinker says, "The female edge in verbal fluency appears so early in life and it is so consistent over time and across cultures that the science of sex differences must be involved."[51] Once again neuroscience helps us understand why. Most men (probably the Action Men) have less developed language centers than women. They actually have eleven percent fewer neurons in the areas of the brain that process language.[52]

We could argue about why this is—whether nature or nurture or, the current favorite, an evolutionary process dating from our prehistoric hunter-gatherer ancestors. We could discuss how to bring these men out of the Stone Age and remake them in our Communication Age image. We could even discuss whether, or to what degree, doing so is necessary for them to know God and fulfill their place in God's plan. But the prior and more important question is, "Has God left Godself without a witness among them?" The galling reality of these men who experienced God non-verbally says, "No! God spoke to these men and they heard—intuitively." Oh, they read their Bibles. They had devotions. But where they really connected with God was in the midst of doing something else, usually outdoors, often away from buildings and cars and roads or anything made by human hands. Rather than insisting that such men must become verbally fluent to become spiritual, we need to learn from their intuitive grasp of God's presence. Rather than discounting such men as non-spiritual we need to learn from them.

We need to spend more time in God's creation rather than inside humankind's creations. In God's creation we shrink. We are more likely to see our place in God's plan. Take John the Baptist. He didn't just visit the wilderness; he *lived* there, facing the challenge of living off the land. He had been the religious rock star everyone wanted to see and many wanted to follow.

50. Schiffer, et al., using "a modified version of the reading the mind in the eyes test in combination with functional magnetic resonance imaging (fMRI) . . . found that men actually had twice as many problems in recognizing emotions from female as compared to male eyes and that these problems were particularly associated with a lack of activation in limbic regions of the brain. . . . Our findings highlight the function of the amygdala in the affective [i.e. emotional] component of theory of mind (ToM) and in empathy, and provide further evidence that men are substantially less able to infer [i.e. intuit] mental states expressed by women . . . " ("Why Don't Men," 1).

51. Pinker, *The Sexual Paradox*, 37.

52. Witelson, "Women Have Greater," 577.

Yet when Jesus came along and people began flocking to him instead, John harbored no jealousy towards him—despite encouragement from those around him to do so (John 3:22–26).

> To this John replied, "A person can receive only what is given them from heaven. You yourselves can testify that I said, 'I am not the Messiah but am sent ahead of him.' The bride belongs to the bridegroom. The friend who attends the bridegroom waits and listens for him, and is full of joy when he hears the bridegroom's voice. That joy is mine, and it is now complete. He must become greater; I must become less" (John 3:27–30).

When we spend all our time inside our creations it is easy to be impressed with ourselves. Rather than seeking our place in *God's* plan, we end up asking God for what we want in *our* plan. Richard Rohr says,

> In the five-day Men's Rites of Passage—that was a focus of my work for fifteen years—so many men felt that prayers and rituals inside of human-scale buildings were rather domesticated and controlled. They often perceived that the salvation offered inside these artificial constructs was also "small" and churchy. Almost without exception, the greatest breakthroughs for our men occurred during extended times of silence in nature, where the human and the merely verbal were not in control, or during rituals that were raw and earthy. Remember that good ritual, like art itself, merely imitates nature.[53]

I am not saying we should abandon our church buildings and go sit in silence in the woods every Sunday. We should, however, creatively consider ways to make space for silence and intuitive connection. One church I served set up a large roughhewn cross (think seven foot tall railroad ties) outside the entrance to the sanctuary for Holy Thursday and Good Friday services. Their tradition had been to beautify the cross by covering it completely with flowers for Easter morning. We decided that year to, instead, set up the cross just inside the altar rail for the Good Friday service. We placed 10-penny nails and several hammers in the trays on the altar rail. After a lay leader read the account of the events Good Friday, I stood and said,

> "What Jesus did on this day, he did for each of us. He went to the cross to set each of us free from our sin. When I look at this cross I know my sin put him there."

---

53. Rohr, "Creation Is the Primary Cathedral," para 5.

I picked up a nail and a hammer, went to the cross, and drove it in three booming strokes. A baritone soloist sang, a capella, the first verse of "What Wondrous Love Is This?" as I knelt at the altar. Then I stood and said,

> "The altar is open if you wish to come and pray. If you prefer to kneel or sit and pray where you are, you are free to do so. The nails and hammers are for your use should you choose. Stay as long as you like. Leave when you are ready. Please preserve the silence for those who stay. Do not speak until you leave the parking lot."

The silence was not complete. The sound of booming hammers, sometimes singly, sometimes severally, resonated through the sanctuary and through my soul, accompanied by the quiet sound of tears. It was two hours before the last person left. He stood beside me as I locked the church doors.

"There are not words," he said, and walked to his car.

When it comes to church talk, more often than we realize, less is more.[54]

---

54. When my daughter read the first draft of this chapter she sent me her memory of that night: "Though it was twenty years ago, I remember the service vividly. The church was dimly lit, the cross laid out in front, not hoisted vertically as we are accustomed to seeing it, but horizontally as if waiting for Jesus to be nailed to it. In the semi-darkness, Dad described in graphic detail the reality of what happens to the body during the most painful method of execution ever conceived, crucifixion. We then listened with fresh and horrified ears to the scriptures describing the events from the Last Supper until Jesus's burial. In silent prayer, we contemplated the meaning of Jesus's sacrifice, taking responsibility for our sins even as we were absolved of them with each pounding of a nail.

That night I dreamt so vividly that I can only describe it as a vision. It was a mob scene, one in which the lives of my friends, family, and community and were threatened. Someone had to die. I volunteered to be crucified in their place as did my father and we were each hung on a cross side by side. At our feet were my mother and brother, just as Mary and John were at the feet of Jesus. There were faceless others by their side, all weeping and pleading. But Dad and I were perfectly happy to make this sacrifice for our family and those faceless others. While we were in physical pain, the most painful part of the experience were the tears shed by my mother and brother. Overriding the entire dream was an enormous feeling of terrible, beautiful, awesome love.

Surprisingly, I did not start awake from this dream as one does from a nightmare. I woke with a new sense of understanding of myself and God's vision of and for me. I understood that I, like my father, have the self-sacrificial spirit of a martyr. That I would go to such lengths for others shocked me even while I understood the truth of that vision. What I did not understand until later was the critical role of my mother and brother and the rest of the community portrayed. Not until recent years have I understood how much I need the support of those at my feet.

That this vision has continued to teach me, even twenty years later, speaks to its authenticity. But how did I become so blessed as to receive it? I believe it is because the act of driving a nail into the cross allowed me to connect with the *reality* of the Crucifixion. Reading or listening to the story is very different experience from actually

THE PENDULUM IS THE PITS

"Less is more" is something to bear in mind when it comes to responding to the missing men as well. The history of the church's efforts to reach the men who had gone missing is littered with pendulum swings to the extremes. Take, for example, the medieval priests who took on concubines or illicit marriages, participated in jousts, and joined in the hard drinking at the taverns at least in part to convince the men in their communities of their manhood.[55] Or consider how the growing momentum of Muscular Christianity and a concurrent urge for the recovery of manliness in the late nineteenth to early twentieth century set the stage for many churches' acceptance of World War I as a "Holy War," despite the presence of Christians in opposing trenches.[56] Such extremes are not limited to the male side of the swing. We saw in chapter 3 how the pendulum has swung in the other direction in times of spiritual awakenings, to the point that the Blessed Margaret Ebner[57] could use highly erotic language to describe her relationship with Christ, apparently without batting an eye.

For most of its existence the church has swung between the poles commonly thought of as masculinity and femininity. In her book, *Dying to Be Men: Gender and Language in Early Christian Martyr Texts*, L. Stephanie Cobb, notes that the early church was adamant about portraying the martyrs, including women, as masculine:

> "This Christian identity based on socially agreed upon virtues was bolstered by the comparison of Christians who would not be expected to embody masculine ideals—specifically, the elderly, the young, women, and slaves—with non-Christians at the peak of manliness. In each case it is the Christian who displays superior masculinity. I am not suggesting that the articulation of any one of these characteristics alone is enough to sustain a masculine social identity, but the portrait of the Christian

---

picking up a nail and driving it into a cross, knowing how such a nail once tore through the flesh and bone of Jesus. Sitting in silence but for the pounding of hammer and nail in a darkened room with the broken, bleeding, weeping Body of Christ allowed me to experience a crucifixion within myself, drawing me so close to God that I could hear his voice in my dreams."

55. Thibodeaux, "Man of the Church," 387–94.

56. Burleigh, *Earthly Powers*, 447–51. The current men's movement's almost exclusive connection with conservative Christianity and politics makes me wonder if we aren't repeating history rather than learning from it.

57. Beatified in 1979 by Pope John Paul II.

> martyr that emerges from the composite picture—including the comparison to non-Christians—is strikingly masculine."[58]

The church in that age almost certainly had no problem reaching not only Action Men, but Action Women as well. But with the church's shift from persecuted to privileged came a swing from masculine to feminine. And so the perpetual pendulum began.

> According to Erich Fromm[59] and many other cultural analysts of religion, "Mary with the infant Jesus became the symbol of the Catholic Middle Ages." . . . Early Christianity was militant and rebellious against authority, Roman or otherwise, and was father-centered.[60] However, the more important point is that the dominance of the cult of Mary coincided with the Dark Ages and with the humanism of the Renaissance, eras that have been described by historians as decidedly more feminine, passive, and anti-scientific than was the Enlightenment that followed.[61]

Unlike Edgar Allan Poe's pendulum that swung *deeper* with each pass,[62] the danger of the gender pendulum in the church is the *width* of its swing. When the swing gets to the extremes, it takes us shallow (see Figure 9.1). Responding to the missing men through men's ministries that rely on male stereotypes does that. I have seen men's retreats with fifty mounted deer heads on the front wall as well as motorcycles, NFL paraphernalia, athletic equipment, fishing tackle and more surrounding the speakers' platform. When I have asked non-church men what they thought of it, the following statement best sums up their response: "It's okay. Better than a bunch of flowers. But, somebody's trying too hard."

The same thought came to mind when I walked into a Christian bookstore recently. A ten-foot long, five-foot tall set of shelves confronted me. Three quarters of it was filled with books whose covers were emblazoned with swords and shields, and "WARRIOR this" and "BATTLE that" in the titles. As I walked through the aisles to the back of the store the theme was repeated over and over. I finally picked up one of the many different warrior/battle prayer guides and flipped it open about halfway through. The first paragraph I saw was about the emotional hurts of the reader and contained two hedges, three qualifiers, and three intensifiers (remember chapter 7?).

58. Cobb, *Dying to Be Men*, 62.
59. Fromm, *The Dogma of Christ*, 69.
60. Ibid. See also Schoenfeld, "Militant and Submissive Religions" 1987, 1989, 1992.
61. Schoenfeld and Mestrovic, "With Justice and Mercy," 373–74.
62. Poe, "The Pit and the Pendulum," 202–203.

Scanning through the book showed more of the same. So here we have a book whose cover shouts, "a book for guys," but whose content reads like a book for women. Using the latest buzzwords while continuing to talk about the same things the same way we have been for forty years will not reach the men who have been voting with their feet. It will just confirm *their* stereotype of church men as a bunch of wannabes. The use of stereotypes begets a response of stereotypes. It keeps the conversation shallow.

Pulling Back from the Poles

If we are to become more effective in ministering among Action Men and Action Women we are going to have to pull back from the extremes. That will be difficult because increasingly over the last four decades the church's attention has been drawn *to* the extremes—to the exceptions at the ends of the distribution. In this the church is merely a reflection of the changes that have been taking place in American culture as a whole. The words "normal," "normative," and "majority" have taken on negative connotations. "Abnormal" has become taboo and been replaced with "special," "exceptional," and "challenged." Such changes are an expression of the so-called "feminization" of American culture that Strauss and Howe say occurs in the period after a spiritual awakening,[63] like the one we had in the late sixties and early seventies. They are also an expression of the concern for inclusiveness that we have seen is the focus of women's attention. What we have failed to recognize is that our attention on including the extremes has caused us to miss, or lose, many in the middle.

Let's look at the swing of the pendulum in a different way. Think of its arc as an inverted normal distribution—a bell curve on its head. (See Figure 9.1.)

---

63. Strauss and Howe, *Generations*, 102.

Figure 9.1: The Pulled Back Pendulum

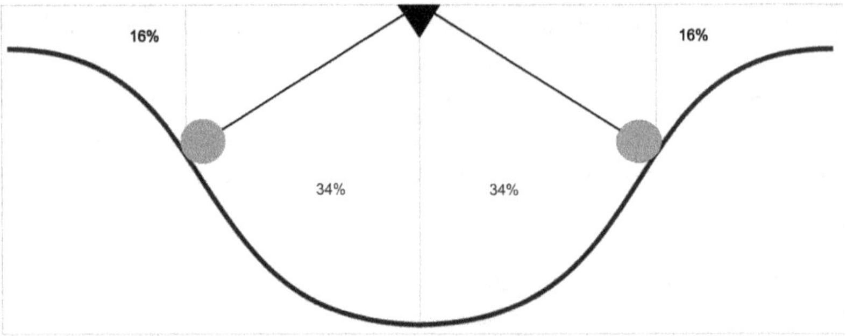

When we minister at the extreme ends of the swing—with an over-emphasis on either the actional and or the relational end—our effectiveness is limited to those who identify with that pole—that's sixteen percent out at either end. Those in the middle say, "That's not for me." For example, a woman who is an elementary school counselor posted in one of our discussions on our "Church Without Balls" Facebook page, "I love my church because the men there are real men—they can cry, they can hug—they can be themselves." The immediate response by a man who has become a "done"[64] was, "Why is it that the definition of being a real man has become being more feminine?" In contrast, some of the staff members from the Pro Football Hall of Fame were in the booth next to Dad and I during our weekly lunch at the sports bar. All of a sudden over the din of the restaurant I heard, "... he asked ... to his church. [Quiet exchanges from others.] I'm a real *guy*. [Quiet exchanges from others.] Yeah, you want the one up there on the platform to be a real guy ... " This man is not your stereotypical jock. He is a congenial person who connects well to everyone in the restaurant whenever he is there. But his "real guy" was clearly different from the elementary school counselor's "real man." He is a man in the middle section of that inverted distribution.[65] But the man on the platform—the embodiment of the church's relational orientation—didn't connect with him.

When we pull back from the poles—whether it is the relational pole or the actional pole—it enables us to minister more effectively to that huge majority, the Action Men plus the Action Women in the middle section of the distribution—that sixty-eight percent you see in the center section in Figure 9.1. How do we do that? As you may have guessed, that is what this whole book has been about. We need to put less emphasis on surface expressions, and more on substance. Having a man-friendly setting for a gathering

---

64. As in "with the church."

65. Remember chapter 3? Sixty-nine percent outside the church are Action Men.

of men—like holding worship in a gym, or group meetings in the driveway around a portable fire pit—is okay as far as it goes. But it has to go beyond that to the character and content of our talk. Anything less is stopping short, like being satisfied with niceness.

If our vocabulary and our themes and our sentence structures do not connect with the Action Man, we will merely inoculate any who do come because of the setting. They will never return, or they'll only show up for the calf fries. The same holds true for mixed gatherings—be they worship, discipleship, administrative, or missional—as well as for personal conversations with individuals or groups. As we expand our vocabulary (chapters 3 and 4); as we soak in those "masculine themes" rather than swimming in a sea of verbal estrogen (chapters 5 and 6); as we rebuild our sentence structures (chapters 7 and 8) so that they reflect our confidence in the God who loves us infinitely and demonstrates it decisively; we will find ourselves connecting, going deep, and engaging in ministry with Action Men and Women. In the process the church will recover its soul. Church talk will no longer make them walk. It will help them act, and in that action connect with the God who is impacting a hurting world with powerful, incarnational, resurrection love.

Appendix A

Research on Gender across the Cultures

Antill, John K., and Graeme Russell. "The Factor Structure Of The Bem Sex-Role Inventory: Method And Sample Comparisons." *Australian Journal of Psychology* 34, no. 2 (1982).
Archer, John. "The Relationship between Gender-role Measures: A Review." *British Journal of Social Psychology* 28, no. 2 (1989) 173–84.
Bem, Sandra L., and Steven A. Lewis. "Sex Role Adaptability: One Consequence of Psychological Androgyny." *Journal of Personality and Social Psychology* 31, no. 4 (1975) 634–43.
Bem, Sandra L. "On the Utility Of Alternative Procedures for Assessing Psychological Androgyny." *Journal of Counseling and Clinical Psychology*, 45, no. 2 (1977) 196–205.
———. "Gender Schema Theory: A Cognitive Account of Sex Typing." *Psychological Review* 88, no. 4 (1981) 354–64.
Campbell, John. *Honour, Family, and Patronage: A Study of Institutions and Moral Values in a Greek Mountain Community.* Oxford: Clarendon, 1964.
Carlsson, M., & Magnusson, E. "Construct Validation of the Bem Sex Role Inventory." *Scandinavian Journal of Psychology,* 21 (1980) 27–31.
Crapanzano, Vincent. *Tuhami: Portrait of a Moroccan.* Chicago: University of Chicago Press, 1980.
Davis, John. *People of the Mediterranean: An Essay in Comparative Social Anthropology.* London: Routledge and Kegan Paul, 1977.
Denich, Bette. "Sex and power in the Balkans." In *Women, Culture, and Society,* edited by Michelle Rosaldo and Louise Lamphere, 243–62. Stanford: Stanford University Press, 1974.
Donnelly, Kristin, and Jean M. Twenge. "Masculine and Feminine Traits on the Bem Sex-Role Inventory, 1993–2012: A Cross-Temporal Meta-Analysis." *Sex Roles,* 2016.
Fitzclarence, L., and C. Hickey. "Real Footballers Don't Eat Quiche: Old Narratives in New Times." *Men and Masculinities* 4, no. 2 (2001) 118–39.
Geertz, Hildred. "The meanings of family ties." In *Meaning and Order in Moroccan society,* edited by Clifford Geertz, H. Geertz, and L. Rosen, 315–86. New York: Cambridge University Press, 1979.

Gilmore, David D. *Manhood in the Making: Cultural Concepts of Masculinity.* New Haven, CT: Yale University, 1990.

Godelier, Maurice. *The Making of Great Men.* Cambridge: Cambridge University Press, 1986.

Gough, H. G. & Heilbrun, A. B. Jr. *The Adjective Checklist Manual:* 1983 edition. Palo Alto, CA: Consulting Psychologists Press, 1983.

Gutmann, Matthew C. Trafficking in Men: The Anthropology of Masculinity. *Annual Review of Anthropology,* 26, (1997) 385–409.

Heilbrun, A. B., Jr. Androgyny as Type and Androgyny as Behavior: Implications for Gender Schema in Males and Females. *Sex roles,* 14(3/4), (1986) 123–39.

Herzfeld, Michael. *The Poetics of Manhood: Contest and Identity in a Cretan Mountain Village.* Princeton: Princeton University Press, 1985.

Hughes, R. N. "Bem Sex Role Inventory Performance in Students: Comparisons between New Zealand, Australian and American Samples." *New Zealand Psychologist,* 8, (1979) 61–6.

Leaper, C. & Ayres, M. M. "A Meta-Analytic Review of Gender Variations in Adults' Language Use: Talkativeness, Affiliative Speech, and Assertive Speech." *Personality & Social Psychology Review,* 11, no. 4, (2007) 328–63.

López-Sáez, Mercedes, J. Fransisco Morales, and Ana Lisbona. "Evolution of Gender Stereotypes in Spain: Traits and Roles." *The Spanish Journal of Psychology,* 11, no. 2 (2008) 609–17.

Mahalingam, Ramaswami. and Sundari Balan. "Culture, Son Preference, and Beliefs About Masculinity." *Journal Of Research On Adolescence,* 18, no. 3, (2008) 541–53.

Maloney, P., J. Wilkof, and F. Dambrot. "Androgyny across Two Cultures: United States and Israel." *Journal of Cross-Cultural Psychology* 12, no. 1 (1981) 95–102.

Martin, Harry J., & Nerella V. Ramanaiah, "Confirmatory Factor Analysis of the Bem Sex Role Inventory." *Psychological Reports,* 62, no. 2 (1988) 343–50.

Maznah, I. R., & Choo, P. F. "The Factor Structure of the Bem Sex Role Inventory." *International Journal of Psychology* 21, (1986) 31–41.

Myers, Anita M., & Gail Gonda. "Utility of the Masculinity-Femininity Construct: Comparison of Traditional and Androgyny Approaches." *Journal of Personality and Social Psychology* 43, no. 3 (1982) 514–22.

Newman, Matthew L., Carla J. Groom, Lori D. Handelman, and James W. Pennebaker. "Gender Differences in Language Use: An Analysis of 14,000 Text Samples." *Discourse Processes* 45, no. 3 (2008) 211–36.

Nilan, Pam. Contemporary Masculinities and Young Men in Indonesia." *Indonesia and the Malay World,* 37, no. 109, (2009) 327–44.

Oswalt, P. A. "An Examination of the Current Usefulness of the Bem Sex-Role Inventory." *Psychological Report:* 94, no. 3 (2004) 1331–6.

Özkan, Türker and Timo Lajunen. "Masculinity, Femininity, and the Bem Sex Role Inventory in Turkey." *Sex Roles* 52, no. 1–2 (2005) 103–10.

Pedhazur, Elazar J., and Toby J. Tetenbaum. "Bem Sex Role Inventory: A Theoretical and Methodological Critique." *Journal of Personality and Social Psychology* 37, no. 6 (1979) 996–1016.

Peng, T. K. "Construct Validation of the Bem Sex Role Inventory in Taiwan." *Sex Roles* 55, no. 11–12 (2006) 843–51.

Reed-Sanders, Delores., Richard A. Dodder, R. A., and Lucia Webster. "The Bem Sex Role Inventory across Three Cultures." *The Journal of Social Psychology* 125, no. 4 (1985) 523–5.

Schenk, J., & Heinisch, R. "Self-Descriptions by Means of Sex-Role Scales and Personality Scales: A Critical Evaluation Of Recent Masculinity and Femininity Scales." *Personality and Individual Differences* 7, no 2 (1986) 161–8.

Spence. Janet. T. "Gender-Related Traits and Gender Ideology: Evidence for a Multifactorial Theory." *Journal of Personality and Social Psychology* 64, no. 6 (1993) 624–35.

Spence. J. T., & Helmreich. R. L. *Masculinity and femininity: Their Psychological Dimensions, Correlates, and Antecedents.* Austin: University of Texas Press. 1978.

Spencer, Paul. *Nomads in Alliance: Symbiosis and Growth among the Rendille and Samburu of Kenya.* London: Oxford University Press. 1973.

Sugihara, Yoko, and Emiko Katsurada. "Gender-Role Personality Traits in Japanese Culture." *Psychology of Women Quarterly* 24, no. 4 (2000) 309–18.

Tabar, R. "'Habiibs' in Australia: Language, Identity and Masculinity." *Journal of Intercultural Studies* 28, no. 2 (2007) 157–72.

Williams, John E. and Deborah L. Best. *Sex and Psyche: Gender and Self Viewed Cross-Culturally.* Newbury Park, CA: Sage. 1990.

Williams, J. E., Satterwhite, R. C., & Best D. L. "Pancultural Gender Stereotypes Revisited: The Five Factor Model." *Sex Roles* 40, nos. 7/8, (1999) 513–25.

Wilson, David, John McMaster, Ruth Greenspan, Lillian Mboyi, Thabis Ncube, Babus Sibanda. "Cross-cultural Validation of the Bem Sex Role Inventory in Zimbabwe." *Personality and Individual Differences* 11, no. 7 (1990) 651–6.

Yan, Xiumei, Meifang Wang, and Qing Zhang. "Effects Of Gender Stereotypes On Spontaneous Trait Inferences and The Moderating Role of Gender Schematicity: Evidence from Chinese Undergraduates." *Social Cognition*, 30, no. 2 (2012) 220–31.

Yim, Jennifer Young, and Ramaswami Mahalingam. "Culture, Masculinity, and Psychological Well-Being in Punjab, India." *Sex Roles* 55, no. 9–10 (2006) 715–24.

Appendix B

Perceptions of Christians

RATIONALE

THE CONSISTENCY WITH WHICH many "masculine" and "feminine" items have loaded on the instrumental/assertive/dominant and expressive/nurturant/submissive factors, respectively, makes it possible to apply this continuum and its items to the question of people's perceptions of Christians. If it is true that being a Christian means being more feminine and/or less masculine, it should be revealed when people rate these gender-related items in terms of their perceptions of Christians. That is, if being a Christian means being feminine then those items rated "most Christian" should be predominantly feminine. If being a Christian also means being less masculine then the items rated "least Christian" should be predominantly masculine. If, on the other hand, gender is not an issue in people's perceptions of Christians then there should be no consistent effect in the rating of the gender items.

In addition to this main effect, it is also possible to compare churched and unchurched person's perceptions, as well as those of men and women. With regard to the latter, if psychological sex type affects persons' responses to gender-related issues and if perception of Christians is such an issue, then it should be revealed in the rating of the items. We should see sextyped women and cross-sextyped and androgynous men aligned together while sextyped men and cross-sextyped and androgynous women should be aligned together.

METHOD

Q Methodology[1] was selected for this study for several reasons. First, it allows the respondent great freedom. S/he is not limited to a numeric scale but rather is able to place items in a quasi-normal distribution wherever s/he chooses. Second, the respondent is able to make comparisons between items and prioritize them according to his/her perceptions, rather than those of the researcher. This will be of great help in answering question of the extensiveness of the feminine Christian stereotype. Third, as a factor analytic approach to analyzing people as variables, Q enables us to discern various patterns of perceptions of Christians, i.e. types of perceivers. This will be of help in discerning possible differences among men and women, psychological sex types, and churched and unchurched persons. Fourth, since Q is concerned with the discovery of types of perceivers rather than representation of the population, large sampling techniques are not necessary.

SAMPLE

Participants were undergraduate and graduate students at a major Midwestern university—twenty men and sixteen women, ranging in age from eighteen to forty-three with a mean age of twenty-five years. Fifteen of the respondents were Catholic, seventeen were Protestant, and two indicated no church affiliation. Thirteen were unchurched (defined as attending twice a quarter or less), while twenty-three were churched (defined as attending once a month or more). Of the thirteen unchurched respondents, ten were male and three were female. Of the twenty-three churched respondents, thirteen were female and ten were male.

PROCEDURE

Out of some 250 adjectives and descriptive phrases used in the sex role and sex stereotyping literature sixty were selected to form the Q deck. These items were selected to form a balanced masculine-feminine design (thirty masculine and thirty feminine items). Because many of the descriptions offered by unchurched men in interviews were negative in spite of the dominance of Christianity in North American culture, the author decided to include a positive-negative dimension in the Q deck. For both masculine

---

1. Stephenson, *The Study of Behavior*, 1953.

and feminine items sixteen positives, nine negatives, and five neutrals were selected (See Table B.1).

Table B.1: Q Deck Items by Gender and Valence

MASCULINE POSITIVE	FEMININE POSITIVE
Take a stand	Devote self to others
Influential	Trusting
Act as a leader	Understanding
Skilled in business	Polite
Dynamic	Aware of others' feelings
Independent	Devout
Strong	Modest
Competent	Have a strong conscience
Logical	Warm
Self-confident	Gentle
Assertive	Home-oriented
Forceful	Sociable
Manly	Cooperative
Adventurous	Sincere
Active	Sensitive to others' needs
Know ways of the world	Helpful
MASCULINE NEGATIVE	FEMININE NEGATIVE
Selfish	Self-punishing
Cynical	Fickle
Argumentative	Wimpy
Feel superior	Easily influenced
Use harsh language	Need approval
Lack tact	Dependent
Dominant	Weak
Mischievous	Naive
Stern	Strong need for security
MASCULINE NEUTRAL	FEMININE NEUTRAL
Like math and science	Submissive
Interested in sex	Express tender feelings
Competitive	Sentimental

| Ambitious | Meditative |
| Aggressive | Cautious |

Each subject was asked to Q-sort the items on the following criterion: "If I were a good Christian, I would (be or do) ... " giving a rank of eleven to the three items s/he considered most like what they would be as a good Christian, a rank of ten to the four items s/he considered to be next most like what they would be as a good Christian, and so on to complete the following forced distribution:

Rank	11	10	9	8	7	6	5	4	3	2	1
Items	3	4	5	6	8	8	8	6	5	4	3

These data were analyzed using Q factor analysis. A principle axis solution with unities in the diagonal was used. The resulting factors were rotated to an orthogonal (Varimax) solution.

RESULTS

The principle axis solution resulted in three factors that accounted for 74 percent of the total variance. After rotation, the three factors individually accounted for 30 percent, 17 percent, and 27 percent of the total variance. Twenty-six percent of the total variance remained uncorrelated. Of the variance held in common by the three factors, 40 percent was accounted for by Factor One, 23 percent by Factor Two, and 37 percent by Factor Three. This solution divided the subjects into three groups or types. Table B.2 gives the subject assignments by type together with each subject's sex and factor loading.

Table B.2: Subject Assignments with Factor Weights by Type

Type 1 (F=11 M=5)			Type 2 (M=5)			Type 3 (M=10 F=5)		
ID	Sex	Factor Weight	ID	Sex	Factor Weight	ID	Sex	Factor Weight
3	F	1.2132	1	M	1.0586	2	F	0.7907
5	M	1.3679	7	M	4.2913	4	M	1.0781
9	M	0.8560	17	M	0.8474	6	M	0.6941
11	F	1.0994	25	M	0.8549	8	M	1.1083
12	F	.0419	27	F	1.3913	10	F	0.8751
13	F	1.6444				14	M	1.0964
15	M	1.2998				18	M	1.4885
16	F	2.3206				19	M	1.3533
20	F	1.0160				21	M	0.6374
22	F	1.4797				26	F	0.9980
23	F	1.1179				28	M	2.8193
24	M	1.3626				29	M	1.0332
30	F	0.9618				32	F	0.7126
31	F	0.5707				34	M	0.7335
33	F	1.1422				36	F	1.7998
35	F	0.7691						

As may be seen from Table B.Three, the three types are highly correlated, with Types One and Three sharing a .885 correlation and Type Two sharing a .689 and a .682 correlation with Types One and Three respectively. This high correlation is further reflected in the fact that a whopping forty-three out of the total sixty items emerge as consensus items, meaning that for those items the average z-scores in each type are within one standard deviation of the average z-scores in the other two types. (See Table B.4.)

Table B.3: Correlations between Types

	Type 2	Type 3
Type 1	0.689	0.885
Type 2		0.682

Table B.4: Forty-three Consensus Items and Average Z-Scores[2] across All Types
(Sextype refers to the gender and valence of each item.)

ITEM	SEX-TYPE	Z SCORE
MOST LIKE A GOOD CHRISTIAN		
Sensitive to others' needs	F+	1.743
Aware of others' feelings	F+	1.681
Trusting	F+	1.582
Devote myself to others	F+	1.469
Understanding	F+	1.381
Sincere	F+	1.372
Devout	F+	1.277
Helpful	F+	1.205
Gentle	F+	1.043
Express tender feelings	Fo	1.024
LIKE A GOOD CHRISTIAN		
Cooperative	F+	0.931
Warm	F+	0.908
Polite	F+	0.857
Sentimental	Fo	0.793
Home-oriented	F+	0.608
Modest	F+	0.578
Sociable	F+	0.475
Meditative	Fo	0.427
Active	M+	0.291

2. A z-score shows where an item lies along a continuum. The closer the number is to zero, the more in the middle it is. The larger the number, whether positive or negative, the more toward the end. So, a z-score of 1.743 is at the "most like" end, and z-score of −1.935 is at the "most NOT like" end of the continuum.

NOT LIKE A GOOD CHRISTIAN		
Logical	M+	-0.019
Know the ways of the world	M+	-0.025
Ambitious	Mo	-0.052
Dynamic	M+	-0.108
Cautious	Fo	-0.142
Assertive	M+	-0.162
Skilled in business	M+	-0.214
Like math and science	Mo	-0.396
Competitive	Mo	-0.437
Manly	M+	-0.442
Adventurous	M+	-0.446
Wimpy	F-	-0.634
Stern	M-	0.655
Dominant	M-	-0.744
Aggressive	Mo	-0.934
MOST NOT LIKE A GOOD CHRISTIAN		
Fickle	F-	-1.037
Feel superior	M-	-1.093
Lack tact	M-	-1.284
Forceful	M+	-1.462
Mischievous	M-	-1.464
Cynical	M-	-1.625
Selfish	M-	-1.917
Use harsh language	M-	-1.935

DISCUSSION

The Stereotypical Christian

The prime area of concern in this study is the general consensus of how people perceive Christians, or the stereotypical Christian, if you will. Since this is our concern, it is logical to look first at the forty-three consensus items. These represent the perceptions of Christians shared across all three types. A review of Table B.5 quickly reveals two important elements in the common perception of Christians. First, with only two exceptions all items identified as "like a good Christian" (z-scores greater than zero) and all those identified as most like a good Christian (z-scores 1.00 or greater) are feminine. In contrast, with only Three exceptions all items identified as "not like a good Christian" (z-scores less than zero) and all but one of those identified as most unlike a good Christian (z-scores -1.00 or less) are masculine.

Clearly the stereotypical Christian (a good one at any rate) is decidedly feminine. It cannot be said from this data, however, that being a Christian means being less masculine, at least in the positive sense. It appears that with regard to the consensus items, the positive masculine characteristics are perceived as not especially like or unlike a good Christian since, though almost wholly on the "not like" side of the distribution, they are all less than .5 standard deviation from the mean. On the other hand, it can be said that the stereotypical Christian is not masculine in the negative sense, since all but one of the items identified as most unlike a good Christian are masculine, and all but one are negative.

All this raises the second element in the common perception of Christians: social positiveness. There is a strong movement from negative to positive valence as one progresses from those items identified as most unlike a good Christian to those identified as most like a good Christian. Given the frequency with which Christians had been described in negative terms by unchurched male interviewees, the author did not anticipate this positive movement to be quite so robust.

Four factors may help to explain this effect. First, a higher proportion of the respondents (64 percent) were churched than was anticipated. We would expect perceptions of Christians by churched people to be positively biased. Second, as mentioned above, Christianity is a strong influence in North American culture and it remains socially desirable to be Christian in one sense or another. Third, this effect may have been enhanced by having the respondents perform the Q-sort egocentrically. Focusing attention on what "I would be like if I were a good Christian" undoubtedly raised the salience of social desirability. This was done in order to overcome resistance to "stereotyping people," a problem which surfaces frequently in stereotyping studies. However, it appears in retrospect to have been a trade-off. The same may be said for the fourth factor—the specification of "a good Christian" rather than simply "a Christian" as the sorting criterion. The rationale for doing this was, again, to overcome resistance to stereotyping. But the presence of the word "good" would naturally have given primacy to those items that were positively valenced.

The question still remains, however, why were only feminine items chosen on the positive end of the distribution and masculine items almost exclusively chosen on the negative end. Why were these particular items chosen and others excluded? A review of the defining consensus items (those with average z-scores whose absolute value is greater than 1.00; See Table B.5) shows that, with the exception of "devout" and "cynical," all are either directly relational or have indirect relational consequences.

Table B.5: Defining Consensus Items and Average Z-Scores across All Types (Sextype refers to the gender and valence of each item.)

ITEM	SEX-TYPE	Z SCORE
Sensitive to others' needs	F+	1.743
Aware of others' feelings	F+	1.681
Trusting	F+	1.582
Devote myself to others	F+	1.469
Understanding	F+	1.381
Sincere	F+	1.372
Devout	F+	1.277
Helpful	F+	1.205
Gentle	F+	1.043
Express tender feelings	Fo	1.024
Fickle	F-	-1.037
Feel superior	M-	-1.093
Lack tact	M-	-1.284
Forceful	M+	-1.462
Mischevious	M-	-1.464
Cynical	M-	-1.625
Selfish	M-	-1.917
Use harsh language	M-	-1.935

If we ask why negatively valenced feminine items were not included as being most unlike a good Christian we find additional evidence for this relational factor. With the exception of "fickle" all the feminine negative items are primarily psychological (e.g. "self-punishing, weak, wimpy, naïve"), whereas the masculine negative items are predominantly relational (e.g. "selfish, lack tact, use harsh language").

So, we may say that the stereotypical Christian is primarily considered relationally positive. More specifically, since the positive defining items can be conceived as applying to the nurturant portion of the expressive/nurturant/submissive dimension discussed above, and since the defining negative items can be conceived for the most part as "not nurturant" (see Table B.5), we may say that the primary element in the consensus perception (or stereotype) of a good Christian is nurturance. That is, a good Christian is "sensitive to the needs of others, aware of other's feelings, trusting, devotes him or herself to others, is understanding, sincere, devout, helpful, gentle, and expresses tender feelings." A good Christian is not, on the other hand, "fickle, forceful, mischievous, cynical, selfish, and does not feel superior, lack tact, or use harsh language."

It is worthy of note that, with the exception of "forceful" and "feel superior" none of the items that can be conceived as applying to the instrumental/assertive/dominant dimension and none of the items that can be conceived as applying to the submissive element of the expressive/nurturant/submissive dimension are to be found among the defining consensus items. We have seen that nurturance defines the consensus perception of a good Christian. We will now see that instrumentality, assertiveness, and submissiveness differentiate among the three types of perceivers.

Type ONE: The Influential Christian

Type One is comprised of eleven women and five men. Thirteen of the sixteen (ten women and three men) are churched, far and away the highest proportion (81 percent) of any of the groups. In addition to the consensus items listed above, (see Table B.4) Type One does not consider a good Christian to be stern, weak, argumentative, or easily influenced.

What differentiates Type One from both Type Two and Type Three is instrumentality. Type One perceivers consider a good Christian to be much more likely to be influential and to take a stand than Type Three perceivers (see Table B.6). When compared with Type Two perceivers they also consider a good Christian to be more likely to act as a leader, be strong, and have a strong conscience (see Table B.7). In other words, Type One perceivers expect good Christians to do something that makes a difference in the world around them.

Table B.6: Items Distinguishing between Types One and Three[3]

ITEM	TYPE 1	TYPE 3	DIFFERENCE
Influential	1.044	-0.374	1.418
Take a stand	1.357	0.173	1.183
Submissive	-0.216	-1.328	1.112
Independent	-0.276	0.901	-1.176

Table B.7: Items Distinguishing between Types One and Two

ITEM	TYPE 1	TYPE 2	DIFFERENCE
Take a stand	1.357	-0.745	2.102
Have a strong conscience	1.584	-0.330	1.914
Act as a leader	1.018	-0.443	1.461
Strong	0.705	-0.497	1.202
Influential	1.044	0.006	1.038
Dependent	-0.474	0.878	-1.352
Have a strong need for security	-0.835	0.534	-1.369
Self-punishing	-0.938	0.550	-1.488
Need approval	-0.778	0.792	-1.570
Naïve	-0.638	1.000	-1.638
Easily influenced	-1.485	0.215	-1.701

This focus on instrumentality as the defining characteristic of a type composed mostly of women appears to fly in the face of the sex role and sex stereotype research. However, when we consider that this type also has the highest proportion of churched persons, including all of the "super-churched" (those who attend more than once a week), this finding is not that surprising. Some Christians are frequently exposed to messages from sermons, church school lessons, devotional materials, small group discussions, etc. stressing the need to "stand up for Christ," or to "live a life holiness and conscience," or to "change the world." Perhaps more intriguing than the fact that Type One persons perceive Christians in this way is that Type Two

3. Distinguishing items are those items whose typal z-scores differ by greater than one standard deviation.

and Three persons do not. Either Type Twos and Threes are unaware that Christians expect this of themselves, or they do not consider them to be effective in accomplishing it. This brings us to Type Two.

Type Two: The Christian as Wimp

All five subjects who comprise this type are men. Three are moderately churched (attend 1–2 times a month), two are unchurched (one attends 1–2 times a quarter, one attends 1–2 times a year). In addition to the consensus items, Type Two considers a good Christian to be cooperative, home-oriented, and naive. Type Two does not perceive a good Christian to be interested in sex, independent, aggressive, or argumentative.

What differentiates Type Two from both Type One and Type Three is a negative evaluation of assertiveness/dominance. Type Two considers a good Christian much more likely to be dependent, naive, easily influenced, self-punishing, and to have a strong need for security and approval than does Type One (see Table B.8). In addition to these, Type Two considers a good Christian much more likely to be weak and submissive, and much less likely to be self-confident, independent, argumentative, interested in sex, and to have a strong conscience than does Type Three (see Table B.8).

Table B.8: Items Distinguishing between Types Two and Three

ITEM	TYPE 2	TYPE 3	DIFFERENCE
Dependent	0.878	-1.159	2.037
Naïve	1.000	-0.789	1.790
Need approval	0.792	-0.986	1.779
Easily influenced	0.215	-1.142	1.358
Submissive	0.008	-1.328	1.337
Weak	-0.203	-1.327	1.124
Self-confident	-0.265	0.759	-1.024
Interested in sex	-1.125	-0.027	-1.098
Argumentative	-1.756	-0.517	-1.239
Have a strong conscience	-0.330	1.510	-1.840
Independent	-1.178	0.901	-2.078

The picture that emerges from these distinguishing items is the classic stereotypical wimp. This further evidenced by the defining items (those with z-scores whose absolute value is greater than 1.00) for this type. Type Two includes more feminine items as being most like a good Christian (including one negatively valenced one: naive, and more masculine items as being most unlike a good Christian than either Type One or Type Three. For Type Two, being a Christian definitely means being more feminine and less masculine.

Type Three. The Independent Christian

Ten men and five women make up Type Three. Seven are churched (four men, Three women) and eight are unchurched (six men, two women). What differentiates Type Three is a negative evaluation of submissiveness. In addition to the consensus items, Type Three considers a good Christian not to be wimpy, easily influenced, dependent, weak, or submissive. Here we have a very different picture from Type Two. For Type Three, Christians are more likely to have a strong conscience and to be independent. Yet Type Three is not willing to go as far as Type One and say that Christians are influential.

CONCLUSIONS

The above results indicate that there is a pervasive stereotype of a good Christian. This stereotype is best described positively by "feminine" nurturing characteristics and negatively by "masculine" anti-social characteristics. This stereotype appears to be modified slightly by two factors: psychological sex type and church participation.

Psychological Sex Type (aka Gender Schematicity)

Though no measure of psychological sex type was taken, demographic data does support the conjecture that this variable did influence the subjects' responses. The first indication is simply the breakdown of men and women in the three types. Types One and Three are virtually mirror images (eleven women to five men and ten men to five women, respectively), while Type Two is exclusively male. This leads us to ask what the members of these groups have in common besides their responses to the Q-sort.

Type One is made up almost exclusively of people whose academic program is concentrated in what might be considered feminine fields, such as elementary education, home economics, family resources, and nursing. The men in Type One are all education or family resources majors, with the exception of one who is undecided. While we cannot identify people's psychological sex type on merely the basis of their academic major, it does suggest that the men in Type One may be either cross-sex-typed or androgynous.

This conjecture is strengthened by the same kind of information for Type Three. Academic majors for this type include journalism, accounting, agriculture, international relations, etc.; fields which, though changing, have been considered traditionally masculine professions. The women in Type Three are all majoring in these areas, with the exception of one math education major. Again, no hard conclusions can be drawn, but this taken together with Type Three's strong emphasis on independence and lack of submissiveness suggest that the women in Type Three may be cross-sex-typed or androgynous.

Type Two is the clearest indication of psychological sex type. All members of the group are male, all are majoring in traditionally masculine fields (engineering, agribusiness, business, and political science), and their responses are strongly stereotypical. These men are clearly masculine sex typed (high masculine, low feminine.)

Church attendance

One of the goals for this study was to begin to explore the impact that perceptions of Christians might have on church participation. What surfaced instead was the impact which church participation has on perceptions of Christians. Church attendance is obviously an influencing factor in Type One. This type was clearly the "churched group" and the perceptions of the group were both the most positive of the three types, and consistent with Christian teaching. This would account for the apparent contradiction of having masculine differentiating items ("take a stand, influential," etc.) for this apparently feminine group.

The kind of data that was anticipated was only mildly evidenced in Type Two. The most negative perceptions were reported here and church attendance was somewhat lower. This is suggestive, but not enough to draw conclusions, and therefore calls for further research.

Appendix C

Gender Schemas and Self-Schemas

RATIONALE

FOR SOME TIME THERE has been a debate about whether such a thing as a gender schema exists, or at least is measured by paper and pencil tests that purport to do so. Spence and her colleagues[1] have consistently maintained that neither the PAQ nor the BSRI measure the global constructs of masculinity and femininity, and cannot do so because they are multidimensional. This would render Bem's[2] unitary gender schema construct invalid. Bem[3] responded that gender schema theory is a theory of process, not content—that persons differentially apply their culture's definition of masculinity/femininity (whatever that may be) to themselves, some accepting it wholesale as a primary criterion for processing information, others adjusting or refusing it. Bem defended the BSRI as a measure of gender schematicity on the basis of historically consistent evidence that instrumentality and expressiveness are culturally designated in North America as expressions of masculinity and femininity, respectively. But there is no assurance that the content of the gender schema has not changed in the time since the BSRI was developed. In other words, Bem's gender schematicity may be no longer valid.

There has also been some question as to what the nature of aschematicity with regard to gender is. Bem has held that both androgynous and

---

1. Spence, et al. "Negative and Positive Components," 1979; Spence and Helmreich, "Androgyny versus Gender Schema," 1981; Spence, "Masculinity, Femininity, and Gender-Related Traits," 1984.
2. Bem, "Gender Schema Theory," 1981.
3. Bem, "The BSRI and Gender Schema Theory," 1981.

undifferentiated persons are aschematic, while Markus and her colleagues[4] and Spence[5] contend that only low androgynous (Bem's undifferentiated) persons are aschematic. We might also ask whether cross sex typed persons are aschematic as well, since they appear to apply the gender schema in reverse.

This analysis sought to answer several questions raised by the Spence/Markus-Bem debate. First, does such a thing as a gender schema exist? If there is a gender schema, it should be revealed when people rate a heterogeneous collection of attributes in terms of how feminine or masculine they are. If the same items were consistently rated as most masculine or most feminine, this would indicate the existence of a commonly held gender schema, thus supporting Bem's position. If several sets of items were consistently rated as most masculine or most feminine, this would indicate the existence of multiple gender schemas, thus supporting the Spence/Markus position. If, on the other hand, there is no consistent effect in the rating of the items, this would indicate a multidimensional definition of masculinity/femininity, again supporting the Spence/Markus position.

Second, are instrumentality and expressiveness still considered expressions of masculinity and femininity in this kinder, gentler America, or have other dimensions augmented or supplanted these? If so, instrumental/expressive items from the heterogeneous collection of attributes should be consistently rated as most masculine and most feminine, respectively. If other sets of items are equally rated as most masculine and most feminine, this would indicate augmentation of the traditional view. If other sets of items are consistently rated as more masculine and more feminine than instrumental/expressive items, this would indicate a supplanting of the traditional view.

Third, if a gender schema exists, what is its relationship to the self-schema? Are the self-schemas of most persons bipolar with respect to gender (i.e. do they simply adopt the gender schema as a template in the formation of their self-schemas, as Bem indicates), or are most people's self-schemas multidimensional with respect to gender? That is, even though they may be able to identify a cultural definition of masculinity/femininity, do they form their self-schemas separate from it and the characteristics they have selected become their personal definition of femininity or masculinity (as Spence believes)? If persons are bipolarly schematic with respect to gender there should be a close match between those items from the heterogeneous collection of attributes rated as most masculine/feminine and those items rated most/least like themselves, consistent with their sex. If persons are multidimensionally schematic with respect to gender, there should not be a close

---

4. Markus, et al., "Self-schemas and Gender," 1982.
5. Spence, "Masculinity, Femininity, and Gender-Related Traits," 1984.

match between items rated culturally masculine/feminine and those rated most/least like themselves, but the specific items "masculine" and "feminine" should be among those rated most/least like themselves consistent with their sex. If they are aschematic with respect to gender there should not be a close match between items rated culturally masculine/feminine and those rated most/least like themselves, and the specific items "masculine" and "feminine" should not be among those rated most/least like themselves.

Fourth, if a gender schema does exist, is the BSRI a valid measure of gender schematicity? According to Bem, the BSRI was designed to present an individual with a heterogeneous collection of attributes and then to assess the extent to which he or she clusters this collection into the two categories designated by the culture as masculine and feminine.[6]

Q methodology[7] provides an excellent means for assessing the validity of the BSRI, since it asks the respondent to sort the attributes into clusters along some continuum. If the BSRI is valid, the respondents' sex type classification (or at least their schematic classification) will bear a marked resemblance to any self-schema types uncovered by Q analysis. If, when given the freedom to actually sort the items into clusters for themselves, the respondents' Q types bear little or no resemblance to the BSRI types then there will be serious doubt as to the validity of the BSRI.

METHOD

This study involved comparing the results from the standard administration and median split scoring of the BSRI items (see Appendix B) with the results of the same respondents' Q sorting of the same items in order to test the validity of the BSRI. Confirmatory factor analysis using principle components with Varimax rotation was computed for the BSRI as a check of the validity of the assumption of the orthogonality of the masculine and feminine constructs. Respondents' self-schemas were measured by Q analysis of their sorts of the items along a continuum ranging from "most like me" to "least like me." Cross-tabulation of psychological sex types with Q self-schema types was performed, with Cramer's V as the measure of association. Gender schema was measured by analysis of the respondents' sorts of the BSRI items along a continuum ranging from "most masculine" to "most feminine," as defined by North American culture. The relationship between gender schema and self-schemas was analyzed by comparing the contents of the gender schema sorts with those of the self-schema sorts.

6. Bem, "Androgyny and Gender Schema Theory," 1984, 194.
7. Stephenson, *The Study of Behavior*, 1953.

SAMPLE

Participants were undergraduate and graduate students at a major Midwestern university It included 46 men and 55 women, ranging in age from 18 to 44 with a mean age of 21.5 years. Ninety-three percent of the participants were white, 6 percent black, 1 percent Asian.

PROCEDURES

The measures were administered to groups of 3–5 respondents in individual corrals in the communication laboratory. The respondents were told they were participating in "a self-perception study." They completed the BSRI first, followed by the self-schema Q sort and then the gender Q sort. The gender Q sort was held until last so as not to bias the ratings on the BSRI or the selection of the self-schema items by making gender salient. Finally, the respondents completed a brief demographic questionnaire.

Gender schematicity was operationalized in terms of the short Bem Sex Role Inventory. Using discriminant function coefficients that predicted the self-schema types in the previous analysis respondents were classified as schematic, cross-schematic, or aschematic.

RESULTS

R Analysis Results

Standard median-split scoring of the BSRI masculine and feminine scales was computed. Median for the masculine scale was 101, while the median for the feminine scale was 97. Respondents were classified (as described in chapter 3) as Feminine ($n = 32$), Masculine ($n = 32$), Androgynous ($n = 20$), and Undifferentiated ($n = 17$). As expected, cross-tabulation of these types with sex of the respondents revealed significant differences between males and females with regard to psychological sex type ($phi = .484$, $p < .000$). Women were more likely than men to be classified as Feminine (49.1 percent vs. 10.9 percent) or Androgynous (23.6 percent vs. 15. percent). Men were more likely than women to be classified as masculine (47.8 percent vs. 18.2 percent) or Undifferentiated (26.1 percent vs. 9.1 percent).

Data from the standard administration of the BSRI was factor analyzed. A minimum of four items with .60 loadings was the criterion for acceptance of a factor. A .30 loading was the minimum criteria for inclusion of additional items on a factor. Principal components analysis with Varimax rotation resulted in two factors consisting of 23 and 24 items that met the criteria (see Table C.1). Fourteen of the 23 items that loaded on Factor One are from the BSRI's feminine list. The remaining items are all from the neutral list. Six of these ("likable, happy, truthful, tactful, helpful, and reliable") are positive relational characteristics. Two of the three remaining items ("conceited and moody") are negative relational characteristics and, coincidentally, have negative loadings. Nearly all masculine items loaded on Factor Two. Three of the exceptions, "soft-spoken, shy, and does not use harsh language," come from the feminine list. They loaded negatively and suggest a retiring relational style. "Flatterable" also comes from the feminine list, and together with the neutral "flatterable," loaded positively and suggests a more flamboyant relational style.

Table C.1: Factor Analysis of the Bem Sex Role Inventory

ITEM	FACTOR 1	FACTOR 2
Feminine	.866	-.229
Tender	.743	-.048
Friendly	.732	.088
Understanding	.731	.054
Compassionate	.725	.062
Warm	.716	.043
Sensitive to others' needs	.686	-.054
Sincere	.680	.087
Eager to soothe hurt feelings	.673	.178
Gentle	.649	-.290
Likable	.613	.093
Cheerful	.578	.031
Affectionate	.576	.141
Happy	.568	-.083
Loyal	.529	.033
Sympathetic	.489	-.005
Truthful	.467	.145
Tactful	.462	.183
Conceited	-.437	.388
Helpful	.434	.111

ITEM	FACTOR 1	FACTOR 2
Moody	-.388	.314
Conventional	.355	-.030
Reliable	.318	.198
Masculine	-.025	.970
Dominant	-.191	.767
Has leadership ability	.182	.737
Acts as a leader	.050	.728
Assertive	.064	.705
Has a strong personality	.209	.654
Willing to take a stand	.202	.639
Aggressive	-.233	.636
Ambitious	.260	.541
Competitive	-.217	.536
Forceful	-.382	.521
Willing to take risks	.152	.518
Independent	.145	.479
Individualistic	-.040	.478
Makes decisions easily	-.050	.472
Self-sufficient	.258	.460
Defends own beliefs	.118	.434
Soft spoken	.035	-.416
Shy	-.318	-.405
Does not use harsh language	.193	-.398
Self-reliant	.337	.372
Theatrical	-.037	.354
Flatterable	.052	.351
Adaptable	.205	.305
Eigen Values:	9.617	8.552
Variance	16.0%	14.3%
Total Variance	=	30.3%

Q Analysis Results

Gender Schema Sort

Respondents sorted the items from the BSRI into the quasi-normal distribution from "most masculine" to "most feminine," as described in Appendix B. These data was then factor analyzed by Q analysis. While a scree test of the principal axis solution suggested the presence of four factors, and a common variance test suggested the presence of two factors, Humphrey's test indicated that only one of these factors was meaningful. Though not statistically significant, the second factor does provide some interesting information. A two-factor solution results in the discernment of two types, which are distinguished by their perception of North American culture's *evaluation* of femininity (i.e. whether negative characteristics are placed on the feminine end of the continuum). Type Two places all of the following characteristics on the feminine end: unpredictable, moody, jealous, inefficient, unsystematic, flatterable, gullible, yielding. There is a .7 or greater standard deviation between Type 2's rankings of these items and Type 1's rankings. Type One places only unsystematic, flatterable, and gullible on the feminine side, and does so only .44 standard deviation or less from the mean. In contrast, Type Two places these three items greater than one standard deviation from the mean. Neither type places any negative items on the masculine end of the continuum. What is interesting is that Type Two is 67 percent female, while Type One is 70 percent male.

The lack of a significant second factor means that all 60 items in the Q sort are consensus items. Table C.2 presents the items together with their z-score rankings, broken down into three groups of twenty for purposes of comparison with the BSRI. These results are remarkable for their almost exact match to Bem's classification of the items as masculine, feminine and neutral. The only difference between the two lists is the exchange of three of the BSRI feminine items (loyal, cheerful, and childlike) for three of its neutral items (helpful, sincere, and moody) in the Q sort.

Table C.2: Items and Descending Array of Z-Scores for Gender Schema

ITEM	Z-SCORE
Masculine	2.061
Dominant	1.897
Aggressive	1.737
Competitive	1.645
Athletic	1.464
Acts as a leader	1.416
Forceful	1.407
Assertive	1.407
Willing to take risks	1.315
Has leadership abilities	1.130
Independent	1.113
Ambitious	1.097
Strong personality	1.082
Self-sufficient	1.071
Self-reliant	1.002
Willing to take a stand	0.988
Makes decisions easily	0.803
Individualistic	0.646
Defends own beliefs	0.644
Analytical	0.629
Conceited	0.467
Solemn	0.115
Jealous	0.109
Reliable	0.106
Unsystematic	0.061
Conventional	0.052
Adaptable	0.048
Childlike	-0.061
Unpredictable	-0.080
Secretive	-0.135
Happy	-0.141

ITEM	Z-SCORE
Likable	-0.149
Tactful	-0.168
Inefficient	-0.243
Truthful	-0.261
Loyal	-0.267
Conscientious	-0.343
Theatrical	-0.364
Friendly	-0.409
Cheerful	-0.422
Shy	-0.616
Helpful	-0.644
Flatterable	-0.662
Yielding	-0.707
Moody	-0.737
Sincere	-0.806
Gullible	-0.826
Does not use harsh language	-0.884
Understanding	-1.085
Warm	-1.138
Soft-spoken	-1.184
Eager to soothe hurt feelings	-1.195
Sympathetic	-1.217
Affectionate	-1.232
Compassionate	-1.311
Loves children	-1.365
Sensitive to the needs of others	-1.459
Gentle	-1.482
Feminine	-2.034

Self-schema Sort

Respondents sorted the items from the BSRI into the quasi-normal distribution from "most like me" to "least like me" as described in chapter 3. This data was then factor analyzed by Q analysis. Both the scree test and the common variance test of the principal axis solution suggested the presence of five factors. However, Humphrey's test indicated that only three of these factors were meaningful.[8] This solution accounted for 52 percent of the total variance. After rotation, the three factors respectively accounted for 21 percent, 15 percent, and 15 percent of the total variance. Forty-eight percent of the total variance remained unexplained. Of the variance held in common by the three factors, 41 percent was accounted for by Factor One, 29 percent by Factor Two, and 30 percent by Factor Three. The three factor solution produced three types. As may be seen from Table C.3, the three types are correlated, with Types One and Three sharing a .604 correlation and Type Two sharing a .479 and a .650 correlation with Types One and Three respectively.

Table C.3: Correlations between Self-Schema Types

	Type 2	Type 3
Type 1	0.479	0.604
Type 2		0.650

The Types

Consensus Items

Five of the defining items (those with z-scores whose absolute value is greater than 1.00) rated "most like me" and seven of the defining items rated "least like me" were ranked similarly enough to be classed as consensus items. It is

---

8. As with the gender schema sort, one of the factors which was not meaningful nonetheless provided some interesting information. It split the males into two types, the Affable Athlete who was a happy-go-lucky macho jock, and the Scrupulous Scout who was a quiet honest dependable analyst. Perhaps the most interesting thing about these two types is that the primary distinguisher between them was how they rated the items "feminine" and "masculine." The Affable Athlete's rating for "feminine" was more than two negative standard deviations from the mean—as if to say "Don't even *think* about calling me feminine." The Scrupulous Scout's rating of for "masculine" was more than two positive standard deviations from the mean—as if to say, "I know I'm not macho, but *please* call me masculine."

here that much of the social desirability bias hypothesized in chapter Three surfaced. All five "like me" items (friendly, reliable, loyal truthful, and likeable) are socially desirable. Five of the seven "not like me" items (gullible, conceited, unsystematic, theatrical, inefficient) are clearly undesirable, and the remaining two (solemn, childlike) were probably considered undesirable, given a sample of college students.

In addition to this effect, the consensus items provide clear evidence that gender was the criterion for distinguishing between the three types. A comparison of the 34 consensus items (see Table 4) with the results of the gender schema sort (see Table C.2) reveals that all twenty of the neutral gender schema items (those with z-scores between 0.500 and-0.500) emerge as consensus items, compared to only eight feminine and six masculine. The use of the gender schema is made even more evident by each of the types.

Table C.4: Thirty-four Self-schema Consensus Items

ITEM	AVERAGE Z
Reliable	1.510
Friendly	1.472
Loyal	1.300
Truthful	1.105
Likable	1.023
Happy	0.869
Helpful	0.836
Defends own beliefs	0.741
Cheerful	0.632
Adaptable	0.579
Self-sufficient	0.568
Self-reliant	0.470
Affectionate	0.464
Individualistic	0.462
Conscientious	0.454
Eager to soothe hurt feelings	0.221
Tactful	0.137
Analytical	0.001
Flatterable	-0.490

ITEM	AVERAGE Z
Moody	-0.503
Conventional	-0.511
Makes decisions easily	-0.514
Unpredictable	-0.619
Yielding	-0.781
Secretive	-0.840
Does not use harsh language	-0.896
Jealous	-0.932
Childlike	-1.033
Gullible	-1.068
Solemn	-1.197
Theatrical	-1.442
Unsystematic	-1.596
Conceited	-1.799
Inefficient	-2.016

Type One: The Caring Companion

Type Ones are strongly person-oriented, with an emphasis on nurturing. They consider themselves to be understanding, sensitive to the needs of others, sincere, compassionate, affectionate, helpful, happy, cheerful, and to love children. They consider themselves to not be dominant, aggressive, forceful, or masculine. These defining items for Type One are taken on the positive side from the defining feminine items of the gender schema sort, while those on the negative side taken are taken from the defining masculine items (compare Table C.2).

This pattern continues in the distinguishing items (those whose typal z-scores are more than one standard deviation greater or lesser than the typal z-scores of other types, and those with the highest and lowest typal z-scores). Type Ones consider themselves more feminine and warm than do either Type Twos or Threes (see Tables C.5 and C.6). They perceive themselves as more gentle, tender, sympathetic, sincere, sensitive to the needs of others, compassionate, understanding, shy, and soft spoken than do Type Twos and more loving of children than do Type Threes. Type Ones have the highest typal z-scores for feminine, warm, sensitive to the needs of others, and compassionate; lowest typal z-scores for "have leadership ability" and "dominant." Given this clear identification with feminine nurturant items and disassociation from masculine items, it is not surprising that Type One is predominantly female ($n = 33$, male $n = 6$).

Table C.5: Items Distinguishing between Self-schema Types One and Two

ITEM	TYPE 1	TYPE 3	DIFFERENCE
Shy	-0.328	-2.067	1.739
Sensitive to others' needs	1.428	-0.102	1.530
Soft-spoken	-0.376	-1.813	1.437
Feminine	0.824	-0.611	1.435
Compassionate	1.203	-0.011	1.214
Warm	0.995	-0.216	1.211
Gentle	0.710	-0.495	1.100
Sincere	1.291	0.165	1.085
Understanding	1.429	0.329	1.060
Forceful	-1.738	-0.687	-1.051
Willing to take a risk	-0.633	0.422	-1.054
Willing to take a stand	0.039	1.178	-1.138
Ambitious	0.404	1.679	-1.275
Acts as a leader	-0.572	0.758	-1.329
Has leadership abilities	-0.119	1.280	-1.399
Competitive	-0.575	0.944	-1.519
Assertive	-0.448	1.235	-1.684
Strong personality	0.129	1.886	-1.756
Independent	0.142	2.164	-2.022
Aggressive	-1.514	0.533	-2.047
Dominant	-1.479	0.590	-2.069

Table C.6: Items Distinguishing between Self-schema Types One and Three

ITEM	TYPE 1	TYPE 3	DIFFERENCE
Feminine	0.824	-2.444	3.268
Warm	0.995	-0.159	1.154
Loves children	1.119	0.038	1.081
Aggressive	-1.514	-0.339	-1.175
Athletic	-0.596	1.520	-2.116
Competitive	-0.575	1.789	-2.364
Masculine	-1.876	1.194	-3.070

Type 2: The Unyielding Leader

Type Twos are virtually the polar opposite of Type Ones. They are definitely not person-oriented. Rather, they are strongly leadership-oriented. They consider themselves to be independent, ambitious, assertive, to have strong personalities and leadership abilities, and to be willing to take a stand and defend their beliefs—all masculine defining items from the genders schema sort. They perceive themselves as not yielding, shy, soft spoken, or secretive, and as not a person who "does not use harsh language"—all, except "secretive," feminine defining items.

As with Type Ones, the pattern continues in the distinguishing items. Type Twos have the greatest typal z-scores for each of the positive defining items above, as well as for "dominant" and "aggressive." They have the lowest typal z-scores for "sensitive to the needs of others," "soft spoken," and "shy." They perceive themselves as more dominant, assertive, independent, ambitious, and more likely to have strong personalities than either Type Ones or Type Threes (see Tables C.5 and C.7). In addition they see themselves as more competitive, aggressive, forceful, more likely to have leadership ability and to act as a leader, and more willing to take risks or to take a stand than do Type Ones.

Table C.7: Items Distinguishing between Self-schema Types Two and Three

ITEM	TYPE 2	TYPE 3	DIFFERENCE
Strong personality	1.886	-0.235	2.121
Feminine	-0.611	-2.444	1.833
Dominant	0.590	-1.191	1.781
Assertive	1.235	-0.222	1.457
Independent	2.164	0.950	1.214
Ambitious	1.679	0.670	1.008
Soft-Spoken	-1.813	-0.489	1.324
Athletic	0.150	1.520	-1.370
Shy	-2.067	-0.104	-1.963
Masculine	-0.889	1.194	-2.082

The exception to this pattern lies in the distinguishing items between Type Twos and Type Threes. Type Twos perceive themselves as more feminine and less masculine than do Type Threes (placing both these items on the negative side). This reflects the fact that, contrary to what we might expect from the almost exclusively instrumental nature of the defining and distinguishing items, Type Two is predominantly female ($n = 20$, male $n = 10$). The ranking of both "feminine" and "masculine" as secondary negatively defining items ($z = -.611$ and $-.889$, respectively) indicates, for the women at least, an awareness that they are going against the grain of the gender schema. It is as if they were saying, "I know with these characteristics I don't fit the feminine mold. But don't call me masculine, either."

Type Three: The Team Player

Type Three is almost exclusively male ($n = 30$, female $n = 2$) and is the one type that does not follow strictly gender schematic lines. Type Threes primarily consider themselves competitive, athletic, masculine (all three of which Type Threes' typal z-scores are the highest), and helpful. They see themselves as definitely not jealous, dominant, forceful, or feminine. They do not consider themselves to have strong personalities (lowest typal z-score). The presence of one feminine gender schema item (helpful) on the positive end of the sort and three masculine gender schema items (dominant, forceful, and strong personality) on the negative side of the sort could suggest that this type is slightly less concerned about the gender schema.

There are, however, indications that this is not the case. Types Two and Three are highly correlated (.650), indicating that many of the characteristics of Type Two are shared by Type Three. Type Threes secondarily define themselves as independent, ambitious, self-sufficient, self-reliant, individualistic, and willing to defend their own beliefs, and act as a leader. Table C.6 shows that the secondary distinguishing items between Types One and Three are the same masculine and feminine gender schema items that distinguish between Types One and Two. Finally, Type Threes have the highest typal z-score for "masculine," and the lowest typal z-score for "feminine"—a clear indication of concern about gender.

Cross-Classification Results

With Q analysis producing only three types as opposed to the four types produced by the standard scoring of the BSRI there are obviously significant differences between the two. It is instructive, however, to examine the results of cross-tabulation of them.

Given the complete identification with nurturant items and rejection of instrumental items by Type One (the Caring Companion), we might expect to find almost all of these respondents in the Feminine cell. Yet this is not the case. Only 66.7 percent are classified as feminine, while 20.5 percent are Undifferentiated, and one is even classified as Masculine. Type Two (the Unyielding Leader) is divided between the Androgynous (36.7 percent) and the Masculine (63.3 percent) cells. This finding is not surprising, given the identification with instrumental items, rejection of nurturant items, and ranking of both "feminine" and "masculine" in the negative third of the distribution. Type Three (the Team Player) is spread across all four BSRI cells, with the greatest number in the Masculine cell (37.5 percent). It is evident that the BSRI and the self-schema sort are not measuring the same thing. Therefore, discriminant analysis was performed on the Q self-schema data to determine the best predictors of the self-schema types, for use in re-analysis of the data in Study Three.

Discriminant Analysis Results

Discriminant analysis using the twenty items from the short form of the BSRI suggested eleven predictors of the self-schema types. Eight of the items were masculine (dominant, competitive, have leadership ability, aggressive, strong personality, willing to take a stand, independent, and forceful), while three were feminine (tender, sincere, compassionate). These eleven items classified 88.12 percent of the cases into their Q self-schema types correctly.

To further test the effectiveness of these predictors, they were used in a discriminant analysis of the BSRI R data to classify the cases into the Q self-schema types. All eleven items continued to be significant predictors and correctly classified 76.24 percent of the cases. This suggests that computing self-schema types from these eleven items' R data would be sufficiently robust to give meaningful results in subsequent analysis.

Computation of these types was accomplished by multiplying each of the eleven items by its discriminant function coefficient for each type (see Table C.8) and summing the products and the constant within each type.

Table C.8: Classification Function Coefficients for Self-Schema Types
(Fisher's Linear Discriminant Functions)

ITEM	TYPE 1	TYPE 2	TYPE 3
Tender	-0.405E-01	-0.538	-1.058
Compassionate	3.848	3.123	3.242
Sincere	6.086	4.813	6.121
Strong personality	2.983	3.637	2.924
Aggressive	-0.236E-02	0.732	0.664
Dominant	-1.818	-1.309	-2.366
Forceful	2.873	2.549	2.312
Take a stand	0.174	0.940	0.320
Leadership ability	0.366	0.959	0.941
Competitive	2.369	2.778	3.792
Independent	1.919	2.578	2.225
(Constant)	-52.760	-60.163	-55.897

This produced three typal scores (one for each type) for every case. Criteria for classification in a given type was a difference score greater than or equal to one between that type and each of the other two, and a difference score less than one between the other two types. This ensured that one type clearly stood out above the other two. Classification by this process resulted in 24.8 percent ($n = 25$) Type One (Caring Companion), 22.8 percent ($n = 23$) Type Two (Unyielding Leader), 20.8 percent ($n = 21$) Type Three (Team Player, and 31.7 percent ($n = 32$) No Type, meaning they could not be purely classified.

If we consider the implications of being "no type" in the context of previous research in androgyny it is evident that further attempts to classify this segment of the sample are warranted. Being "no type" in this case means that a person combines enough characteristics from either two or all three types to prevent pure classification. Thus, a person might combine elements of Types One and Two, and be characterized as a "Caring Leader," or they might be a "Caring Player," combining Types One and Three. These would be androgynous types. Or they might combine elements of Types Two and Three, forming a masculine type characterized as a "Team Leader." Finally, they might be a "Caring Team Leader," combining all three in another androgynous type. These combinations were computed using criteria similar to those above (i.e. two difference scores greater than 1 and one less than 1 for the dual types; no difference scores greater than 1 for the triple type). This resulted in six Type Four "Caring Leaders," ten Type Five "Team Leaders," six Type Six "Caring Players," and ten Type Seven "Caring Team Leaders."

Because of their nurturant vs. instrumental dimension and the identification of that dimension with femininity/masculinity in the gender schema sort, the seven self-schema types (three pure, plus four combination) may be reduced to a three-fold gender schematic taxonomy of self-schemas. Female Caring Companions (Type One) and male Unyielding Leaders (Type Two), Team Players (Type Three) and Team Leaders (Type Five) would be labeled schematic. Though Type Five is a combination type, it is not androgynous because it combines two masculine schematic types. Male Caring Companions (Type One) and female Unyielding Leaders (Type Two), Team Players (Type Three) and Team Leaders (Type Five) would be labeled Cross-schematic; because they are androgynous, Caring Leaders (Type Four), Caring Players (Type Six), and Caring Team Leaders (Type Seven) would be labeled aschematic regardless of sex.

Applying the taxonomy to this sample produced the following results: 70 percent of the respondents were schematic, 11.9 percent were cross-schematic, and 19.1 percent were aschematic. For purposes of comparison the same type of transformation was performed on the BSRI data. Results were significantly different ($p < .001$): schematic = 48.5 percent, cross-schematic = 14.9 percent, aschematic = 36.6 percent. The taxonomy was cross-tabulated with sex of the respondent to test for differences in gender schematicity between the sexes, with highly significant results ($p < .000$). Females were 50.9 percent schematic, 21.8 percent cross-schematic, and 27.3 percent aschematic, while males were 93.5 percent schematic, 0 percent cross-schematic, and 6.5 percent aschematic. There were no significant differences between males and females on the comparable BSRI taxonomy.

The findings of Seyfried and Hendrick,[9] Shaffer and Johnson,[10] Hayes and Leonard,[11] and Feinman's[12] status characteristic theory suggesting that there is greater freedom for women to become like men than for men to become like women (discussed in chapter 2) thus receive greater support from the gender schematic taxonomy developed above than from the BSRI taxonomy.

DISCUSSION

There can be no doubt about the existence of a single, pervasive gender schema, given the results of the gender schema sort, the nature of the three basic self-schema types, and the exclusive use of masculine and feminine items to differentiate them. Examination of the defining items of the gender schema sort and their role in identifying the self-schema types does give something of a different slant as to the nature of the factors that define femininity and masculinity in North American culture. As discussed in chapter 2, femininity has been defined in previous research as an expressive/nurturant/submissive dimension. Yet the defining feminine items from the gender schema sort (see Table C.2) and Type One (see Table C.5) are only indirectly related to emotional expressiveness. Femininity's relationship to submissiveness is similarly indirect, based primarily its negative relationship to the power dynamic of masculinity (see below). The primary defining factor for femininity, then, could be termed "nurturance." But even that is not a good characterization. It too much connotes mothering, and of all the items in the list only "loves children" is explicitly related to that behavior. Rather, a better description would be "affiliative," or as suggested in the label for Type One, simply "caring."

For masculinity two issues emerge which define masculinity in the gender schema sort and distinguish Types Two and Three. The first is "power." Independent, strong personality, ambitious, leadership ability, acts as a leader, dominant, assertive, aggressive, takes a stand, defends beliefs—all items that have connotations of power. The other issue is the running mate of power: "competition," expressed in items such as competitive (of course), athletic, ambitious, and willing to take risks.

These characterizations parallel the findings of Tannen[13] that women use language to build and strengthen relationships, whereas men use

9. Seyfried, and Hendrick, "When Do Opposites Attract?" 1973.
10. Shaffer, and Johnson. "Effects of Occupational Choice," 1980.
11. Hayes and Leonard. "Sex-related Motor Behavior," 1983.
12. Feinman, "Why Is Cross-Sex-Role Behavior More Approved," 1981.
13. Tannen, *You Just Don't Understand*, 1990.

language as a means of competition and the acquisition of power. Spence[14] has said that femininity and masculinity are vague, global constructs about which everybody is concerned but the content of which no one is certain. The results of this study suggest that people are indeed concerned about masculinity and femininity, and that they are quite clear about what these constructs are. Bem[15] appears to be correct—a single gender schema does exist, and is remarkably resilient, having changed hardly at all in the years since the introduction of the BSRI.

However, the results of this study suggest that the standard scoring procedure for the BSRI does not accurately represent how, or the extent to which, the gender schema is incorporated into the self-schemas of other than the most schematic persons. Recall that the intent of the BSRI is to measure a person's tendency to cluster items according to cultural gender appropriateness. Yet the BSRI gives not whether a person rates masculine, feminine and neutral characteristics higher or lower than each other at all, but rather whether a person rates him or herself higher or lower than *other people* rate themselves on masculine and feminine characteristics.

It is not surprising that the results of the self-schema sorts are so different from the results of the BSRI. The BSRI types are based on between respondent comparisons on each item, whereas the self-schema types are based on between item comparisons for each respondent. The second is more consistent with gender schema theory. If gender schematicity is defined as the tendency to process information in terms of cultural gender appropriateness, then the question is not whether one sees her or himself as more, say, assertive than the next person does. Rather it is whether a person sees him or herself as more assertive than, say, adaptable, or more sincere than self-sufficient.

The case of the undifferentiated is instructive in this regard. In Bem's model (at the suggestion of Spence and Helmreich) undifferentiated people are aschematic (or low androgynous). This is because they rate themselves below the median on both the masculine and feminine scales. It is assumed that this is because such persons perceive themselves primarily in ways other than those expressed by the items on the BSRI. This may not necessarily be the case, however. Some undifferentiated persons may be given to lower scores in general. This would explain why a classification of undifferentiated is highly correlated with low self-esteem scores. This suggestion is supported by the fact that over 30 percent of the schematic and cross-schematic respondents in this study had typal scores below the median for

14. Spence, "Masculinity, Femininity, and Gender-Related Traits," 1984.
15. Bem, "Androgyny and Gender Schema Theory," 1984.

each type and yet the difference scores for many of them ranged from five to seventeen, indicating strong schematic differentiation. This illustrates how the self-schema sort and subsequent computation of the types using discriminant coefficients more accurately portray the extent to which a person is gender schematic.

The self-schema sorts also helped to reveal how the gender schema is incorporated into the self-schema. For example, until now it has not been clear whether or not feminine sex typed males and masculine sex typed females were schematic, since they appear to process information along gender schema lines, but in the opposite direction. Do they do this blissfully unaware that they are "going against the flow?" The data suggest that they are very aware of that fact. Such an awareness may be anything but bliss, and could have a profound effect on the individual's behavior. Such was the case with several of the cross-schematic women. After completing the gender schema sort, a number of the women expressed anger about it. Brief informal interviews to discover the reason for their anger produced minor variations on the theme, "Because society tells me I'm supposed to be 'like this' and I'm not like that and I don't want to be!" For some, awareness of their cross-schematicity might spark a defiant response. For others it might lead to a careful, and painful, editing of their behavior. It might lead still others to seek out a community of like-minded people where they could be themselves without hesitation. These responses might be very different from those of a schematic or aschematic person. It is, therefore, important to include cross-schematics in the analysis, rather than including them with the schematics as has been the practice since the introduction of Bem's[16] gender schema theory and continues today's successor, "gender identity salience."

CONCLUSIONS

Unquestionably, the gender schema is an important element in how the respondents in this study process information. Fully 70 percent of them were gender schematic and another 11.9 percent were cross-schematic. This means that 81.9 percent of the respondents incorporated the gender schema into their self-schemas in one way or another. Of special interest for this discussion is the fact that over 93 percent of the male respondents were schematic. It has often been noted that sex stereotypes are very restrictive for women, and certainly that is true. But for the men in this study, the gender strait jacket is extremely tight.

16. Bem, "Gender Schema Theory," 1981.

Appendix D

Detailed Comparison of Values Sought in Pastors vs. Industry Leaders

THE PERCENTAGES FOR INDIVIDUAL characteristics are shown graphically below. The columns in each cluster are as follows, left to right:

Cluster 1 = Caring, Honest, Independent;

Cluster 2 = Cooperative, Broad-minded, Determined;

Cluster 3 = Spiritual, Inspiring, Courageous;

Cluster 4 = Self-controlled, Intelligent, Straight-forward;

Cluster 5 = Loyal, Competent, Forward-looking;

Cluster 6 = Supportive, Mature, Imaginative;

Cluster 7 = Fair-minded, Dependable, Ambitious.

APPENDIX D

Figure D.1: Values Most Sought in Pastors by Laity

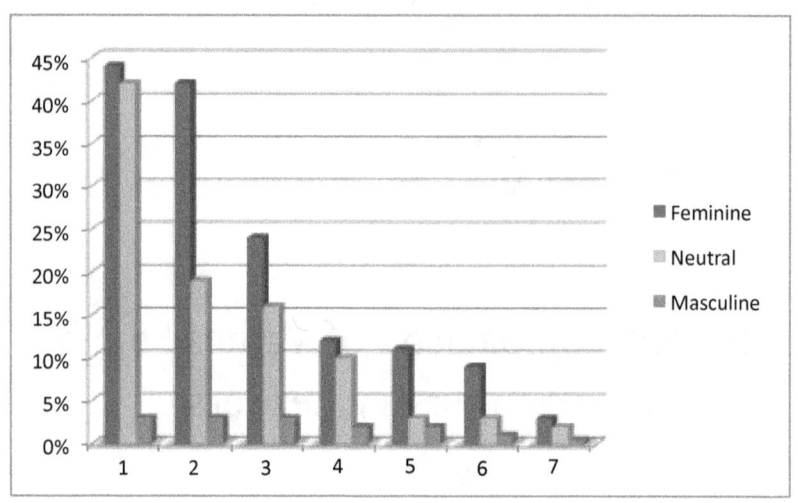

Figure D.2: Values Sought in Leaders of Business and Industry

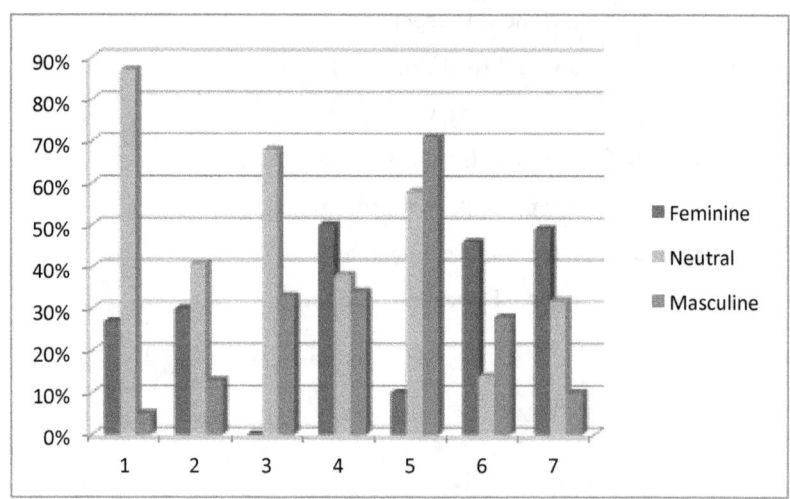

Appendix E

Men, Gender Schemas and Responses to Christian Messages

RATIONALE

BEM[1] CONTENDS THAT ONE'S self-concept (or self-schema) is intimately linked to his/her gender schema. Because one's self-schema is often the primary means s/he uses to form impressions of others[2] one's gender schema becomes extremely important in person perception. In other words, information that is relevant to one's gender schema is more likely to be attended to and processed into memory. Hamilton[3] has suggested that stereotypes may be formed and maintained in part because of the mechanism of illusory correlation occurring during schematic information processing. Briefly, perceivers erroneously judge schema-(or stereotype-) consistent information to have occurred more frequently than schema-neutral or inconsistent information. As a result, stereotypes can be maintained even in the face of many disconfirming examples, since it takes many more instances of disconfirmation than confirmation to overcome the effect of illusory correlation. In addition, Snyder[4] has found that people tend to seek out information which confirms the hypotheses they have about others (i.e. schemas) and ignore information which contradict them.

    1. Bem, "Androgyny and Gender Schema Theory," 1984; "Gender Schema Theory: A Cognitive Account," 1981.
    2. Spence, "Masculinity, Femininity, and Gender-Related Traits," 1984; Catrambone and Markus, "The Role of Self-Schemas," 1987.
    3. Hamilton, *Cognitive Processes*, 2015.
    4. Snyder, "On the Self-Perpetuating Nature," 1981.

Applying this to the case at hand, since androgynous men tend to use some feminine communicative behaviors, both verbal and nonverbal, and feminine men tend to use even more,[5] the mere presence of a higher than normal proportion of aschematic and cross-schematic men in the church population, if it exists, would virtually guarantee that unchurched men would come into contact with sufficient numbers of churched men who fit the feminine Christian stereotype to keep it solidly in place.

If the Christian message is, in fact, generally perceived as being more feminine than masculine, it therefore should be less attractive to those men for whom cultural stereotypes of masculinity are important. Conversely, it should be more attractive to those men who share at least some of the same concerns, and perhaps employ some of the same vocabulary. In other words there should be a higher proportion of cross-schematic men and a lower proportion of aschematic and schematic men than normal in the church population.

In addition, men who are active in the church would be encouraged to adopt the principle concerns expressed in the Christian message (as formulated by the North American church) as personal priorities and to utilize language appropriate to them. If all the above holds true, unchurched men should be confronted with confirmatory examples of "feminine" Christian men saying "feminine" Christian things frequently enough and disconfirming instances of masculine Christian men with sufficient infrequency to maintain their negative, low status stereotype and thus remain unattracted to the church. This leads to the following hypotheses:

> H1. The sample of churched men will contain a higher proportion of aschematic and cross-schematic individuals than the sample of unchurched men.
>
> H2. Churched men in general will endorse stereotypically feminine message behavior more than will unchurched men.
>
> H3. Schematic and aschematic churched men will endorse stereotypically feminine message behavior more than their unchurched counterparts.
>
> H4. Since cross-schematic men have already chosen to ignore societal constraints, there will be no significant difference in message behavior between cross-schematic churched and unchurched men.

---

5. Hayes and Leonard, "Sex-related Motor Behavior," 1983; LaFrance and Carmen, "The Nonverbal Display," 1980; Bem and Lenny, "Sex Typing and the Avoidance," 1976.

H5. The difference between churched and unchurched aschematic men will be significantly greater than the differences between churched and unchurched men of other sex-types.

DESIGN

The study consisted of three parts. Parts One and Two test Hypotheses One and Two respectively, while Part Three tests Hypotheses H3, H4, and H5. Thus, in Part One church participation serves as an independent variable and psychological sex type serves as a dependent variable. In Part Two, church participation is the independent variable and cross-sex-typed message behavior is the dependent variable. In Part Three both church participation and psychological sex type are independent variables, and cross-sex-typed message behavior

OPERATIONALIZATIONS

Churchedness/unchurchedness was operationalized in terms of participation in church activities. Subjects indicated their level of participation on the following scale:

_____ Not at all, _____ One to three times per year, _____ One to three times per quarter, One to four times per month, _____ More than four times per month.

Those who reported participating in religious activities once a month or more were classified as churched, while those who reported participation of three times a quarter or less (i.e. less than once a month), regardless of claimed church membership were classified as unchurched. This definition of churchedness is more restrictive than that which is often used. For example, in their regular Religion in American Life survey, the Gallup organization classifies respondents who claim membership in a church and report participation at least once in a six-month period as churched. This study's admittedly etic definition of churchedness was adopted for two reasons: One, it is assumed that less consistent levels of participation in church life indicate lower levels of existential commitment to concerns expressed in church communication and that therefore those who participate infrequently (i.e. less than twelve times per year) would be less likely to use messages expressing such concerns themselves. Two, such a definition provides a more stringent test of the hypotheses since a violation of the above assumption would result in no significant differences between the churched and unchurched subjects' responses.

Gender schematicity was computed by use of the formula developed in the discriminant analysis of the Bem Sex Role Inventory Principal components analysis with Varimax Form) in the previous study, "Gender Schemas and Self Schemas" (see Appendix C). This computation classified respondents as gender schematic, cross-schematic, or aschematic.

Cross-sex-typed message behavior is operationalized in terms of themes of communitas,[6] and stereotypically feminine concerns[7] drawn from church-related communication. Ten statements containing themes such as expressiveness, nurturance, support, submission, humility, and sacrifice were developed from Biblical passages, sermons, and Christian education materials. These were worded so as to be the type of statements that might occur in a conversation between two friends and were presented as such (see Table E.1). Subjects were asked to rate each statement in terms usage with a male and a female friend, as well as each statement's "independence, assertiveness, sensitivity, and gentleness" (see below).

Table E.1: "Cross-Sex-Typed" Messages
Each statement is followed by the church-related source from which it was adapted.

1. "Don't keep your worries, fears, and problems bottled up inside. We need to share our feelings with each other." (Adult Sunday School lesson)
2. "You come to realize at some point that you are not in charge of your life." (Senior High Sunday School lesson)
3. "Nobody can go it alone. You have to learn to lean on other people to make it in this world." (Adult Sunday School lesson)
4. "You should always refuse to get into a fight. Even if there seems to be no way to avoid it, you should always 'turn the other cheek.'" (Junior High Sunday School lesson)
5. "I'd like to support people, to nurture them so they can be all they want to be." (Sermon)
6. "We all need forgiveness. I do. You do. It's the only way we can get a fresh start." (Sermon)
7. "The greatest need we have is the need for love. You need to know you are loved and to love others." (Sermon)
8. "It's important to be humble. You should put other people first and think of them as better than you." (Philippians 2:3, NIV)

---

6. Turner, *The Ritual Process*, 1977.

7. Lakoff, "Language and Woman's Place." 1973, 1975; Rasmussen and Moelly, "Impression Formation," 1986.

9. "Though it may mean having less money and prestige, serving others should be a person's central goal in life." (Small group Bible study guide)
10. "It's not so much what you do or accomplish that really matters. It's the kind of person you are." (Sermon)

SAMPLE

In order to increase variability and ensure the severest test of the hypotheses, the sample of churched men were drawn primarily from the student body of a local seminary (n = 93). If the propositions set forth in the rationale above were going to be evidenced anywhere, it should be in such a sample. These men would be among those most attracted to the church's message and most likely to endorse its use. If the hypotheses are not supported in this sample it should fairly well disconfirm the "theory." In order to maintain, as much as possible, parity in educational level and life stage, the sample of unchurched men was drawn from students in the graduate school of a major Midwestern university (n = 98). Average age of the samples was 31.4 years for the seminary sample and 29.8 years for the university sample. Both samples were almost exclusively white middle class. The possibility of unchurched seminary students and churched university graduate students was controlled for by the church participation question in the demographic section. Unchurched seminary students (n = 5) and churched university graduate students (n = 31) were included in the unchurched and churched groups respectively

PROCEDURE

Respondents were told they were participating in a study examining the relationship between self-perceptions and perceptions of messages. They completed survey booklets containing the following measures in the following order:

1. The Bem Sex Role Inventory (short form). This form has been shown to have greater reliability than the original form of the BSRI.[8] Subjects rate ten masculine characteristics and ten feminine characteristics of a 7-point scale, 1 being "Never or almost never true of me" and 7 being "Always or almost always true of me."

8. Wheeless & Dierks-Stewart, "The Psychometric Properties," 1981; Wheeless & Duran, "Gender orientation," 1982.

2. The cross-sex-typed message use measure. All subjects received the same messages and rated each message on two 7-point semantic differential scales in terms of likelihood of personal use with a) a male friend and b) a female friend, respectively. A rating of 1 indicated "Not likely to use" and a 7 "Very unlikely to use." Indices of usage with males and females were computed by summing the appropriate items. Indices had a minimum of 10 and a maximum of 70, with a midpoint of 40.

3. The cross-sex-typed message characteristic measure. Each message was rated on a variation of the adjective sex role index which Rasmussen and Moelly[9] developed to test responses to short stories. This also uses a semantic differential scale, with 1 indicating that the adjective is not very characteristic of the message and 7 indicating that it is very characteristic of the message. Two masculine items (independent and assertive) and two feminine items (sensitive and gentle) were selected from the adjective sex role index for use in this study. This was to provide a test of validity for the messages. If they were perceived as feminine messages the means for the two feminine adjectives should be higher than those for the two masculine items.

RESULTS

Validity and Reliability Checks

Confirmatory factor analysis using principal components with Varimax rotation was computed for the BSRI and the message characteristic indices as a check of the validity of the assumption of a masculine-feminine continuum underlying them. A minimum of four items with .60 loadings and others with at least .30 loadings were the criteria for inclusion on the respective factors. As expected, nearly all feminine items loaded on Factor One and nearly all masculine items loaded on Factor Two for both measures. (See Tables E.2 and E.3.)

Table E.2: Factor Analysis Of Bem Sex Role Inventory

ITEM	FACTOR 1	FACTOR 2
warm	.828	.029
tender	.789	.029

9. Rasmussen and Moelly, "Impression Formation," 1986.

ITEM	FACTOR 1	FACTOR 2
gentle	.272	-.048
eager to soothe hurts	.715	.025
sensitive to others needs	.696	.012
helpful	.691	.147
compassionate	.663	-.048
understanding	.643	.031
friendly	.633	.115
sincere	.511	.168
assertive	.018	.788
have a strong personality	.094	.759
aggressive	.047	.730
dominant	-.188	.689
forceful	-.219	.647
act as a leader	.363	.626
willing to take a stand	.202	.577
have leadership ability	.373	.567
competitive	.207	.472
independent	-.054	.312
Eigenvalues	5.649	3.685
Variance	28.2%	18.4%
Total variance	=	46.7%

Table E.3: Factor Analysis of Cross-Sex-Typed Message Characteristics

ITEM	FACTOR 1	FACTOR 2
gentleness (service)	.753	-.008
gentleness (love)	.725	.141
sensitivity (love)	.721	.160
sensitivity (service)	.654	-.061
sensitivity (nurture)	.640	.160
gentleness (humble)	.634	.013

APPENDIX E

ITEM	FACTOR 1	FACTOR 2
sensitivity (kind of person)	.621	.092
sensitivity (forgiveness)	.617	.106
gentleness (nurture)	.582	.185
sensitivity (humble)	.560	.039
gentleness (forgiveness)	.557	.023
gentleness (turn cheek)	.548	-.125
sensitivity (share feelings)	.543	.039
gentleness (kind of person)	.533	.143
gentleness (share feelings)	.509	.001
sensitivity (turn cheek)	.459	-.018
sensitivity (dependent)	.455	.287
gentleness (dependent)	.414	.240
gentleness (not in charge)	.212	.207
assertiveness (forgiveness)	.066	.680
assertiveness (love)	.142	.678
independence (love)	.132	.666
assertiveness (service)	.065	.635
independence (forgiveness)	.099	.631
assertiveness (humble)	.072	.616
independence (not in charge)	.019	.583
assertiveness (not in charge)	.025	.547
assertiveness (kind / person)	.116	.526
independence (humble)	-.024	.526
independence (service)	.076	.512
independence (dependent)	-.094	.509
independence (nurture)	.055	.462
assertiveness (turn cheek)	.059	.439
assertiveness (share feeling)	.072	.384
independence (share feeling)	.053	.381
assertiveness (nurture)	.337	.367
independence (turn cheek)	.084	.344

ITEM	FACTOR 1	FACTOR 2
sensitivity (not in charge)	.255	.333
independence (kind / person)	.283	.315
Eigenvalues	8.128	4.772
Variance	20.3%	11.9%
Total variance	=	32.2%

Reliability coefficients (Cronbach's alpha; Cronbach, 1951) computed for the BSRI were .88 for masculine and .86 for feminine. Alpha scores for the cross-sex-typed message characteristic indices were .82 for independence, .84 for assertiveness, .79 for sensitivity, and .78 for gentleness. Alpha scores for the cross-sex-typed message usage indices were .88 for "Use with a male friend" and .86 for "Use with a female friend."

Gender Schematicity and Churchedness

Hypothesis H1, that the sample of churched men would contain a higher proportion of aschematic and cross-schematic individuals than the unchurched sample was tested by means of cross-tabulation with phi as the test of significance. Analysis revealed that of the churched sample (n = 119), forty-four were schematic (37 percent), forty were cross-schematic (33.6 percent), and thirty-five were aschematic (29.4 percent). Of the unchurched sample (n = 72), forty-six were schematic (63.8 percent), eight were cross-schematic (11 percent), and eighteen were aschematic (25.2 percent). The difference in the proportion of aschematic and cross-schematic individuals in the sample of church men compared to the non-church sample was tested by means of cross-tabulation with chi-square test of significance. Chi-square Likelihood Ratio value was 15.108 (df = 3) and was significant at the .001 level.

Churchedness and Message Behavior

Hypothesis H2, that churched men in general would endorse stereotypically feminine message behavior more than would unchurched men, was tested by means of t-test. Table E.4 presents the mean endorsement ratings for the Male Usage Index, the Female Usage Index, and a difference score computed by subtracting the mean male usage score from the mean female usage score.

Table E.4: Usage: Mean Ratings and Difference Scores

Subjects	Use with male	Use with female	Difference	T (Signif.)
Unchurched	32.82	36.39	3.57	-5.71 (.000)
Churched	46.66	47.56	.91	-2.30 (.023)
T (Significance)	-7.31 (.000)	-6.15 (.000)	3.60 (.000)	

As the table suggests, churched men did endorse the cross-sex-typed messages for use with men at a significantly higher level ($t(164) = -7.31$, $p < .000$), as they did for use with women ($t(158) = -6.15$, $p < .000$), than did unchurched men. In addition, while both unchurched and churched men considered the messages more appropriate for women than for men as indicated by the difference scores ($t(71) = -5.71$, $p < .000$; and $t(118) = -2.30$, $p = .02$ respectively), the unchurched men considered the difference in appropriateness to be significantly greater than did the churched men ($t(127) = 3.60$, $p < .000$).

Message characteristic ratings (see Table E.5) provide a basis for interpreting these findings. The unchurched men rated the messages as slightly more independent ($M = 38.40$) than the unchurched men ($M = 34.85$; $t(158) = -.215$, $p = .033$) and strongly more assertive ($M = 48.90$) than the unchurched men ($M = 37.56$; $t(139) = -7.7$, $p < .000$). This indicates that the churched men perceived the messages as being more masculine than did the unchurched men. Ratings for the feminine characteristics reveal that churched men considered the messages slightly more sensitive ($M = 47.70$) than did unchurched men ($M = 44.33$; $t(145) = -2.27$, $p = .025$) and insignificantly more gentle ($M = 46.39$) than unchurched men ($M = 44.26$; $t(136) = -1.36$, ns). These lower differences coupled the greater difference on the masculine indices raised the churched men's male usage ratings disproportionately.

Table E.5: Message Characteristic Mean Ratings

Characteristic		Unchurched	Churched	T (Sig.)
Independence	M	34.84	38.40	-2.15
	SD	10.78	11.52	(.033)

Characteristic		Unchurched	Churched	T (Sig.)
Assertiveness	M	37.56	48.90	-7.17
	SD	10.94	9.95	(.000)
Sensitivity	M	44.33	47.70	-2.27
	SD	10.09	9.70	(.025)
Gentleness	M	44.26	46.39	-1.36
	SD	10.76	9.65	ns

Gender Schematicity, Churchedness, and Message Behavior

Hypotheses H3, and H4 were tested by means of two-way analysis of variance of the usage indices (gender schematicity by churchedness), with follow-up analyses utilizing one-way analysis of variance with multiple comparisons. Table E6 gives the cell means and standard deviations for each usage index.

Table E.6: Message Usage Cell Means by Gender Schematicity and Churchedness

Cell	n		Use with male	Use with female
Schematic				
Unchurched	72	M	30.93	34.80
		SD	12.96	12.99
Churched	44	M	42.65	44.23
		SD	15.77	15.68
Cross-schematic				
Unchurched	8	M	37.62	40.00
		SD	10.00	9.61
Churched	40	M	48.63	48.11
		SD	9.87	9.26
Aschematic				
Unchurched	18	M	33.53	37.56
		SD	10.97	10.58

Cell	n		Use with male	Use with female
Churched	35	M	50.76	52.15
		SD	12.02	8.65
Entire Sample	191	M	41.44	43.35
		SD	14.66	13.47

A 3 (gender schematicity) X 2 (churchedness) analysis of variance using unique sums of squares revealed significant main effects for gender schematicity on the male usage index (F(2,190) = 5.11, p < .007) and on the female usage index (F(2,190) = 4.23, p < .016), as well as for churchedness on the male usage index (F(2,190) = 45.94, p < .000) and on the female usage index (F(2,190) = 33.68, p < .000). Multiple classification analysis on the male usage index indicated that the model accounted for 25.1 percent of the variance (gender schematicity beta = .20; churchedness beta = .43). Multiple classification analysis on the female usage index indicated that the model accounted for 19.9 percent of the variance (gender schematicity beta = .19; churchedness beta = 38). No interaction effect was found.

In order to identify the significantly different groups, each cell was recoded as a binary variable and entered in a one way analysis of variance utilizing Tukey's alternate multiple comparisons test (Tukey-b). This procedure uses conservative measures to guard against finding significant differences merely as a result of performing a high number of comparisons. Table E.7 represents the breakdown of significantly different groups (p < .050).

Table E.7: Multiple Comparisons of Usage and Assertiveness Ratings

	Male Usage				Female Usage				Assertiveness	
Group	1	3	5	2	1	3	5	2	1	3
1										
3										
5										
2	*	*			*				*	*
6	*	*	*		*	*			*	*
4	*	*	*	*	*	*	*	*	*	*

(*) denotes pairs of groups significantly different at the .050 level.

Group 1 = Unchurched Schematic

Group 2 = Churched Schematic
Group 3 = Unchurched Aschematic
Group 4 = Churched Aschematic
Group 5 = Unchurched Cross-schematic
Group 6 = Churched Cross-schematic

DISCUSSION

Hypothesis H1 regarding the schematicity of the respective samples was partially supported. While there was no significant difference between the churched and unchurched aschematic cells (29.4 percent and 25.2 percent respectively), the difference was in the predicted direction. More importantly, the difference between the churched and unchurched schematic cells (37 percent vs. 63.8 percent respectively) and cross-schematic cells (33.6 percent vs. 11 percent respectively) is strongly supported. This suggests that the church is, in fact, less attractive to schematic men and more attractive to cross-schematic men. When this is coupled with cross-schematic men's greater willingness to use cross-sex-typed messages (to be discussed below), it increases the likelihood that unchurched men will be confronted with examples which confirm the feminine Christian stereotype.

Hypothesis H2's prediction that the churched men as a whole would endorse stereotypically feminine message behavior more than would the unchurched men was strongly supported. It is clear that churched and unchurched men perceive statements containing some of the primary themes of the Christian message (as the North American church has formulated it) very differently. The unchurched men, especially those for whom masculinity is important, consider them decidedly unmasculine and inappropriate for use with a man. The churched men consider them fairly masculine, especially when viewed in terms of assertiveness, and about equally appropriate for use with a man or a woman. Of all the unchurched men, only the cross-schematics rated the messages above the midpoint of the scale, indicating an endorsement, and that only for use with a woman. They were also the only ones to agree with the churched men in rating the messages above the midpoint on assertiveness. This may indicate a sensitivity to the style of the messages as opposed to their content. None of the churched men rated the messages below the midpoint on the scale, indicating a rejection. This means that all of the churched men indicate that they would use statements in conversations with men which all the unchurched men consider altogether inappropriate for such use, as indicated by both usage and message characteristic ratings.

Hypothesis H3, that schematic and aschematic churched men would endorse cross-sex-typed messages more than their unchurched counterparts, was fully supported. However, Hypothesis 4's prediction that cross-sex-typed churched men would not differ significantly from cross-sex-typed unchurched men in usage rating was not supported. This hypothesis was based on Falbo's[10] thesis that cross-sex-typed persons are consciously defiant, so to speak, of cultural gender norms. Thus, we would expect to see an endorsement of the cross-sex-typed messages in the unchurched sample. That this was not the case provides additional evidence for the interpretation of cross-schematics—that they are, indeed, conscious of their lack of fit with the gender schema, and that at least some are uncomfortable with it. Into this situation steps the church, or more likely the person steps into the church, whose message fits the person's self schema, and the person is affirmed—so much so that, alone of all the types, the churched cross-schematics do not vary their usage rating between males and females. Thus it appears that the church's encouragement operates for churched men across all three schema types, resulting in parallel increases (though to varying degrees) in usage ratings over those of their unchurched counterparts.

Finally, Hypothesis H5, which predicted that the difference between churched and unchurched aschematic men would be greater than the differences between churched and unchurched men of other schema types, was also supported on both indices. This hypothesis was based on the same assumption which was just illustrated–that the emphasis of the church on the themes contained in the messages plus its encouragement to engage in such message behavior would free the aschematic men from the constraints of social disapproval placed upon them by North American culture,[11] enabling them to express what they actually felt. Just such an effect is evident in the data: The aschematics have the highest usage rankings among the churched men, while the cross-schematics have the highest among the unchurched men. The size of the effect can be seen in the mean difference scores for the churched and unchurched schema types: For the schematics it is 10.5; for the cross-schematics, 9.5; for the aschematics, 16.5.

It is the varying degree to which the respective schema types feel the constraints of social disapproval that explains why aschematics would

---

10. Falbo, "Relationships between Sex," 1977.

11. Lee and Scheurer, "Psychological Androgyny," 1983; Feinman, "Why Is Cross-Sex-Role Behavior More Approved," 1981; Shaffer and Johnson, "Effects of Occupational Choice," 1980; Cowan and Koziej, "The Perception of Sex-Inconsistent Behavior," 1979; Seyfried and Kendrick, "When Do Opposites Attract," 1973.

increase their usage rating more than the other types. As discussed above, cross-schematics, though uncomfortable, feel the constraint less than aschematics. Indeed, Falbo (1977) contends that androgynes (aschematics) would be cross-sex-typed if it weren't for social constraint. Obviously, schematics feel the constraint the most, as is evidenced by the fact that the churched schematics' usage ratings are the lowest of the three on both indices. Indeed, they are not significantly different, statistically speaking, from the unchurched cross-schematics' ratings. In other words, though they do endorse the cross-sex-typed messages, they are the least comfortable of the churched men with doing so. The aschematics, of course, fall somewhere in the middle. Their overall usage rating increases the most, but even with that increase, aschematics retain the distinction in gender appropriateness, rating the messages higher for use with women. Apparently even so-called aschematics are not so aschematic after all.

The findings of this study have important implications for church communicators who are concerned about lack of participation in the church's life by men. If it is true that all good communication is receiver-oriented and is adapted to the perceptions of the receiver, then church communicators will need to consider carefully the influence of gender schematicity on unchurched men's perceptions of both the men and the messages which are identified with church.

Appendix F

Responses of Men and Women to Masculine and Feminine Christian Message

RATIONALE

IN PREVIOUS STUDIES (SEE Appendices B and E) the author found 1) a strong consensus perception of Christians as both feminine and unmasculine; 2) the ten primary themes of the Christian faith identified by focus groups all came from American culture's feminine set; 3) churched men strongly endorsed use of messages with these feminine themes for both men and women, and there was no significant difference between their usage ratings for men and for women, whereas unchurched men did not endorse the messages, but perceived them as significantly more appropriate for women; 4) the more an unchurched man identified with the cultural definition of masculinity, the lower he rated theses messages for use with men; 5) gender aschematic or "combination" unchurched men made the largest distinction between use with men and use with women, whereas aschematic churched men made no significant distinction and had highest message-use rating for both men and women. Apparently aschematic men outside the church feel the need to edit their communication to fit cultural norms, while aschematic men inside the church feel free to express themselves fully.

Gender appropriateness, then, is shown to be a primary measure by which unchurched men assess statements containing Christian themes. Yet churched men report they would make such statements to other men, while unchurched men consider them altogether inappropriate for use with men. These findings suggest that the contemporary quest for inclusive language has been far too limited in scope. For men outside the church, the issue of inclusive language appears to extend beyond the use of male-referent nouns and pronouns to the very themes Christians choose to communicate.

METHOD

To test this hypothesis the author constructed 10 additional conversational statements using masculine themes that also express a Christian worldview. The ten themes chosen for the Masculine Christian Worldview Statements were those with the highest loadings on the masculine factor in the previous study's factor analysis of the Bem Sex Role Inventory (see Appendix C). These statements were then incorporated into the "Conversational Perceptions Survey" used in the previous research (see Table F.1).

Table F.1: "Masculine" Themed Christian Worldview Statements
Numbers represent each statement's order in the Conversational Perceptions Survey.

3. "I want to be somebody who makes a difference. I want to make the world a little better than it was." (Influence)
6. "You've got to have somewhere to belong. You need a team you're a part of." (Belonging or Teamwork)
7. "There's got to be a purpose in life—a plan you fit into." (Purpose or Position)
9. I want to be known as a person with integrity. It's time we re-discovered the idea of honor." (Character)
12. "At some point you've got to have the courage to stand up for what is right." (Courage)
13. "There's something more asked of us than most of us realize. We are called to live on a higher plane than we do." (Challenge)
16. "You have to try to live up to your potential. That's the only way life is worth living." (Fulfillment)
18. "Some things you just have to do because they're your responsibility. If you don't, you let people you care about down." (Responsibility or Duty)
19. "You have to be tough with yourself sometimes. It may hurt or it may be hard, but you just have to 'suck it up' and do it." (Discipline or Perseverance)
20. "I want to be somebody who can find the strength to face any challenge." (Strength or Power)

SAMPLE

A balanced sample of non-church men (n = 46, age 18–64, M = 37), non-church women (n = 42, age 19–66, M = 39), and church men (n = 43, age 28–68, M = 40) and church women (n = 45, age 24–70, M = 42) rated the statements as in the author's previous studies. Separate indices consisting of the sum of the mean scores for the ten feminine statements' use and the sum of the mean scores for the ten masculine statements' use, with men and with women respectively were computed. As with the previous, male-only study, measure of the respondents' gender schematicity was taken. Though the sample is not yet of sufficient size to provide predictive power for the 3 (gender schematicity) x 2 (churchedness) x 2 (sex) factorial design, it would provide a check of consistency with the previous study's results.

In order to identify the significantly different groups each combination was recoded as a binary variable. Combining churchedness with sex of respondents gives four binary variables: unchurched men, unchurched women, churched men, and churched women. These four variables were entered in a one-way analysis of variance, utilizing Tukey's alternate multiple comparisons test. This procedure (also known as Tukey-b) uses conservative measures to guard against finding significant differences merely as a result of performing a high number of comparisons.

RESULTS

Two-way analysis of variance of the scores for the indices of feminine statements' use and masculine statements' use showed main effects for both churchedness and sex of the respondents. That is, there were significant differences between the responses of churched and unchurched persons, and between men and women (see Table F.2).

Table F.2: Usage Ratings for Feminine and Masculine Christian Statements by Churched and Unchurched Men and Women

		Col. 1 Fem. with Man	Col. 2 Masc. with Man	Col. 3 Fem. with Woman	Col. 4 Masc. with Woman
Unchurched Women	M SD	41.16a 13.18	49.58b,eg 11.46	50.03eg 11.79	55.50dg 10.35
Unchurched Men	M SD	42.36a 13.35	52.50 11.12	44.00c 11.82	51.82d 10.25
Churched Women	M SD	47.78 12.28	53.96fh 11.76	53.88fh 11.29	57.76dh 10.14
Churched Men	M SD	49.89a 11.54	58.50b 8.81	51.94 10.36	56.40d 9.35
	F (Sig.)	4.22 (.0067)	4.70 (.0036)	4.89 .0028)	2.16 (ns)

DISCUSSION

Churched men were significantly more likely than were either unchurched men or women to use feminine Christian statements with a man (c.f. Column 1,a). This finding is consistent with the earlier study. Churched women were not significantly different from the other groups in their rating of the feminine statements with men.

Only churched men and unchurched women were significantly different in rating masculine statements for use with men (c.f. Column 2,b). The difference seems to be a function of the women's perception of appropriate statements from a woman to a man, as evidenced they their strong endorsement of these same messages for use with other women (Compare Row 1, Columns 2 and 4). This is an important finding, as it suggests that the gender schema remains a factor in the evaluation of the masculine messages. The unchurched women strongly endorsed these messages' use with women, but were significantly less likely to use them with a male friend. Thus, they identify with the themes expressed, though they consider them inappropriate for a woman to say to a man.

It is also important that unchurched men did not differ significantly from churched men with regard to the use of masculine messages with men (or women) while they did differ with regard to the use of the feminine messages. Unchurched men were significantly less likely than any other group to use the feminine statements, even with women. They clearly do not identify with the feminine themes. Unchurched women, in contrast, strongly endorsed the feminine statements, as did the churched men and women (c.f. Column 3,c), but *only* for use with women.

There were *no* significant differences between any of the groups with regard to the use of the masculine messages with women (c.f. Column 4, d). All strongly endorsed their use. A review of the message characteristic ratings helped to explain why. It revealed that these messages were perceived as something a sensitive and a gentle person would say as much as an independent and an assertive person. A highly important finding is that both the unchurched and churched women's strongest endorsements were for the use of the masculine statements with a woman. In addition, there is no significant difference between the unchurched women's or the churched women's ratings for the masculine statements with a man and feminine statements with a woman (compare Columns 2, e&f and 3 e&f), but there is a significant difference between their ratings for the masculine statements with a man and the other two ratings (compare Column 4, g&h with Columns 2 and 3, g&h).

CONCLUSIONS

In sum, then, this study confirmed the findings of the previous studies with regard to unchurched men's response to feminine Christian messages—messages which Christian men indicated they are likely to use. The addition of churched and unchurched women to the sample, and masculine statements to the survey enables us to see these findings in a more complete context. It reveals that unchurched women also consider the feminine messages inappropriate for use with a man, but that both men and women, churched and unchurched identify strongly with the masculine statements and consider them appropriate for use with both men and women, particularly when in a conversation with a person of their own sex.

Bibliography

Abell, Aaron I. *The Urban Impact on American Protestantism 1865-1900*. Cambridge, MA: Harvard University Press, 1943.
Andersen, Mark B., and Jean M. Williams. "Gender Role and Sport Competition Anxiety: A Re-examination." In *Research Quarterly for Exercise and Sport* 58 1 (1987) 52-56. doi:10.1080/02701367.1987.10605420.
Anderson, Rindy C., and Casey A. Klofstad. "Preference for Leaders with Masculine Voices Holds the Case of Feminine Leadership Roles." In *PLoS ONE* 7 12 (2012). doi:10.1371/journal.pone.0051216.
Apple, William. "Effects of Pitch and Speech Rate on Personal Attributions." In *Journal of Personality and Social Psychology* 37 5 (1979) 715-27. doi:10.1037//0022-3514.37.5.715.
Arlis, Laurie P. *Gender Communication*. Englewood Cliffs, NJ: Prentice Hall, 1991.
Aromäki, Anu S., et al. "Testosterone, Sexuality and Antisocial Personality in Rapists and Child Molesters: A Pilot Study." In *Psychiatry Research* 110 3 (2002) 239-47. doi:10.1016/s0165-1781(02)00109-9.
Aronovitch, Charles D. "The Voice of Personality: Stereotyped Judgments and Their Relation to Voice Quality and Sex of Speaker." In *The Journal of Social Psychology* 99 2 (1976) 207-20. doi:10.1080/00224545.1976.9924774.
Athenstaedt, Ursula, et al. "Gender Role Self-Concept and Gender-Typed Communication Behavior in Mixed-Sex and Same-Sex Dyads." In *Sex Roles* 50 1/2 (2004) 37-52.
Banse, Rainer, and Klaus R. Scherer. "Acoustic Profiles in Vocal Emotion Expression." In *Journal of Personality and Social Psychology* 70 3 (1996) 614-36. doi:10.1037//0022-3514.70.3.614.
Barna, George. *Futurecast: What Today's Trends Mean for Tomorrow's World*. Carol Stream, IL: BarnaBooks, 2011.
Baxter, Judith, "Is It All Tough Talking At The Top?: A Post-Structuralist Analysis of The Construction Of Gendered Speaker Identities Of British Business Leaders Within Interview Narratives." In *Gender & Language* 2 2 (2008) 197-222.
Bem, Sandra Lipsitz. "Androgyny and Gender Schema Theory—A Conceptual and Empirical Integration." In Sonderegger, T. B., editor(s), *Nebraska Symposium*

on Motivation 1984—The Psychology of Gender. University of Nebraska Press, Lincoln, NB, 1985.

———. "The BSRI and Gender Schema Theory: A Reply to Spence and Helmreich." Psychological Review 88, no. 4 (1981) 369–71.

———. "Gender Schema Theory: A Cognitive Account of Sex Typing." Psychological Review 88, no. 4 (1981) 354–64.

Bem, Sandra L., and Ellen Lenney. "Sex Typing and the Avoidance of Cross-Sex Behavior." Journal of Personality and Social Psychology 33, no. 1 (1976) 48–54.

Bernstein, Elizabeth. "Why Verbal Tee-Ups Like 'To Be Honest' Are a Signal of Insincerity." In The Wall Street Journal. 2014. Accessed January 20, 2014. http://www.wsj.com/articles/SB10001424052702303802904579332751950927282.

Borkowska, Barbara, and Boguslaw Pawlowski. "Female Voice Frequency in the Context of Dominance and Attractiveness Perception." In Animal Behaviour 82 1 (2011) 55–59. doi:10.1016/j.anbehav.2011.03.024.

Brodie, Graham D., et al. "Explaining the Impact of Attachment Style on Evaluations of Supportive Messages: A Dual-Process Framework." In Communication Research 38 2 (April 2011) 228–47.

Bronson, Po, and Ashley Merryman. NurtureShock: New Thinking about Children. New York: Twelve, 2009.

———. Top Dog: The Science of Winning and Losing. New York: Twelve, 2013.

Brooks, John H., and John R. Reddon. "Serum Testosterone in Violent and Nonviolent Young Offenders." In Journal of Clinical Psychology 52 4 (1996) 475–83. doi:10.1002/(sici)1097-4679(199607)52:43.0.co;2-d.

Bruce, Deborah, "Wave II of the U. S. Congregational Life Survey: First Results." Paper presented at the annual meeting of the Society for the Scientific Study of Religion and the Religious Research Association, Denver, Colorado, October, 2009.

Burgoon, Judee K. "Attributes of the Newscaster's Voice as Predictors of His Credibility." In Journalism & Mass Communication Quarterly 55 2 (1978) 276–300. doi:10.1177/107769907805500208.

———. "Nonverbal Behaviors, Persuasion, and Credibility." In Human Communication Research 17 1 (1990) 140–69.

Burleigh, Michael. Earthly Powers: The Clash of Religion and Politics in Europe from the French Revolution to the Great War. New York: HarperCollins, 2005.

Burleson, Brant R., et al. "Guys Can't Say That to Guys: Four Experiments Assessing the Normative Motivation Account for Deficiencies in the Emotional Support Provided by Men." In Communication Monographs, 72 4 (2005) 468–501.

Cahill, Larry, and Anda Van Stegeren. "Sex-related Impairment of Memory for Emotional Events with β-adrenergic Blockade." In Neurobiology of Learning and Memory 79 1 (2003) 81–88.

———. "The Influence of Sex versus Sex-related Traits on Long-term Memory for Gist and Detail from an Emotional Story." In Consciousness and Cognition 13 2 (2004) 391–400.

Canli, Turhan., et al. "Sex Differences in the Neural Basis of Emotional Memories." In Proceedings of the National Academy of Sciences 99 16 (2002) 10789–794.

Carli, Linda L. "Gender, Language, and Influence." In Journal of Personality and Social Psychology 59 5 (1990) 941–51.

Carney, Dana R., et al. "Power Posing: Brief Nonverbal Displays Affect Neuroendocrine Levels and Risk Tolerance." In *Psychological Science* 21 10 (2010) 1363–368. doi:10.1177/0956797610383437.
Cheney, Sheldon. *Men Who Have Walked with God: Being the Story of Mysticism through the Ages, Told in the Biographies of Representative Seers and Saints, with Excerpts from Their Writings and Sayings*. New York: Alfred A. Knopf, 1945.
Cheng, Joey T., et al. "Listen, Follow Me: Dynamic Vocal Signals of Dominance Predict Emergent Social Rank in Humans." In *Journal of Experimental Psychology: General* 145 5 (2016) 536–47. doi:10.1037/xge0000166.
Cobb, L. Stephanie. *Dying to Be Men: Gender and Language in Early Christian Martyr Texts*. New York: Columbia University Press, 2008.
Coccaro, Emil F., et al. "CSF Testosterone: Relationship to Aggression, Impulsivity, and Venturesomeness in Adult Males with Personality Disorder." In *Journal of Psychiatric Research* 41 6 (2007) 488–92. doi:10.1016/j.jpsychires.2006.04.009.
Collins, Sheila. *A Different Heaven and Earth*. Valley Forge: Judson, 1974.
Condry, John C. "Gender Identity and Social Competence." In *Sex Roles* 11 5–6 (1984) 485–511.
Cowan, Gloria, and Joanne Koziej. "The Perception of Sex-Inconsistent Behavior." *Sex Roles* 5, no. 1 (1979) 1–10.
Csinos, David M. "Will Boys Be Boys and Girls Be Girls? Correcting Gender Stereotypes Through Ministry with Children." In *Priscilla Papers* 24 2 (2010) 23–28.
Cuddy, Amy J. C., et al. "Preparatory Power Posing Affects Nonverbal Presence and Job Interview Performance." In *Journal of Applied Psychology* 100 4 (2015) 1286–295. doi:10.1037/a0038543.
Curtis, Brent, and John Eldredge. *The Sacred Romance: Drawing Closer to the Heart of God*. Nashville: Thomas Nelson, 1997.
Dabbs, James M., and Alison Mallinger, "High Testosterone Levels Predict Low Voice Pitch among Men." In *Personality and Individual Differences* 27 4 (1999) 801–04. doi:10.1016/s0191-8869(98)00272-4.
———, and Robin Morris. "Testosterone, Social Class, And Antisocial Behavior In A Sample Of 4,462 Men." In *Psychological Science* 1 3 (1990) 209–11. doi:10.1111/j.1467-9280.1990.tb00200.x.
———, et al. "Saliva Testosterone and Criminal Violence in Young Adult Prison Inmates." In *Psychosomatic Medicine* 49 2 (1987) 174–82. doi:10.1097/00006842-198703000-00007.
———. "Testosterone and Occupational Choice: Actors, Ministers, and Other Men." In *Journal of Personality and Social Psychology* 59 6 (1990) 1261–5.
Davis, Casey W. *Oral Biblical Criticism: The Influence of the Principles of Orality on the Literary Structure of Paul's Epistle to the Philippians*. Vol. 172. Bloomsbury, 1999.
Davis, Woody L. "Men and the Church: What Keeps Them Out and What Brings Them In." In *The Journal of the Academy for Evangelism in Theological Education* 3 (1991) 46–61.
Dittes, James E. *Driven by Hope: Men and Meaning*. Louisville, KY: Westminster John Knox Press, 1996.
Donnelly, Kristin, and Jean M. Twenge. "Masculine and Feminine Traits on the Bem Sex-Role Inventory, 1993–2012: A Cross-Temporal Meta-Analysis." In *Sex Roles*, 2016. doi:10.1007/s11199-016-0625-y.

Drexler, Peggy, and Linden Gross. *Raising Boys without Men: How Maverick Moms Are Creating the next Generation of Exceptional Men*. Emmaus, PA: Rodale, 2005.

Durik, Amanda M, et al. "The Effects of Hedges in Persuasive Arguments: A Nuanced Analysis of Language." In *Journal of Language & Social Psychology* 27 3 (2008) 217–34.

Evans, Sarah, et al., "The Relationship between Testosterone and Vocal Frequencies in Human Males." In *Physiology & Behavior* 93 4–5 (2008) 783–88. doi:10.1016/j.physbeh.2007.11.033.

Fahy, Patrick J. "Use of Linguistic Qualifiers and Intensifiers in a Computer Conference." In *American Journal of Distance Education* 16 1 (2002) 5–22.

Falbo, Toni. "Relationships between Sex, Sex Role, and Social Influence." *Psychology of Women Quarterly* 2, no. 1 (1977) 62–72.

Feinberg, David R., et al. "Manipulations of Fundamental and Formant Frequencies Influence the Attractiveness of Human Male Voices." In *Animal Behaviour* 69 3 (2005) 561–68. doi:10.1016/j.anbehav.2004.06.012.

Feinman, Saul. "Why is cross-sex-role behavior more approved for girls than boys?" In *Sex Roles* 7 3 (1981) 289–300.

Foote, George W. *Flowers of Freethought, Volume* 2. Edmonton: Pioneer, 1894. Original from the New York Public Library, Digitized April 16, 2008.

Forbes. "TED Talks Are Wildly Addictive For Three Powerful Scientific Reasons." Accessed February 25, 2014. http://www.forbes.com/sites/carminegallo/2014/02/25/ted-talks-are-wildly-addictive-for-three-powerful-scientific-reasons/#5cbc11b451e9/.

Fromm, Erich. *The Dogma of Christ, and Other Essays on Religion, Psychology, and Culture*. New York: Holt, Rinehart and Winston, 1963.

Gerra, Gilberto, et al. "Neurotransmitters, Neuroendocrine Correlates of Sensation-Seeking Temperament in Normal Humans." In *Neuropsychobiology* 39 4 (1999) 207–13. doi:10.1159/000026586.

Giles, Kevin. *The Trinity & Subordinationism: The Doctrine of God & the Contemporary Gender Debate*. Downers Grove, IL: InterVarsity, 2002.

Gilmore, David D. *Manhood in the Making: Cultural Concepts of Masculinity*. New Haven, CT: Yale University Press, 1990.

Goodwin, Marjorie Harness. "Directive-Response Speech Sequences in Girls' and Boys' Task Activities." In *Women and Language in Literature and Society*, edited by Sally McConnell-Ginet, et al. New York: Praeger, 1980. 157–73.

Gough, Harrison G., and Alfred B. Heilbrun, Jr. *The Adjective Checklist Manual:* 1983 edition. Palo Alto: Consulting Psychologists, 1983.

Gray, Elizabeth. D. *Patriarchy as a Conceptual Trap*. Wellesley, MA: Roundtable, 1982.

The Guardian. "Women Told to Speak Their Minds to Get On in Boardrooms." Accessed August 3, 2012. http://www.guardian.co.uk/uk/2011/jun/19/women-language-boardroom-study/.

Gurian, Michael, and Barbara Annis. *Leadership and the Sexes: Using Gender Science to Create Success in Business*. San Francisco: Jossey-Bass, 2008.

Hale, James Russell. *The Unchurched: Who They Are and Why They Stay Away*. San Francisco: Harper & Row, 1980.

Hamilton, David L. *Cognitive Processes in Stereotyping and Intergroup Behavior*. New York: Psychology Press, 2015.

Hayes, Steven C., and Susan R. Leonard. "Sex-related Motor Behavior: Effects on Social Impressions and Social Cooperation." Archives of *Sexual Behavior* 12, no. 5 (1983).

Hertz, Rosanna. *Single by Chance, Mothers by Choice: How Women Are Choosing Parenthood without Marriage and Creating the New American Family*. New York: Oxford University Press, 2008.

Hess, Beth B., and Myra Marx Ferree. *Analyzing Gender: A Handbook of Social Science Research*. Newbury Park, CA: Sage, 1987.

Hardesty, Nancy. *Inclusive Language in the Church*. Nashville: Abingdon, 1987.

Hoffman, Shirl J. *Good Game: Christianity and the Culture of Sports*. Waco, TX: Baylor University Press, 2010.

Institute of Education Sciences, National Center for Education Statistics, U.S. Department of Education. Accessed June 12, 2015. http://nces.ed.gov/fastfacts/display.asp?id=372.

Jakupcak, Matthew, et al. "Masculinity and Emotionality: An Investigation of Men's Primary and Secondary Emotional Responding." In *Sex Roles* 49 (2003) 111–20.

Jansz, Joeren. "Masculine Identity and Restrictive Emotionality." In *Gender and Emotion: Social Psychological Perspectives*, edited by A. H. Fischer, 166–186. New York: Cambridge University Press, 2000.

Jespersen, Otto. *Language: Its Nature, Development and Origin*. London: Allen and Unwin, 1922.

Johnson, Fern L. *Speaking Culturally: Language Diversity in the United States*. Thousand Oaks, CA: Sage, 2000.

Jones, Benedict C., et al. "A Domain-specific Opposite-sex Bias in Human Preferences for Manipulated Voice Pitch." In *Animal Behaviour* 79 1 (2010) 57–62. doi:10.1016/j.anbehav.2009.10.003.

Jones, Tony. "Some (Honestly) Bad Reformed Theology Defending Hierarchies." Accessed July 24, 2013. http://www.patheos.com/blogs/tonyjones/2013/07/24/some-honestly-bad-reformed-theology-defending-hierarchies/.

Jordan, Robert, and Brandon Sanderson. *Towers of Midnight*. New York: Tor, 2010.

Keller, Helen. *Let Us Have Faith*. New York: Doubleday, & Doran, 1940.

Key, Mary Ritchie. *Male / Female Language*. Lanham: Scarecrow Press; 2nd edition, 1975/1996.

Klofstad, Casey A., et al. "Sounds like a Winner: Voice Pitch Influences Perception of Leadership Capacity in Both Men and Women." In *Proceedings of the Royal Society B: Biological Sciences* 279 1738 (2012) 2698–704. doi:10.1098/rspb.2012.0311.

Kouzes, James M., and Barry Z. Posner. *Credibility: How Leaders Gain and Lose It, Why People Demand It*. San Francisco: Jossey-Bass, 1993.

Kunjufu, Jawanza. *Adam! Where Are You?: Why Most Black Men Don't Go to Church*. Chicago, IL: African American Images, 1994.

Kurtz, James P., and Marvin Zuckerman. "Race And Sex Differences On The Sensation Seeking Scales." In *Psychological Reports* 43 2 (1978) 529–30. doi:10.2466/pro.1978.43.2.529.

Kyratzis, Amy, and Şeyda Deniz Tarım. "Using Directives to Construct Egalitarian or Hierarchical Social Organization: Turkish Middle-class Preschool Girls' Socialization about Gender, Affect, and Context in Peer Group Conversations." In *First Language* 30 3–4 (2010) 473–92.

Ladd, George Eldon. *The Presence of the Future; the Eschatology of Biblical Realism*. Grand Rapids, MI: Eerdmans, 1974.

Lafrance, Marianne, and Barbara Carmen. "The Nonverbal Display of Psychological Androgyny." *Journal of Personality and Social Psychology* 38, no. 1 (1980) 36–49.

Lakoff, Robin Tolmach, and Mary Bucholtz. *Language and Woman's Place: Text and Commentaries*. New York: Oxford University Press, 2004.

Lawrence, Brother, and Douglas V. Steere. *The Practice of the Presence of God*. Nashville: Upper Room, 1950.

Leaper, Campbell, et al. "Self-Disclosure and Listener Verbal Support in Same-Gender and Cross-Gender Friends' Conversations." In *Sex Roles* 33 5–6 (1995) 387–404.

Lee, Aldora G., and Vernene L. Scheurer. "Psychological Androgyny and Aspects of Self-Image in Women and Men." *Sex Roles* 9, no. 3 (1983) 289–306.

Lewis, Clive S. *Mere Christianity*. Glasgow: Fount Paperbacks, 1977.

Lindsey, A. Elizabeth, and Walter R. Zakahi. "Perceptions of Men and Women Departing from Conversational Sex Role Stereotypes During Initial Interaction." In *Sex differences and similarities in communication: Critical essays and empirical investigations of sex and gender in interaction* (1998) 393–412.

Liu, Hugo, and Rada Mihalcea, R. "Of Men, Women, and Computers: Data-Driven Gender Modeling for Improved User Interfaces." Paper presented at the International Conference on Weblogs and Social Media (ICWSM), Boulder, CO. March, 2007. Accessed January 13, 2014. http://pdf.aminer.org/000/240/077/women_gender_and_computers.pdf/.

Lummis, Adair T. "Men's Commitment to Religion: Perceptions of its Nature, Nurture, and Consequences." Paper presented at the annual meeting of the Society for the Scientific Study of Religion, Norfolk, Virginia, October, 2003. Accessed January 13, 2014. http://hirr.hartsem.edu/bookshelf/lummis_article2.html/.

———. "A Research Note: Real Men and Church Participation." In *Review of Religious Research* 45 4 (2004) 404. doi:10.2307/3511994.

Markus, Hazel, et al. "Self-schemas and Gender." In *Journal of Personality and Social Psychology* 42 1 (1982) 38–50.

Mason, Gail, and Mischa Barr. "Attitudes Towards Homosexuality: A Literature Review." Sydney Institute of Criminology, Sydney Law School, University of Sydney January 2006 Australian Hate Crime Network. Accessed February 24, 2015. http://sydney.edu.au/law/criminology/ahcn/australian_materials.shtml#M.

Mayew, William J., et al., "Voice Pitch and the Labor Market Success of Male Chief Executive Officers." In *Evolution and Human Behavior* 34 4 (2013) 243–48. doi:10.1016/j.evolhumbehav.2013.03.001.

McConnell-Ginet, Sally, et al., eds. *Women and Language in Literature and Society*. New York: Praeger, 1980.

Macnamara, Jim. *Media and Male Identity: The Making and Remaking of Men*. Basingstoke: Palgrave Macmillan, 2006.

Mead, Margaret. *Male and Female: A Study of the Sexes in a Changing World*. New York: William Morrow & Co. 1949, 1975.

Merryman, Ashley. "Losing Is Good for You." The New York Times. 2013. Accessed September 25, 2013. http://www.nytimes.com/2013/09/25/opinion/losing-is-good-for-you.html.

Miller, Alan S., and John P. Hoffmann. "Risk and Religion: An Explanation of Gender Differences in Religiosity." In *Journal for the Scientific Study of Religion* 34 1 (1995) 63–75.

———. "Going To Hell In Asia: The Relationship Between Risk And Religion In A Cross Cultural Setting." In *Review of Religious Research* 42 1 (2000) 5–18.
Mills, Sara. *Gender and Politeness*. Cambridge: Cambridge University Press, 2003.
Milne-Tyte, Ashley. "Women's Words vs. The Message Their Voice Sends." Femme-O-Nomics.com. Accessed August 3, 2012. http://femme-o-nomics.com/2011/07/womens-words-vs-the-message-their-voice-sends/.
Moon, Christine, et al. "Language Experienced *In Utero* Affects Vowel Perception After Birth: A Two-Country Study." In *Acta Paediatrica* 102 2 (2013) 156–60.
Moore, Beth. *Breaking Free*. Nashville: Broadman and Holman, 2000.
Mulac, Anthony, et al. "The Gender-Linked Language Effect: An Empirical Test Of A General Process Model." In *Language Sciences* 38 (2013) 22–31.
———. "A General Process Model of the Gender-Linked Language Effect: Antecedents for and Consequences of Language Used by Men And Women." Conference Papers—International Communication Association Annual Meeting, 1–42. San Diego, CA: 2003.
Murphy, Bróna. *Corpus and Sociolinguistics: Investigating Age and Gender in Female Talk*. Amsterdam: John Benjamins. 2010.
Murrow, David. *Why Men Hate Going To Church*. Nashville: Thomas Nelson. 2005, 2011.
Musson, David J. "Male and Female Anglican Clergy: Gender Reversal on the 16PF5?" In *Review of Religious Research* 43 2 (2001) 175–83.
Newman, Matthew L. et al. "Gender differences in language use: An analysis of 14,000 text samples." In *Discourse Processes* 45 3 (2008) 211–36.
News, BBC. "The Unstoppable March of the Upward Inflection?" BBC News. Accessed August 11, 2014. http://www.bbc.com/news/magazine-28708526.
Office of Research of the General Council on Ministries. *Pastoral Leadership: Admired Values and Essential Skills Identified by United Methodist Laity*. Dayton: United Methodist, 1993.
Osinga, Frans P.B. *Science, Strategy and War: The Strategic Theory of John Boyd*. London: Routledge. 2006.
Oswalt, Patricia A. "An Examination Of The Current Usefulness Of The Bem Sex-Role Inventory." In *Psychological Reports: PR* 94 3 (2004) 1331–336.
Palomares, Nicholas A. "Gender Schematicity, Gender Identity Salience, and Gender-Linked Language Use." In *Human Communication Research* 30 4 (2004) 556–88.
———. "Explaining Gender-Based Language Use: Effects of Gender Identity Salience on References to Emotion and Tentative Language in Intra-and Intergroup Contexts." In *Human Communication Research* 34 2 (2008) 263–86.
Parker, Kathleen. *Save the Males: Why Men Matter Why Women Should Care*. New York: Random House, 2008.
Pennebaker, James W. et al. "Psychological Aspects of Natural Language Use: Our Words, Our Selves." In *Annual Review of Psychology* 54 1 (2003) 547–77.
———. "Testosterone as a Social Inhibitor: Two Case Studies of the Effect of Testosterone Treatment on Language." In *Journal of Abnormal Psychology* 113 1 (2004) 172–75.
Phys.org-News and Articles on Science and Technology. "Men Become the Main Target in the New Gender Wars." Accessed November 19, 2016. http://phys.org/news/2006-11-men-main-gender-wars.html.

Pinker, Susan. *The Sexual Paradox: Men, Women and the Real Gender Gap*. New York: Scribner, 2008.

Podles, Leon. *The Church Impotent: The Feminization Of Christianity*. Dallas: Spence, 1999.

Poe, Edgar Allan. "The Pit and the Pendulum." In *The Complete Stories and Poems of Edgar Allan Poe*, 196–206. Garden City, NY: Doubleday, 1966.

Puts, David A. et al. "Dominance and the Evolution of Sexual Dimorphism in Human Voice Pitch." In *Evolution and Human Behavior* 27 4 (2006) 283–96. doi:10.1016/j.evolhumbehav.2005.11.003.

———. "Masculine Voices Signal Men's Threat Potential in Forager and Industrial Societies." In *Proceedings of the Royal Society B: Biological Sciences* 279 1728 (2011) 601–09. doi:10.1098/rspb.2011.0829.

———. "Men's Voices as Dominance Signals: Vocal Fundamental and Formant Frequencies Influence Dominance Attributions among Men." In *Evolution and Human Behavior* 28 5 (2007) 340–44. doi:10.1016/j.evolhumbehav.2007.05.002.

Rasmussen, Jeffrey Lee, and Barbara E. Moely. "Impression Formation as a Function of the Sex Role Appropriateness of Linguistic Behavior." *Sex Roles* 14, no. 3-4 (1986) 149–61.

Reuther, Rosemary Radford. "Feminist Interpretation: A Method of Correlation." In *Feminist Interpretation of the Bible*, edited by Letty M. Russel. Philadelphia: Westminster, 1985.

Rice, Kate. "Say Hello to My Little Friend." In *The Daily Nexus*. Accessed February 14, 2017. http://dailynexus.com/2004-01-21/say-hello-to-my-little-friend.

Robbins, Mandy, et al. "The Personality Characteristics of Methodist Ministers: Feminine Men and Masculine Women?" In *Journal for the Scientific Study of Religion* 40 1 (2001) 123–28.

Rohr, Richard. "Creation Is the Primary Cathedral." Center for Action and Contemplation. Accessed November 15, 2015. https://cac.org/creation-primary-cathedral-2016-11-15/.

———. "Jesus' Invitation: Follow Me." Center for Action and Contemplation. Accessed October 18, 2016. https://cac.org/jesus-invitation-follow-2016-10-18/.

———. "Passing from Death to Life Now." Center for Action and Contemplation. Accessed October 18, 2016. https://cac.org/passing-death-life-now-2016-05-22/.

Russell, Letty M. *Growth in Partnership*. Philadelphia: Westminster, 1987.

Sax, Leonard. *Why Gender Matters: What Parents and Teachers Need to Know about the Emerging Science of Sex Differences*. New York: Harmony, 2006.

Schaller, Lyle. *It's a Different World: The Challenge for Today's Pastor*. Nashville: Abingdon, 1987.

Scherer, Klaus R. "Personality Markers in Speech." In K. R. Scherer & Howard Giles, eds. *Social Markers in Speech*. Cambridge: Cambridge University Press, 1979. 147–210.

Schiffer, Boris, et al. "Why Don't Men Understand Women? Altered Neural Networks for Reading the Language of Male and Female Eyes." In *PLoS ONE* 8 4 (2013). doi:10.1371/journal.pone.0060278.

Schnabel, Landon. "How Religious Are American Women and Men? Gender Differences and Similarities." In *Journal for the Scientific Study of Religion* 54 3 (2015) 616–22. doi:10.1111/jssr.12214.

Schoenfeld, Eugen. "Justice: An Illusive Concept in Christianity." In *Review of Religious Research* 30 3 (1989) 236. doi:10.2307/3511508.

———. "Militant and Submissive Religions: Class, Religion and Ideology." In *The British Journal of Sociology* 43 1 (1992) 111. doi:10.2307/591203.

———. "Militant religion." In *Religious Society* edited by William Swatos, 125–37. Westport, CN: Greenwood, 1987.

———, and Stjepan G. Mestrovic. "With Justice and Mercy: Instrumental-Masculine and Expressive-Feminine Elements in Religion." In *Journal for the Scientific Study of Religion* 30 4 (1991) 363. doi:10.2307/1387274.

Schwartz, H. Andrew, et al. "Personality, Gender, and Age in the Language of Social Media: The Open-Vocabulary Approach." In *PLoS ONE* 8 9 (2013). doi:10.1371/journal.pone.0073791.

Selnow, Gary W. "Sex Differences in Uses and Perceptions of Profanity." In *Sex Roles* 12 3–4 (1985) 303–12.

Seyfried, B. A., and Clyde Hendrick. "When Do Opposites Attract? When They Are Opposite in Sex and Sex-Role Attitudes." *Journal of Personality and Social Psychology* 25, no. 1 (1973) 15–20.

Shaffer, David R., and Robert D. Johnson. "Effects of Occupational Choice and Sex-Role Preferences on the Attractiveness of Competent Men and Women." *Journal of Personality* 48, no. 4 (1980) 505–19.

Snyder, Mark. "On the Self-Perpetuating Nature of Social Stereotypes". In D. L. Hamilton (Ed.). *Cognitive Processes in Stereotyping and Intergroup Behavior*, 183–212. Hillsdale, NJ: Lawrence Erlbaum, 1981.

Spence, Janet T. "Masculinity, Femininity, and Gender-Related Traits: A Conceptual Analysis and Critique of Current Research" *Normal Personality Processes Progress in Experimental Personality Research*, 1984, 1–97.

———, and Robert L. Helmreich. "Androgyny versus Gender Schema: A Comment on Bem's Gender Schema Theory." *Psychological Review* 88, no. 4 (1981) 365–68.

———, et al. "Negative and Positive Components of Psychological Masculinity and Femininity." *Journal of Personality and Social Psychology*, 37 (1979) 1673–1682.

Spurgeon, Charles H. "The Battle of Life." Accessed 2/26/15. http://www.spurgeon.org/sermons/3511.htm.

Stark, Rodney. "Physiology and Faith: Addressing the 'Universal' Gender Difference in Religious Commitment." In *Journal for the Scientific Study of Religion* 41 3 (2002) 495–507.

Stephenson, William. *The Study of Behavior: Q-Technique and Its Methodology*: (3. impr.). Chicago: University of Chicago Press, 1956.

Strauss, William, and Neil Howe. *Generations: The History of America's Future 1584–2069*. New York: William Morrow, 1991.

Sullins, D. Paul. "Gender and Religion: Deconstructing Universality, Constructing Complexity." In *American Journal of Sociology* 112 3 (2006) 838–80. doi:10.1086/507852.

Surratt, Sherry, and Jenni Catron. *Just Lead!: A No-whining, No-complaining, No-nonsense Practical Guide for Women Leaders in the Church*. San Francisco: Jossey-Bass, 2013.

Tannen, Deborah. *You Just Don't Understand: Women And Men In Conversation*. New York: Ballantine, 1990.

Taylor, Shelley E. *Tending Instinct: Women, Men and the Biology of Nurturing*. New York: Times, 2002.

Thibodeaux, Jennifer D. "Man of the Church, or Man of the Village? Gender and the Parish Clergy in Medieval Normandy." In *Gender & History* 18 2 (2006) 380–99. doi:10.1111/j.1468-0424.2006.00434.x.

Tigue, Cara C. et al. "Voice Pitch Influences Voting Behavior." In *Evolution and Human Behavior* 33 3 (2012) 210–16. doi:10.1016/j.evolhumbehav.2011.09.004.

Turner, Victor. *The Ritual Process: Structure and Anti-Structure*. Ithaca, NY: Cornell University Press, 1982.

Tyre, Peg. *The Trouble with Boys: A Surprising Report Card on Our Sons, Their Problems at School, and What Parents and Educators Must Do*. New York: Crown, 2008.

Weeks, Justin W., et al. "The Sound of Fear: Assessing Vocal Fundamental Frequency as a Physiological Indicator of Social Anxiety Disorder." In *Journal of Anxiety Disorders* 26 8 (2012) 811–22. doi:10.1016/j.janxdis.2012.07.005.

Wheeless, Virginia Eman, and Kathi Dierks-Stewart. "The Psychometric Properties of the Bem Sex-Role Inventory: Questions Concerning Reliability and Validity." *Communication Quarterly* 29, no. 3 (1981) 173–86.

Wheeless, Virginia Eman, and Robert L. Duran. "Gender Orientation as a Correlate of Communicative Competence." *Southern Speech Communication Journal* 48, no. 1 (1982) 51–64.

Williams, John E., and Deborah L. Best. *Sex and Psyche: Gender and Self Viewed Cross-Culturally*. Newbury Park, CA: Sage, 1990.

Witherington, Ben, and Darlene Hyatt. *Paul's Letter to the Romans: A Socio-rhetorical Commentary*. Grand Rapids, MI: W.B. Eerdmans, 2004.

Witelson, Sandra. F., et al. "Women Have Greater Density of Neurons in Posterior Temporal Cortex." In *Sex and the Brain*, edited by Gillian Einstein, 577–89. Cambridge, MA: MIT Press, 2007.

Wittels, Peter, et al. "Voice Monitoring to Measure Emotional Load during Short-term Stress." In *European Journal of Applied Physiology* 87 3 (2002) 278–82. doi:10.1007/s00421-002-0625-1.

Wolff, Richard, *The Church on TV: Portrayals Of Priests, Pastors and Nuns On American Television Series*. New York: Continuum International, 2010.

Wren, Brian. *What Language Shall I Borrow? God-Talk in Worship: A Male Response to Feminist Theology*. New York: Crossroad, 1989.

Zwart, Abby. "Brother Lawrence: Carmelite lay brother." Christian Classics Ethereal Library. Accessed December 1, 2016. http://www.ccel.org/ccel/lawrence.

Subject Index

accomplishment, 82, 103, 194, 195
achievement, 45n11, 99, 102n36, 103
Action Men/Women, 43–48, 59, 62, 67, 89–92, 107, 153–54, 189, 198, 201–2, 206–9
actional vs. relational, 79, 116, 119, 126, 186, 189, 198–99, 208
Adjective Checklist, 42n8, 43n9, 212
agenic, 42–43, 46–47, 93, 199
amygdala, 188, 198, 202n50
androgyny, 42–43, 90n6, 104, 199n42, 211, 212, 214, 227–31, 245, 247, 252, 265
Anglican clergy, 17
Annis, Barbara, 189n12, 195, 199n41
approval-seeking, 149

balance, 18, 32n10, 46, 47n15, 63, 67, 68–69, 74, 83, 104, 119, 121, 126, 131, 134, 136, 179
Barna, George, 9, 23
Bem Sex Role Inventory (or BSRI), 41, 42n8, 93n9, 211–13, 228–32, 254–56, 267
Bem, Sandra, 42n8, 93n9, 211, 228, 251
Bernard of Clairveaux, 52
Bishop of Pakistan, 60
Blessed Margaret Ebner (*see* Ebner, Blessed Margaret)
Boyd, David, 35
Bozos, 47–48, 179–80

brain chemistry, 195, 198
Bridal Mysticism, 52
British Methodists, 17
Bronson, Po, 194
Brother Lawrence, 80, 200
Burleson, Brant, 153
Buttprints in the Sand, 66–67

Church Without Balls, 79, 208
class meetings, Methodist, 64
Cobb, L. Stephanie, 205
Collins, Sheila, 98
colostomy bag on the body of Christ, 22
Combination Men/Women, 43, 89–95, 154
comfort zone, 22, 138
communalness, 137, 146–48, 159
communitifiers, 147, 163, 169
competition, 98, 193–99, 246
Conversational Perceptions Survey, 93, 267
credibility, 14, 108, 142, 146, 159, 161, 172,m 178
Cuddy, Amy, 192–93
culture, 186
culture, church, 18, 20, 22, 29, 34, 40–42, 51, 56, 73, 102, 161, 185
Euro-American/Western, 37, 98

SUBJECT INDEX

culture, North American, 12, 54, 110, 146, 148, 207, 215, 221, 231, 264
Dabbs, James, 17n32, 192n23
discipline, 58, 64, 78–79, 81, 83, 93, 94, 97, 177
discipleship, 104, 188, 209
Dittes, James, 98, 104
Drexler, Peggy, 190

Ebner, Blessed Margaret, 54, 205
Emerging Church Movement, 146
emotionality, 51, 59, 107, 151, 153, 171–72, 188–91, 206
empty adjectives, 51–52, 72–74
enmeshment, 56, 79–80
estrogen, 41, 67, 136, 209
evangelism, 102, 184

Facebook, 48–50, 62–63, 76n984, 150–53, 208
feminine Christian themes, 109, 111, 115, 117, 127, 133, 169
Feminine Register, 50, 70–73, 83, 136, 149, 169, 171, 178
Fromm, Erich, 206
fruit of the Spirit, 92, 131

Gallup survey, 23, 253
gender appropriateness, 92, 247, 265–66
gender associations, 12n23, 34, 42
gender mix, 10n17, 23, 28–32, 38, 46, 177
gender schema, 41–45
Gender Schematicity, 44–45, 88–95, 189, 228–47, 254–65, 268
Gender-Linked Language Effect, 136–37
generational cycle, 10, 107, 186
Giles, Kevin, 101
Gilmore, David, 45, 79, 212
Goodwin, Marjorie Harness, 147
Gray, Elizabeth Dodson, 100
Great Commission, 184–87
Greek manuscripts, 156–58, 160
Gurian, Michael, 189n12, 195, 198

Hardesty, Nancy, 18, 101
hedges, 138–39, 143, 159, 163
Heilbrun, Richard, 42n8, 43n9
hierarchy, 72, 98–101, 195
Hildegard of Bingen, 53
Hoffman, Shirl James, 194, 195
holiness, 55, 129, 186, 224
Hunter, George G. III, xv, xviii

inclusive language, xvii, 18, 84–86, 92, 102–5, 147, 167
Ingersoll, Robert, 4
Institutional Church Movement, 5, 186
instrumental, 42–43, 46, 214, 223–24, 228–29, 242–45
intensifiers, 149–50, 159, 163, 171, 206
intimate/intimacy, 46, 51, 53–55, 71, 76–77, 79, 112, 114, 165, 170
Isaacs, Susan, xiv, 78

Jesus Daily, 62, 66, 151
Jones, Tony, 100, 156n47

Keller, Helen, 61
Kouzes and Posner, 14–15

Lakoff, Robin Tolmach, 50–51, 71, 136, 145–49, 151
Ladd, George Eldon, 185n7
Lawrence, Brother (see Brother Lawrence)
lectionary, 111, 119–27
Lewis, C. S., 183
Lummis, Adair, 46–48, 199

Macnamara, Jim, 190
Manas, Meagan, 184
Markus, Hazel, 154n42, 229, 251n2
martyrs, 205
masculine Christian themes, 109–11, 127, 134
Mead, Margaret, 99
Men and Religion Forward Movement, 5, 186
men's ministry, 7, 20, 36, 152, 154
Men's Bible Study Movement, 5
Merryman, Ashley, 193

Miller and Hoffman, 59–60
Moore, Beth, 53, 156
Murrow, David, xiii, 3, 35, 37n14
Muscular Christianity, 205
nature/nurture, 1, 202
neurological gender differences, 188, 191
niceness, 137, 183, 187, 209

OODA Loop, 35

paralanguage, 170–78
Parker, Kathleen, 190
particularity-generality dichotomy, 140–41
patriarchy, 85, 98, 102n35, 190
Pennebaker, James, 45n11, 138
perceptions of Christians, 9, 11–13, 86, 182, 214
perseverance, 83, 93, 94, 110, 127, 177
personal relationship, 46, 55–56, 71, 79n12, 80
Pinker, Susan, 202
pitch, voice (*see* voice pitch)
Podles, Leon, xiv, 52–54
power posing, 192
powerless language, 136, 143, 149, 151–63
Powerless Language Indicators, 155–78
Pro Football Hall of Fame, 73, 208
profanity, 74, 150n23
psychological sex type, 41n3, 42n8, 214, 215, 226–27, 230, 231, 253
psycho-social captivity of ministry, 10, 188, 189

Q Methodology, 93n9, 215, 230
qualifiers, 140–43, 159
quest-ments and state-tions, 146–47, 159

Radford-Reuther, Rosemary, 102
rapport vs. report talk, 51
Rejected by eHarmony, xiv, 78
Relation Men/Women, 43, 89–92
relational/communal, 42–43, 102, 184
relationships, 45–46, 51, 56–58, 67–69, 77, 98, 103, 140, 195, 246

risk aversion, 59–60
Ritchie-Key, Mary, 50–51
Rohr, Richard, 162, 203
romantic emotions, 52–56, 69, 71, 75–77
Russell, Letty, 100

s'Mothering, 56–62, 71, 78–79
sacrifice, 79, 82, 109, 111, 196, 204n54, 254
safety, 45, 59–60, 78–79
Save the Males, 190
Sax, Leonard, 180
Schaller, Lyle, xv, 4
schema, 12n23, 42n8, 88n4, 93, 95, 154, 224–48
Schuller, Robert, 20–21
sermon analysis, 111, 127, 165
shared action, 80
sharing, 63, 80, 86, 103
small groups, 29–30, 63–65
social desirability, 221, 238
sooo, 150–51, 171
Spurgeon, C. H., 81
Stark, Rodney, 19n38
Strauss and Howe, 10, 47n15, 207
stereotypes, 10, 41, 137, 186–88, 206–7, 248, 251–52
Sunday, Billy, xiii, 5
Sunday School, 6, 28–30, 63, 86
super-polite language, 138, 147–49, 159–63

tag question, 146–47
Tannen, Deborah, 51, 103n37, 246
TED talks, 155–57, 169
tentativeness, 137, 145
testosterone, 17, 45n11, 47, 67, 192–93
Turner, Victor, 254n6
Tyre, Peg, 191, 198

U.S. Congregational Life Survey, 9
uncertainty signals, 143–46, 159, 163
Ungame, The, 194
universal gender difference in religion, 19
uptalk, 145–46, 163, 170

values sought in pastors, 14, 149–50
verbal estrogen, 41, 209
vocal italics, 149–55, 159, 163, 171
voice pitch, 171–72, 178, 192–93

Warren, Rick, 49, 77, 155
weakness/brokenness, 62–67
Wesley, John, 104, 128, 131
Williams and Best, 15n28, 3n9, 97n21

wimps, 11, 18, 83n14
Witherington, Ben, 57n31
women pastors, 17–18
Words Matter, 84–85
world of men, the, 359
World Values Survey, 19
Wren, Brian, 98

youth ministry, 24

Scripture Index

OLD TESTAMENT

Genesis

1:27	98
2:15	99
2:18–24	111
3:4	56
3:5	100
50:15–21	121

Exodus

3:1–15	119
12:1–14	121
14:19–31	121
16:2–15	122
17:1–7	122
20:1–4, 7–9, 12–20	122
32:1–14	123
33:12–23	123

Leviticus

19:1–2, 15–18	123

Deuteronomy

30:9–14	127
34:1–12	123

Joshua

3:7–17	124
24:1–3a, 14–25	124

Judges

4:1–7	124

1 Samuel

16:1–16	22

2 Samuel

7:1–11, 16	126

Psalms

1	123
8:3–5	100
19	122
19:1–6, 13–17	123
23	123
25:1–9	122
26:1–8	119
43	124
70	124
78:1–4, 12–16	122
78:1–7	124
80:1–7, 17–19	125
80:7–15	122
85:1–2, 8–13	125
89:1–4, 19–26	126
90:1–8, (9–11), 12	124
95:1–7a	125
96:1–9, (10–13)	123
100	124
103:(1–7), 8–13	121
105:1–6, 37–45	122
105:16, 23–26	119
106:1–6, 19–23	123
107:1–7, 33–37	124
123	124
126	125
148	126

Isaiah

5:1–7	122
25:1–9	123
40:1–11	125
45:1–7	123
61:1–4, 8–11	125
61:10—62:3	126
64:1–9	125

Jeremiah

15:15–21	119

Ezekiel

18:1–4, 25–32	122
33:7–11	121
34:11–16, 20–24	124

Amos

5:18–24	124

Jonah

3:10—4:11	122

Micah

3:5–12	124

Zephaniah

1:7, 12–18	124

NEW TESTAMENT

Matthew

7:28–29	161
8:5–13	81
10:34	103
11:7–15	93
11:19	185
13:18–23	69
14:22–33	22
16:21–28	119
18:15–20	121
18:21–35	121
20:1–16	122
21:23–32	122

21:33–46	122
22:14	123
22:15–22	123
22:34–46	123
22:38–39	124
23:1–12	124
23:27	124
25:1–13	124
25:14–30	124
25:31–46	125
28:19–20	184

Mark

10:2–16	111
11:1–8	125
13:24–37	125

Luke

1:26–38	126
1:46b–55	126
2:22–40	126
7:2–10	103
8:40–49	81
9:54	160
10:7	38
10:25–37	127
17:5–10	93
24:49	161

John

1:6–8, 19–28	125
1:9	127
3:16	168
3:22–26	203
3:27–30	203
4	103
10:10	131
12:44—17:26	101
14:16	161
15:5–7	131
17:13–19	37

Acts

2	161
4:13	161
9:1–9	108
10	103

Romans

5:10	55
8:18–39	93
10:10	131
12:1–2	64
12:2	185
12:10	196
12:9–21	119
13:8–14	121
14:1–12	121
16:25–27	126

1 Corinthians

1:3–9	125
9:22	103
9:24–27	93
12:1–31	94
12:28	101
13	161

2 Corinthians

1:5	83
5:19	55
12:9	65

Galatians

4:4–7	126
5:22–23	93

Ephesians

1:15–23	125
4:11–13	58
4:11–16	93
6:4	58
6:13	66
6:18–19	161

Philippians

1:21–30	122
2:1–13	122
2:3	254
3:4b–14	122
3:7–14	93
4:1–9	123

Colossians

1:9–16	127
1:24	83
1:28	57

1 Thessalonians

1:1–10	123
1:2–10	93

2:1–8	123
2:9–13	124
4:13–18	124
5:1–11	124
5:16–24	125

1 Timothy

5:18	124

2 Timothy

3:5	100

Hebrews

2:9–11	165
10:24	196

James

1:22—2:26	93

2 Peter

3:8–15a	125

www.ingramcontent.com/pod-product-compliance
Lightning Source LLC
Chambersburg PA
CBHW071234230426
43668CB00011B/1436